Help Wanted

How Companies Can Survive and Thrive in the Coming Worker Shortage

Kevin R. Hopkins

Susan L. Nestleroth

Clint Bolick

McGraw-Hill, Inc.
New York   St. Louis   San Francisco   Auckland   Bogotá
Caracas   Hamburg   Lisbon   London   Madrid
Mexico   Milan   Montreal   New Delhi   Paris
San Juan   São Paulo   Singapore
Sydney   Tokyo   Toronto

Library of Congress Cataloging-in-Publication Data

Hopkins, Kevin R.
    Help wanted: how companies can survive and thrive in the coming
    worker shortage / Kevin R. Hopkins, Susan L. Nestleroth, Clint
    Bolick.

        p.   cm.
    ISBN 0-07-030341-X
    1. Manpower planning—United States.   2. Employment forecast-
ing—United States.   I. Nestleroth, Susan L.   II. Bolick, Clint.
III. Title.
HF5549.5.M3H66   1991   658.3'01—dc20   90-31479
                                                                CIP

1 2 3 4 5 6 7 8 9 0   DOC/DOC   9 6 5 4 3 2 1 0

ISBN 0-07-030341-X

The sponsoring editor for this book was Barbara Toniolo, the editing supervisor
was Marion B. Castellucci, the designer was Naomi Auerbach, and the
production supervisor was Suzanne W. Babeuf. This book was set in Baskerville.
It was composed by McGraw-Hill's Professional & Reference Division
composition unit.

Printed and bound by R. R. Donnelley & Sons Company.

To our parents,
who taught us the value of work,
and to
Martin Anderson,
who taught us how to think
K.R.H.
S.L.N.

To Ricky Silberman,
my friend and mentor
C.B.

About the Authors

KEVIN R. HOPKINS is a senior fellow with the Hudson
Institute, an internationally renowned research institution
specializing in studies of the future. He is also president of
The Workforce 2000 Group, a management consulting firm
in Arlington, Virginia. He recently directed the Hudson
Institute's *Opportunity 2000* project, an in-depth
investigation into corporate strategies for meeting the
coming worker shortage. Previously, he served in the White
House as an economic adviser to the President.

SUSAN L. NESTLEROTH is a human resources specialist with the
Hudson Institute and was research director for its
Opportunity 2000 project. She is coauthor, with Mr.
Hopkins, of *Another Country: Poverty in the United States*
and *Real Equality*, a study of minority economic
advancement.

CLINT BOLICK is founding director of the Landmark Legal
Foundation's Center for Civil Rights in Washington, D.C.
He served as an attorney with the U.S. Justice Department's
Civil Rights Division and the U.S. Equal Opportunity
Commission. He is author of *Unfinished Business: A Civil
Rights Strategy for America's Third Century* and *Changing
Course: Civil Rights at the Crossroads*.

Contents

Preface

This is a book about how American business can stay competitive in the 1990s. But it isn't about the Japanese. It isn't about the trade deficit. It isn't even about some grand new management theory.

It is about *people*.

Ever since Ben Wattenberg warned in his book *The Birth Dearth* a few years ago that the growth of the United States population was slowing down, academics and national policymakers have been aware of the dramatic changes in store for the country in the wake of the shrinking number of young people entering the work force. But the same degree of understanding has not yet filtered its way through the business world.

While corporate executives, managers, and new business owners have been preoccupied with raising capital, opening new markets, and fending off the threat of foreign imports, an even more pressing challenge has emerged right here at home. During the 1990s, the United States will face an unprecedented shortage of workers. With the number of new workers at its lowest point since the Great Depression, there will be far more jobs available than there will be people to fill them. And the problem will only grow worse as the decade goes on.

At the same time, employers will have to cope with another, even more vexing shortage: a shortage of *skills*. Young people entering the work force in the coming decade will be less skilled, in some ways, than ever before. As many as one-third of the new workers will lack even the most basic abilities, such as reading, simple mathematics, and communications skills. They will have to be reschooled before they can be retrained.

Yet businesses will have no other choice. All the fancy management theories notwithstanding, no company will be able to survive in the 1990s without *people*—people in the right numbers and with the right skills. For the firms that prepare themselves to meet this challenge, the company work force will be more than the means to a good product. Quality workers will be business's most important tool for building up productivity, capturing new markets, and staying ahead of the competition. In short, quality workers will become the number one competitive advantage, bar none.

But for firms that don't prepare, that wait for the shrinking supply of workers to come to them, the labor shortages of the 1990s will be something else entirely—financial disaster.

Take your choice: prosperity or calamity.

Help Wanted is a guidebook for achieving the first and avoiding the second. It gives you detailed, advance warning about the lay of the land in the labor market of the coming decade, advising you what to beware of and where your greatest opportunities may lie. Then it takes you step-by-step through each new source of workers, your key to surviving and thriving during the emerging labor shortages. Its hundreds of real-world, *working* examples show you just how to locate, recruit, train, and retain the kind of workers you will need not just to keep up, but also to move ahead.

Other books tell you how to manage your work force for productivity, and that is important. But *Help Wanted* is the only book of its kind that tells you how to make sure you have the workers there to manage in the first place.

We believe this is the most important challenge American business will face in the 1990s. How well the country addresses this issue will play a major part in solving the other national problems that concern us so much—productivity, economic growth, trade and budget deficits, and leadership in the world economy.

But for individual companies, the issue is much more straightforward. You either will have the workers to do the job, or you won't.

The good news is that any firm that puts itself to the task can come out a winner. There is only one stipulation: You can't wait. To beat the new decade's worker shortages, you have to begin planning *now*. And then you have to begin putting the plans into practice, without delay.

No book can give you every answer to every problem that you will face along this road. But we hope that *Help Wanted*, in its own small way, can help you get started.

Acknowledgments

As with all books, *Help Wanted* could not have been written without the assistance and advice of many people whose names are not listed on the front cover. But our debt in this case is greater than that of most authors, for this book would not exist without the generous cooperation of the more than 100 company personnel officials, equal opportunity officers, program managers, and corporate executives who talked with us during the course of this study. Their ideas and efforts to bring the new work force into the economic mainstream were the most important resource for this book. While we cannot thank each individual by name here, the value of their contributions is evident in our many citations, throughout this book, of both their words and their accomplishments.

We would, however, like to mention the names of a few people who were especially helpful to us, whether by making us aware of new work force strategies, providing us with useful leads, or commenting on portions of the text. In particular, we would like to thank: Joann Milano, at the time a human resources manager at PepsiCo's Taco Bell Division; Jeffrey Norris of the Equal Employment Opportunity Council; Fritz Rumpel and Neil Woods of Mainstream, Inc.; Professor Nancy Hensel of the University of Redlands; Michael Kennedy of Associated General Contractors; Dr. Malcolm Lawton of the Santa Clara Valley Rehabilitation Center; former U.S. Labor Department officials Roger D. Semerad, Arnold H. Packer, Marilia A. Robbins, and Robert Planansky; OFCCP Regional Administrators Manuel Villarreal and Carmen McCulloch, as well as Myra Stratton of OFCCP's San Francisco office; the staff of the Task Force on Women, Minorities and the Handicapped in Science and Technology; Martin Artiano; Richard Jackson; Sylvia Martins; and Dean White.

We also owe a tremendous debt to former U.S. Assistant Secretary of Labor Fred W. Alvarez, and U.S. Labor Department officials Willis Nordlund and Cynthia Deutermann, who worked with us on *Opportunity 2000*. They helped us to refine the direction of that study and focus our research toward the interests of those it was designed to benefit—the companies, their top managers, their EEO officers, and their personnel. We also would like to thank the management and staff of the Hudson Institute, particularly Vice President William B. Johnston and the staff of the institute's library, who were instrumental in seeing the *Opportunity 2000* report to completion.

Thanks to the miracle of modern word processing, we were able to type the final manuscript ourselves. But at various earlier stages of the project, a number of people provided timely clerical support, including: Melody Campbell, Jackie Chase, Ruth Doerflein, Bettylou Reed, Donna Rouse, and Joyce Stabile. Mary Chlopecki supplied first-rate research assistance on a number of occasions, for which we express our appreciation. We would also like to thank LaPorta's Restaurant in Alexandria, Virginia, purveyors of some of the finest cuisine in the Washington area, who kept us well fed during the course of this project.

Naturally, we owe a multitude of thanks to our editors at McGraw-Hill, William Sabin and Barbara Toniolo, who helped make *Help Wanted* both more readable and to the point. Also, *muchas gracias* to Ben Kamsler of H. N. Swanson, Inc., who handled financial matters for us so that we could concentrate, undistracted, on finishing the manuscript, and who also provided useful editorial suggestions.

Lastly, and most importantly, we would like to thank our parents, who very early in life taught us the meaning of work, the value of acquiring a good education, and the importance of striving against the odds.

1

Snapshots of a Shrinking Work Force

A funny thing happened on the way to the 1990s. The laws of economics went into reverse.

Anyone who has watched economic trends over the years can't help but have noticed: when inflation went down, unemployment went up. The relationship has been so predictable, for so long, that it has acquired its own name. Economists call it the "Phillips curve." Political candidates call it the "misery" in the "misery index." Editorial writers call out with judgments against "using unemployment to fight inflation."

Or at least they used to. The editorial writers have been mysteriously silent of late. Since the end of the last recession, both inflation and unemployment have been headed fitfully downward—*at the same time*. By the laws of economics, these things should not be happening.

But they are. By mid-summer 1989, the nation's jobless rate had dipped to 5.2 percent, just above the 14-year low set four months before, and has remained in that range since then. Even as early as mid-1987, the rate was less than 4 percent in 31 major urban areas throughout 19 states. The number of "discouraged workers," at fewer than a million, was also at a 10-year low. And while the average unemployed worker in Japan is out of work for three months, and in Europe for six months, in the United States the figure is below seven weeks.

All this is taking place, mind you, in the seventh year of an economic expansion, when inflation itself—despite some recent upswings—is hovering at rates unheard of since the early 1970s.

Just what is going on here?

What is going on is something called a worker shortage. There are, to put it bluntly, too few workers for too many jobs. The economy is continuing to grow as fast as it has in the past, but the labor force isn't, leaving employers—in the words of one business analyst—in the "unaccustomed position of scrambling for workers."

And matters will get worse. Says William B. Johnston, author of the landmark study *Workforce 2000* and one of the shrewdest observers of work force trends in the United States: "The labor market of the next decade will be the 1970s turned on its head. There will be a spreading surplus of jobs and spreading shortages of workers to fill them."

For a generation of hourly wage earners for whom the loss of a job has been an ever present worry, this prospect may seem farfetched, a vestige of the "feel good" ethics of the early 1980s. And for national policymakers, for whom the unemployment problem has been a front burner political issue for years, the idea of a worker shortage may be altogether inconceivable, even a little surreal.

But it's coming. In fact, in many areas, it's already here. Mark Goldstein admonishes in *Industry Week:* "Don't bother waiting for the 1990s to watch America's work force unravel. It's happening before our eyes. All across the country, in almost every part of the economy, the seams that have held the work force fabric together for the last 40 years are coming loose."

Canada's Anne Ironside is even more direct. "We're looking," she says, "at the collapse of the job system as we've known it."

Welcome to the Worker Shortage

If all this sounds incredible, consider these recent reports from the front lines:

- By the late 1980s, Disneyland (perhaps the most coveted teenage job site in southern California) was unable to fill 200 of its 2000 jobs. The situation has not improved since then.

- Across the country, in Danbury, Connecticut, the opening of a shopping mall was delayed by five weeks because of a severe shortage of workers.

- Texas' Zapata Gulf Marine, a supplier of offshore oil rigs, has had to mothball several ships because it can't find chief engineers to operate them.

- In Hyannis, Massachusetts, owners of the popular Denny's restaurant were forced to close up shop just before the start of the summer beach rush because they could hire only 13 of the 70 employees they needed.

To employers caught in the grip of these shortages, their inability to fill out their staffs is anything but an illusion and is already driving many to extraordinary measures. For instance:

- A Pawtucket, Rhode Island, pizza shop, strapped for order takers, advertises jobs at the previously unheard-of wage of $10 an hour.

- Gary Snow, president of an electronics manufacturing firm in nearby Bethany, Connecticut, "risked everything" to move the company to upstate New York because he couldn't find workers, even at high wages.

- California retailers, facing severe staff shortages, have turned to adolescents to fill clerk positions; as a result, labor-law violations involving 14- and 15-year-olds have more than doubled in recent years. At least one state, Connecticut, has taken the more direct approach, officially lowering the statewide minimum age for most jobs from 16 to 15.

- Companies ranging from Wendy's to Stop & Shop, from Hollywood's Universal Studios to construction firms in booming Fairfax and Prince William Counties in Virginia are busing in workers from surrounding areas, often up to two hours away, just to meet their hiring needs.

- Even the federal government, the nation's biggest employer, has gotten into the act. Reversing long-time policy, the federal Office of Personnel Management (OPM) has proposed to allow federal agencies to use temporary-help firms to fill some job slots. Admits Connie Horner, OPM's former director, the personnel office is making the recommendation now because the problem of finding employees "is only going to get worse over the next two decades."

All available evidence suggests that Connie Horner is right. The days of long queues for every job opening are coming to an end. It's a completely new world for people who hire people—and for executives, entrepreneurs, managers, and workers as well. Selectivity is being replaced with extended searches, and hiring lines with worry lines. And it's not going to change any time soon. For the foreseeable future, the worker shortages are here to stay. Employers who once had to worry about turning job applicants away, warns former U.S. Labor Department official Marilia Robbins, are suddenly going to find they need "all the workers they can get."

Who Will Flip the Hamburgers?

Every titanic social change seems to start with a small rumble. For the coming worker shortage, the first rumble may have been in the fast-food industry. Long a favored source of summer jobs and after-school work, fast-food outlets have been feeling the worker pinch for nearly a decade because of the shrinking pool of teenagers. But for much of the time, the shortage has been little more than that—just a pinch. Few companies felt the need to respond in any systematic way, except perhaps by recruiting a little more aggressively.

The McDonald's Corp. was one of the exceptions. In the late 1970s, the company's executives began putting numbers together that showed, beyond question, how severe their future labor crunch would be. Shortly afterward, they started designing a rehirement program, a carefully mapped out strategy for bringing retirees back into the work force.

The program has been an undisputed success. Step under the Golden Arches today, and you're almost as likely to see a senior citizen behind the counter as you are a teenager. By all reports, these older workers are solid, stable, and highly capable and have blended in well with the younger work force. What's more, while many other fast-food restaurants struggle to fill positions, most McDonald's are fully staffed.

But if McDonald's took the lead in recognizing the emerging worker shortages, other top fast-food merchants were not far behind. Wendy's, the hamburger giant that goes head-to-head with McDonald's in many markets, began to experience serious recruiting difficulties when it started keeping many of its restaurants open past midnight. Even where teens were available, says marketing public relations manager Linda Packer, it was "tough to find a 17-year-old to work until 1 a.m. and then go to school in the morning." So Wendy's turned to the elderly as well. The company now employs a large contingent of older workers, and many of the restaurants located near retirement areas are staffed almost exclusively by the elderly.

Other companies are taking different but just as innovative approaches:

- Hardee's, the North Carolina-based hamburger chain, is recruiting inner-city youths for its suburban restaurants.
- Burger King, another industry leader, promises tuition assistance to students with three months of experience and at least C-average grades.
- Kentucky Fried Chicken boasts a stock option program for entry-level workers.
- Vie de France pays as much as $1000 in educational expenses for employees seeking a high school or college degree.
- Some franchises even offer sign-up bonuses of $50 or more.

These efforts are coming just in time, if they aren't already too late. Hardee's John Merritt predicts that the industry is "going to face a crisis in the next ten years." Indeed, if hiring practices don't change dramatically, *crisis* could be too mild a description. A study prepared by Arthur D. Little, Inc., at the request of the National Restaurant Association, determined that the food-service industry as a whole could face a shortage of as many as 1 million workers by 1995. If that happens, the pet phrase of labor force analysts—"Who will flip the hamburgers?"—will become far more than a rhetorical question for fast-food executives.

From Hotel Workers to Home Builders—Labor Shortfalls

The food-service industry isn't alone in veering toward a labor shortfall. The problems confronting the hotel and hospitality industry are similar, if less often noticed by the general public. Already, argues David R. Murphy, a human resources expert with the Marriott Corp., "in terms of competent hourly employees, the situation is critical in much of the nation."

For example, the Cambridge, Massachusetts, Hyatt Regency, a popular hotel just north of Boston, has had trouble filling "virtually every position," from "pastry makers to administrative assistants," according to personnel director Susan Wall. Help-wanted advertisements that once drew 125 applications now are lucky to bring in one-fifth that many. Another chain had to close two floors in one of its hotels because the company couldn't hire enough housekeepers.

The murmurs of troubles like these have been enough to awaken the hospitality industry leaders to the dimensions of the worker shortage. Employee-short Marriott Corp., for instance, has turned to a variety of nontraditional sources of labor, including people with physical and mental disabilities, homemakers, retirees, minorities, the economically disadvantaged, new immigrants, and workers displaced from their jobs in other industries. But at this point, with worker shortages already building, the transition will not be easy. "You don't need a crystal ball," warns Anthony Marshall, "to predict that as competition for employees becomes more intense, the industry will be forced to offer higher wages and broader benefit packages." If that is the last resort that hotels have for attracting workers, it clearly will be an expensive one.

Not surprisingly, grocery stores, also heavily dependent on entry-level workers, are experiencing labor pains as well. Von's, a major California grocer, couldn't attract enough students to its 16-hour-a-week shifts. In hopes of bringing in homemakers and older workers looking for more substantial income, it doubled the available hours and let employees set their own schedules. The chain is also among the increasing number of grocery outlets using the least expensive means of help-wanted advertising: placing copies of job announcements in shoppers' bags right alongside the chicken and the Cheerios. And, in the logical extension of bar code pricing and electronic scanners, some grocery stores are even experimenting with robot checkers to take the place of their human counterparts. *Store wars* meets *Star Wars*.

At the other end of the food production and distribution process, agricultural growers throughout the country are suffering from worker shortages that threaten crops already plagued by periodic droughts, cold snaps, and union dissent. During the summer of 1988, more than one-third of Oregon's $30 million strawberry crop was left to rot because of a shortage of migrant workers, and Oregon's Governor Neil Goldschmidt predicted that the state could "lose as much as $300 million of [the] $1 billion annual crop of fruits, vegetables, and flowers"— problems that have eased little since then. Also in jeopardy were Michigan's cherry, peach, and apple harvests; North Carolina's tobacco; and Texas' poultry. And in one of California's garlic fields at midseason, *Newsweek* reported, "the only movement was an old collie searching for shade."

Elsewhere, employers in industries ranging from retail to garment making to truck driving are having trouble recruiting workers nationwide. Some 90 percent of the country's long-distance haulers, for instance, have experienced such problems. But the shortages aren't confined to lower-skilled or entry-level positions. The inventory of worker-short professions reads like a career counselor's A-list: scientists, engineers, pilots, nurses, computer systems analysts, corporate managers, accountants, and auditors.

And even in the often bulging skilled manufacturing and construction trades, workers are scarce. "It's unbelievable," says Steven P. Tocco, executive director for the Associated Builders and Contractors'

Massachusetts–Rhode Island chapter. "Open shop or union, there's a shortfall."

Not every industry or region of the country is strapped for workers, of course. Some, like oil and gas in the South and Southwest, remain gripped by recession, with thousands of employees let go, while others, particularly manufacturers in the Rust Belt of the Upper Midwest, are just now recalling large numbers of veteran laborers laid off in the early 1980s.

But these examples increasingly are the exceptions. By now, a large share of the nation's companies, of all sizes and in nearly every major industry, are seeing signs of shrinking job queues and impending recruitment problems. For them, the coming worker shortage is just around the corner. For a growing number of others, however, it is already here.

Workers Who Can't Read, Write, or Count

Unfortunately, there's more to the worker shortage than just a falloff in the *number* of potential employees. Equally troubling is the continuing decline in the *quality* of the American work force. Not only are there too few workers to meet the demand, but there are too few *good* workers as well.

Louis V. Gerstner, Jr., chairman of RJR Nabisco, the food and tobacco conglomerate, is one of the corporate world's most thoughtful advocates of the need for a highly skilled labor force, and what he has found on his travels around the country is anything but encouraging. "Almost every business leader I have talked with," he reports, "has told me that the quality of their potential work force is the most important issue they face."

David T. Kearns, chairman of the Xerox Corp., is one of those business leaders. The shortage of good workers, he says, has all "the makings of a national disaster." James E. Burke, chief executive officer of Johnson & Johnson, sees the problem as "the American dream turned nightmare." Corporate America, says *The New York Times*, "has seen what the nation's schools are producing and it is alarmed."

It's not hard to see why employers might feel this way. Look at some of the skills problems they are confronting:

- In recent years, the New York Telephone Company has had to test as many as 60,000 workers to find just 3000 who were qualified. The Minneapolis, Minnesota, firm Campbell-Mithun Advertising finds that it must interview 20 secretarial and 10 mail clerk applicants to come up with a single worker who is qualified.

- Half a continent away, fully 132 of 187 businesses in high-growth Manchester, New Hampshire, have struggled with serious deficiencies in the quality of their new employees. Nationwide, a 1988 survey by the U.S. Department of Labor found two-thirds of businesses reporting the same difficulties.

- In order to make use of the growing number of underqualified workers in the shrinking teenage labor pool, McDonald's Corp. has had to "deskill" many of its jobs, for instance by putting pictures of food rather than prices on its cash registers. New York's Chemical Bank, burdened with interviewing up to 40 applicants to find a single person qualified even to be *trained* as a teller, has had to let its standards for new workers slip.

- More than one-quarter of the U.S. Army's current recruits are unable to read training manuals written at a seventh-grade reading level. The same is true at Domino's Pizza, which has had to spend $50,000 on reading lessons so that its apprentice bakers can understand dough-making instructions. And IBM had to teach thousands of employees in its Burlington, Vermont, factories basic high school algebra before they could operate a new computer system.

- But forget these higher-order basic skills. A survey by New York's Center for Public Resources found that large numbers of employees in a variety of businesses had difficulty understanding even oral instructions and expressing their ideas. "The frightening part," says Jerry Janka, manager for instructional resources at Motorola, Inc., "is that we're seeing the problem among *all* entry-level applicants. Often, the ones with high school diplomas have the same deficiencies as those without."

These examples are only the first wave of what *Time* magazine has termed the "skills gap"—the growing discrepancy between the demands of the workplace and the capabilities that today's job applicants bring to it. The skills gap is the handmaiden of the shortage in the absolute number of workers. If one or the other problem did not exist, then perhaps the challenges posed would be more bearable or more easily overcome.

But the combination in time of both *quantity* and *quality* deficiencies is an incendiary mixture that threatens the competitive potential of millions of American businesses. It will, without question, cause a great deal of heartache in the next several years for executives, program and personnel managers, entrepreneurs, and workers alike.

David Kearns, the Xerox Corp. CEO and, with Denis Doyle, author of the provocative book *Winning the Brain Race*, is right on target when he warns: "The American work force is in grave jeopardy. We are running out of qualified people. If current demographic and economic trends continue, American business will have to hire a million new workers a year who can't read, write or count."

One could only add: *if they can find them.*

A Scouting Party Report

This book is meant to help you find these workers and, where necessary, "build them" from scratch. It is a scouting party report from the inhospitable territory of the coming labor and skills shortages, designed to show corporate leaders, company planners, personnel officers, small business owners, potential employees—indeed, anyone with a practical interest in working or hiring someone to work—what the employment landscape will look like in the the next decade and how to conquer it.

It's a one-size-fits-all book. Whether your company is a multimillion-dollar electronics firm or a start-up day-care center, a business that's been in the family for three generations or a new manufacturing idea that's still a gleam in your entrepreneurial eye—*Help Wanted* is intended to provide real-world answers and examples that can guide your personnel, training, promotion, and other work-related policies and help you turn the coming worker shortages into an unbeatable competitive edge.

Our message is an optimistic one: there *are* ways of getting—and keeping—good workers, if you're willing to:

- Think creatively.
- Experiment with new and perhaps unfamiliar ideas.
- Give the matter of developing your employees as much attention as acquiring financial capital, raw materials, innovative products, and market share.

But with this optimism, there is also one small warning: *Don't wait too long to start.*

Why *Help Wanted?*

The ideas that inspired *Help Wanted* grew out of a three-year study called *Workforce 2000,* an undertaking described by then Secretary of

Labor William Brock as a "Manhattan Project for skills." In February 1986, the U.S. Department of Labor asked Hudson Institute, a public policy research organization well known for its forecasting studies, to examine the long-term trends in the United States labor force. Bill Johnston, former research director for the New York-based Conference Board, was given the project lead. To help manage the study, he chose Arnold H. Packer, a former assistant secretary of labor, who is also one of the nation's top experts in employment and training policy.

At about the same time, the U.S. Department of Health and Human Services commissioned Hudson Institute to investigate, among other things, the factors that keep poor people from participating more fully in the labor market. One of the current authors (Hopkins) directed this project, and another (Nestleroth) was the principal research assistant. A few miles away, *Help Wanted*'s third author (Bolick) was putting the finishing touches on his own book dealing, in large part, with the employment problems of minority workers.

These events converged in the summer of 1987. Just as Hopkins, Nestleroth, and Bolick were announcing their findings to the public, Johnston and Packer were completing the benchmark volume of *Workforce 2000*, a report that, over the next several months, became a veritable bible for the employer and personnel-management communities. It captured, in the words of *The Futurist* magazine, "worldwide attention among government and private-sector policymakers."

But *Workforce 2000* raised as many questions as it gave answers. Company officials, once recognizing the dramatic labor force changes in store for the next decade, began to ask: *What can we do to prepare?* After hearing these pleas, the Labor Department proposed a follow-up study that would address the issue. Assistant Secretary of Labor Fred W. Alvarez again asked Hudson Institute to do the work, and Hopkins, Nestleroth, and Bolick, in close collaboration with *Workforce 2000*'s Johnston and Packer, took on the chore of cataloging the strategies that more than 150 companies across the country were already putting into place to meet the coming worker shortages.

The product of that effort was a volume called *Opportunity 2000*, which quickly became the Labor Department's guidebook for showcasing innovative worker-recruitment and management strategies and for suggesting how other companies might take advantage of them. It was, in the words of one observer, the "how-to" to *Workforce 2000*'s "what-for."

Help Wanted builds on all of these studies, but it goes one step further. More than just providing general information, it is designed to show employers of all kinds what they can do specifically to survive and *thrive* in the coming worker shortage. To paraphrase Tom Peters, it is more than a how-to or nice-to-do book. It is a must-do manual for companies that wish to remain competitive in the 1990s—and for job applicants who want to know what they should expect of the worker-oriented employer of the future.

And it isn't just theory. *Help Wanted* is intended, more than anything, to be a practical guide for making your way through the coming worker shortages. An investigation into the work force practices of companies that *are* successfully beating the worker and skills shortages, it is meant to serve as a ready resource of strategies that firms can apply in planning for and meeting their own labor force needs. While many of the businesses profiled are large, almost all of their methods can be replicated on a smaller scale or through cooperative ventures.

What's more, these experiences can be an inspiration for all kinds of employers who, in the months and years ahead, will face the same challenges that these other farsighted firms have already begun to overcome.

The Old Ways and the New

These will not be easy times, especially for those companies that are left behind and for those workers who don't take full advantage of the coming opportunities to upgrade their skills. "The years of picky hiring are over," laments Elizabeth Ehrlich, writing in the September 19, 1988, issue of *Business Week,* and she is right. What once was the employer's great luxury has gone the way of leisurely innovation and easy market dominance. Adds Roger Semerad, the former assistant secretary of labor who was *Workforce 2000*'s top government lieutenant, "the labor market will be unlike anything employers have faced in the past." The old ways of recruiting, managing, and promoting employees simply won't do.

Well, so be it. American economic success has never rested on stagnation and smug satisfaction in the past, and there is no reason to expect it to do so in the future. Even if there were no Japan, no South Korea, and no Europe 1992, the economic laurels still would go to the American companies who were first in line with the best ideas and most skillful development of capital. The only difference is that, in the 1990s, corporate capital will have to include every bit as large a share of the human as well as the financial kind.

For executives and managers unused to investing aggressively in people, even for those experienced in the practice, searching for and building up good workers will no longer be a routine journey through familiar terrain, complete with consensus agendas and up-to-the-minute schedules. It will be more like a safari, where success—and survival—go only to those who know intuitively what to expect, where they're going, and how safely to get there.

This book, we hope, will give you a few good ideas where to start.

2
The New Worker

"The signs are everywhere," proclaims business reporter Mark Czarnecki. But it's not just help-wanted signs, those red-and-white placards announcing firms' desperate need for workers. There are also signs of a slowly changing attitude on the part of senior corporate planners and managers toward the impending worker and skills shortages. Clifford Ehrlich, senior vice president for human resources at the Marriott Corp., reflects the insurgent view among corporate executives when he declares that "if today's management thinks that the labor surplus they grew up with will continue, they're in for a shock."

No longer can it be said that it's business as usual for American business; companies all across the country are starting to wake up to the worker crisis that waits just outside their doors.

Waking Up to the Challenge

But waking up to a challenge is one thing. Responding effectively, and in time to beat one's competitors, is a much more difficult chore. There were, for instance, scores of books and articles on the market about Japanese industry's threat to the American economy, as early as Herman Kahn's *The Emerging Japanese Superstate* in 1970, before the implications of the Japanese challenge became common knowledge in the United States.

Still, it took many major American companies more than a decade to streamline their operations and redesign their products before they could meet their more efficient Asian counterparts head-to-head. Other firms still have not adjusted. This is one of the main reasons, as John Naisbitt, Tom Peters, and other godfathers of the corporate restructuring movement have argued, why some once vibrant American industries are in perhaps irreparable decline.

But the original Japanese challenge was largely one of superior organization and production. Belatedly, many American firms are starting to implement some of the techniques—ranging from completely automated manufacturing to just-in-time inventory control, from team production to continuous, short-cycle innovation—that have given Japanese firms such a strong competitive edge. If this transformation has been long in coming, the delays have been due more to companies' resistance to change than to inherent limitations in responding. Imposing a new organizational structure requires far more will than waiting. Even deficiencies in financial capital or raw materials usually can be overcome without undue strain—just look at what Japan has accomplished with essentially no indigenous natural resources.

The same is not true, however, of comparative advantages (or disadvantages) stemming from differences in the quantity or quality of *human* capital. Unlike financial or natural resources, human resources aren't traded on the open market by multinational vendors. Unlike corporate structure, people are highly inflexible entities; their capabilities and dispositions cannot be molded or redesigned at the whim of a board of directors.

And, perhaps most important, unlike other production inputs, even when the number or skills of workers can be increased, these changes cannot be brought about overnight. Inculcating even the most basic "basic skills," such as job-specific literacy or simple math capabilities, can take several weeks to several months. More complex skills, such as technical knowledge in specialized fields or the ability to conceive and communicate abstract ideas, arise only after many years of experience and training.

As a result, companies expecting to face deficiencies in the number and quality of workers at any point during the next decade cannot afford to wait until the moment of crisis before acting. In order to be equipped for the future worker and skills shortages, firms must begin preparing *now* for the changes to come.

A Lesson Learned in Boston

This need to be prepared is a lesson already being learned in the most leading of America's leading edge industries, the computer sector. Route 128 in Boston, the epicenter of the once booming East Coast computer-making industry, was the backbone of the "Massachusetts miracle" in the early 1980s. Now, the February 8, 1989, issue of *The*

Wall Street Journal reports, the arcing highway runs through a "convalescent community of high-tech has-beens."

Not only did they fail to anticipate the consumer demand for smaller computers (a serious bit of shortsightedness in itself), but the firms also fell "victim to [their] own success" by growing faster than local labor markets could keep pace. The combination of labor shortages and inadequate planning for their future work forces left companies with only one hiring alternative—higher wages—which crippled their ability to compete with lower-cost firms on the West Coast and overseas.

If this quick fall from grace could beset such a success-story sector as computers, then the same troubles clearly could visit firms in less glamorous industries where the psychic rewards from work and the public acclaim and interest are less pronounced. Does your company need to worry? The answer is: you do. Virtually every business, in nearly every industry, that plans to employ workers in the 1990s must be concerned about the approaching labor shortages.

This is the newest commandment of corporate life, and it needs to become ingrained in the mind of every executive, every planner, every entrepreneur, and every human resources manager in corporate America: *The worker shortage is coming, it will affect your company, and you either can plan and act ahead of time to preserve your company's strength, or you can wait and, like the computer giants of Route 128, be overwhelmed.*

Put more bluntly, to paraphrase a popular television commercial, you can either pay up now or you can (much more painfully) pay up later.

America's New Workers

To prepare for change, one obviously must understand the nature of the change. Fortunately, it's not hard to assess what the future work force is going to look like. More than 85 percent of people who will be on the job in the year 2000 already are of working age today, and *everybody* who will be available for work over the next decade has already been born.

To see the future, then, one need only walk around a little in the present—to the street corners and playgrounds, the high schools and trade schools, the immigration offices and day-care centers. There, the picture of the future work force becomes clear, and it is a portrait much different from that of the 1950s or 1960s—even from that of the current day.

American Demographics magazine calls them "America's New Workers." Their faces look out from all corners of the *Workforce 2000* portrait. These are the people who will fill up your secretarial pools and hiring halls in the coming decade, the people who will respond to your help-wanted ads and job-fair flyers. They are older. More female. More minority. More apt to be from a foreign country. And fewer in number.

They are part of an accelerating transformation of United States society and the United States economy that, as Bill Johnston and Arnold Packer predict in *Workforce 2000,* "will produce an America that is in some ways unrecognizable from the one that existed only a few years ago."

A number of key trends, in fact, are already apparent. Among them:

1. The population and the work force will grow much more slowly in the years ahead.

2. The number of young workers entering the work force will decline.

3. The average age of the population and the work force will rise.

4. The majority of new entrants into the work force will be women.

5. An increasing number of workers will have dependent-care responsibilities at home.

6. Members of minority groups will account for a much larger share of new work force entrants.

7. More immigrants will enter the work force than at any time in the past 70 years.

8. Worker skill levels will fall short of those demanded by new jobs.

These eight fundamental trends will shape your needs and options in the next decade's labor market and govern whether your firm is able to remain neck and neck with the competition—or will lose out. Here's a closer look at each of them:

1. The Population and the Work Force Will Grow Much More Slowly in the Years Ahead

New England is America's future in a microcosm.

A drug store chain in the region leaves many of its part-time positions unfilled because of a lack of applicants. "There is definitely an employment problem," says the company's corporate vice president for human resources. "It is difficult to have an adequate applicant stream even to fill a [single] job."

A women's sportswear manufacturer in Fall River, Massachusetts, has been turning business away. "I could put 40 people to work today," complains owner Aaron Mittelman, "and when I filled up my empty machines, I'd buy 30 more machines and hire 50 more workers." But the workers are nowhere to be found, even at better-than-average wages.

Adds Gladys Cerruto, president of a sheet-metal plant in nearby Torrington, Connecticut, "I've never seen it as tight as it is now, and we've been in business for 35 years."

These conditions, bad as they are, aren't expected to ease soon, short of a major recession. For instance, looking toward the year 2000, the regional economic forecaster for Nassau and Suffolk Counties on Long Island projects that, for every ten new jobs created on the Island during the period, only four new workers will join the labor force. The reason for these shortages is all too clear: during the years 1970–1980, the population in the Northeastern United States rose by less than 1 percent. This near standstill in population growth translated directly into slowdowns in labor force additions, and, as a result, workers became increasingly—sometimes prohibitively—scarce.

But what has been happening in New England is lying in wait for businesses in much of the rest of the United States. The overall United States population grew by an average of only 1 percent a year during the 1970s and 1980s. That rate will slip to three-quarters of 1 percent a year during the 1990s, falling to a microscopic one-half of 1 percent by the end of the century. By then, there will be a total of 275 million Americans, just 15 percent over the 1985 level, representing the smallest increase in population since the years of the Great Depression.

Why has population growth slowed so much? More than any other factor, the baby boomers simply aren't having many kids. Among adults born in the 1940s and early 1950s, marriages and first children have been postponed and overall family sizes have shrunk. From a high of 3.8 children per woman in 1957, United States fertility in 1972 slipped below the population replacement rate of 2.1 and, in the years since, has averaged only about 1.8.

Blame it on the two-career family, declining real wages, or changing values; it doesn't matter. Fewer births mean fewer people.

Predictably, these population patterns will spill over into the work force. The total number of workers between the years 1985 and 2000 will climb by about 22 percent, from 115 million to 141 million people, less than two-thirds of the rise during the previous 15-year period. As a result, there will be comparatively fewer people added to the work force than at any time since the 1930s.

The bottom line is enough to sends shivers down the spine of any employer who plans to be on the lookout for new workers in this decade: There will be 10 million *fewer* people entering the work force in the 1990s than in the 1970s, and this in an economy twice as big as in the 1970s.

2. The Number of Young Workers Entering the Work Force Will Decline

Youth is filled with its rites of passage: driver's licenses, sexual initiations, graduations, and, of course, first real jobs. Although teenagers' lives vary markedly depending on where they grow up, their first jobs almost all seem to have one characteristic in common: they pay the minimum wage.

Strange thing, though. The minimum wage isn't the minimum anymore.

Though scheduled to rise to $4.25 an hour by April 1991, up from $3.35 an hour that had been in force since 1981, the nationwide minimum wage has become almost irrelevant for many of the most common entry-level jobs. For instance:

- Burger King and other fast-food outlets in Massachusetts often pay up to $7 an hour for starting help, and jobs go begging.

- A steak house chain in Atlanta is offering $4.50 an hour for busboys.

- The Sheraton Needham Hotel in Boston must pay hotel service workers between $6 and $7 an hour.

- Farm workers' wages in some parts of the West and Upper Midwest have climbed to $6 an hour, nearly 30 percent above the norm.

The official minimum wage, in other words, is increasingly being replaced with a wage set by shrinking supply and rising demand. As Robert Zagami, president of the Needham, Massachusetts, firm Information Technology, Inc., wryly notes, "the minimum wage in Massachusetts is whatever McDonald's is paying this week."

When Young Workers Disappear. This change in the wage structure of entry-level jobs has a little to do with the worker shortage in general and a lot to do with a very critical component of the shortage: the growing scarcity of *young* workers. Among all demographic groups, youth and young adults are the shortest in supply. The country, as Keith McKnight puts it, is "running out of kids."

This should come as little surprise to anyone who has been watching developments in major school systems. Between 1970 and 1980, the number of grade-schoolers fell by 15 percent and, by the end of the decade, the same thing was starting to happen among high school students. As a result, as long ago at the late 1970s, school districts had started laying teachers off and schools in a number of metropolitan areas were closing down or consolidating.

Now, that retrenchment has hit the labor force, and its effects will be felt for a generation. The decline in the number of teenagers available for work is most obvious because labor shortages started among this group first and were already apparent by the onset of the 1980s. These reductions will continue through 1992, during which time the total of teens aged 16 to 19 will have dropped by 1.5 million.

Still to come are even larger falloffs in the number of workers aged 20 to 29, the pool of young people that firms most frequently dip into for new hires. According to projections from the U.S. Bureau of Labor Statistics, the number of workers aged 20 to 24 will fall by 2.4 million between 1986 and 1997 before starting to rise again, while the number of workers aged 25 to 29 will decline by 2.9 million, a drop that will persist through the year 2000.

This dwindling supply of young workers will have a number of immediate effects. Among them, according to the *Workforce 2000* team:

- Companies that have depended in the past upon younger workers for quick expansion will be unable to rapidly enlarge their work forces to respond to new market openings.

- Large-scale entrepreneurship will grow problematic, and the "overnight creation of a Federal Express, an MCI, or an Apple Computer Company may become much more difficult" if not impossible in some circumstances.

- "Creative destruction," in which a company uses aggressive, just-hired young people to start up a new corporate unit while retiring older workers in a sunset division, may no longer be cost efficient.

- Young workers' wages will rise across-the-board, in the unskilled as well as the highly skilled job categories.

Perhaps more than any other work force trend, this "disappearance" of 1 in every 6 young adults from the labor market will force employers and would-be entrepreneurs to plan ahead. After all, the only way to hire workers who aren't there is to look elsewhere—and to find these new sources of labor before the competition does.

Be that as it may, from the workers' point of view at least, there *is* one happy side to this problem. As Northwestern University economist Andrew Sum notes, "just about every kid who wants a job" will be able to find one. For any young person with determination and training in the 1990s, the career ladder will be that much easier to climb aboard.

3. The Average Age of the Population and the Work Force Will Rise

As smaller cohorts of young people are entering the working-age population, the ranks of the middle- and older-age groups will swell. Between now and the end of the century, while the 20- to 29-year-old group will shrink by 17 percent, the number of people aged 35 to 47 will climb by 38 percent and the number between the ages of 48 and 53 will jump by 67 percent.

As might be expected, similar developments will take place in the labor force. During the years 1985–2000, the number of workers aged 35 to 54 will rise by as much as 25 million people—a sum equal to all the net additions to the work force projected to take place before the end of the century. The average age of the work force also will climb, reaching a median of 39 years by the year 2000. Hudson Institute's Bill Johnston fittingly terms this development the "middle-aging of the work force."

There is good reason to expect that this "middle-aging" not only will open up new opportunities for workers wanting to change professions at midcareer but also will help clear away at least some of the worries about worker shortages. Examples of senior citizens staying on the job, even going back to work once they have retired, abound:

- Dan Wheeler, a 71-year-old retiree, has enthusiastically taken up the job of fast-food merchant at an Akron, Ohio, McDonald's.
- Sixty-three-year-old Hank Siewert, also once retired, is back in the job market as a shoe salesman for the California department store chain Mervyn's.
- Albert B. Putnam, 66, who was a supervisor in the brake-and-steering unit of Bendix Corp. before a heart condition forced him to leave this demanding job, is now back at work as a part-time checker in Martin's Super Markets in South Bend, Indiana.
- Leon Levitt, 81, was retired only six months from his job as a salesman before he returned to a new career as a trainee machinist, meanwhile cutting back his weekly hours from 55 to a mere 49.

Clearly, in the right circumstances, older workers can fill in many of the gaps left by the shrinkage of the younger-aged work force. But two important considerations need to be kept in mind. One is that while some older persons want to remain on the job, others—many others, in fact—do not. This is especially true among older men. Between the years 1972 and 2000, the proportion of men aged 55 to 64 who are part of the labor force will decline from 80 to 63 percent, a drop of more than one-fifth. For men 65 or over, the expected falloff is even greater, from 24 to 10 percent. Just because there are more older people in the population theoretically available for work does not mean they will be actively seeking jobs, or even that they readily will accept a position if it is offered.

A second consideration is that many older workers may be less willing or less able to adapt to fast-paced changes in technology or to take the risks necessary for rapid company growth. For example, an older worker may resist relocation because it would mean the disruption of long-established community ties; this is one reason why older workers are only about one-third as likely to transfer as younger ones. A middle-aged person who has spent a number of years in a given occupation also may face difficulties in switching careers and is, again, just one-third as likely to make this change as a younger person.

None of this diminishes the importance of the role older workers will play in alleviating the coming labor force shortages, says Dr. Marjorie Honig, an economics professor at New York City's Hunter College and a respected expert on demographic trends. But making the best use of this group of workers will be neither as easy nor as automatic as employing the overabundant supply of younger workers has been in the past. As with beating labor shortages in general, making the "older worker" option work will require companies to devote a great deal more effort—and creativity—to planning ahead.

4. The Majority of New Entrants Into the Work Force Will Be Women

Any American who owned a television set in the 1950s and 1960s would recognize the All-American family portrayed on such domestic comedies as *The Adventures of Ozzie and Harriet, Leave It to Beaver, Father Knows Best,* and *The Donna Reed Show.* Father worked in an office while Mother stayed back at the house to raise two or three clean-cut youngsters and to take care of the family's suburban home. While this scenario by no means described conditions in every household, it did reflect the lives of a majority of American women: fewer than 35 percent worked outside the home in 1950 and fewer than 40 percent did so in 1960.

But the situation has changed markedly over the last two decades. Between the years 1965 and 1988, the proportion of women in the civilian labor force rose from 39 to 57 percent. Even more astounding has been the increase in labor market participation by younger women: by the mid-1980s, among women aged 20 to 30, more than 80 percent were in the labor force.

These trends will persist, and in some respects will accelerate, for the rest of the century. Between 1985 and 2000, white males, who only a generation ago were the dominant demographic group in the labor market, will account for but 1 of every 7 net *additions* to the work force—a mere 15 percent.

The vast majority of new entrants, by contrast, will be women, some two-thirds of all new workers through the early 1990s. All told, the number of women in the labor force will rise by 25 percent, representing 13 million new workers—a rate of growth twice as fast as that among men. By the year 2000, women will account for 47 percent of the work force and 61 percent of all American women will be employed outside the home.

Obviously, these women will play a critical role in helping companies to prosper amidst the coming worker shortages. Notes Lotus Development Corporation's Sandra Gunn, who has started two divisions in her first four years with the company, "When you're growing at 500 percent a year, you grab whoever walks in the door who can get the work done."

But as with older workers, the switch won't be automatic. For instance, much higher percentages of the available women employees are already at work now than was the case just a decade or two ago. As Samuel Preston, director of the University of Pennsylvania's Population Studies Center, points out, the rates of increase of new female entrants into the work force has been slowing in recent years and will stabilize sometime in the 1990s. Thus, he says, women workers "will take up some of the slack, but not all."

There is also the matter of preferences. A recent Gallup poll yielded some disturbing findings for employers expecting a surge of women to replace the declining cohorts of white male and young labor market entrants on their payrolls. According to the survey, among women with children (the largest share of the potential female work force):

- Only 13 percent wanted to hold full-time jobs with regular hours (even though more than half were doing so).
- Three-fifths wanted only part-time work.
- One in six preferred having no paid employment.
- Only one-half felt they adequately could meet their responsibilities to their children if they worked full-time.

All the same, women still will account for the overwhelming majority of new workers. But employers looking to women to fill in the gaps in their work forces will have to be diligent in devising ways to make work (especially full-time work) an attractive and rewarding option for those women who would rather be on the job only part-time or not at all. Perhaps most important, employers will need to make clear that women who make these sacrifices will have the same chance of moving into fast-track careers that men have enjoyed for so long.

5. An Increasing Number of Workers Will Have Dependent-Care Responsibilities at Home

There is another side to the story that more women are working: as indicated, more mothers are working as well. By the mid-1980s:

- Fully 61 percent of all women with children were in the labor force, more than twice the 1960 level of 28 percent.

- Of all mothers of children under age 6, 54 percent held jobs outside the home, up from 19 percent in 1960.

- For women with children 3 years old or younger, more than one-half were in the work force, compared to only one-third a decade earlier.

Who Will Care for the Children?   With developments like these, it shouldn't be surprising, as the *Workforce 2000* team forecasts, that "day care, like health care during the 1970s, will claim a rising share of national income" or that adequate provision of day care, as former U.S. Secretary of Labor Ann McLaughlin has repeatedly argued, will become one of the top work force issues of the 1990s.

A recent poll by the Wilmington, Delaware, Du Pont Co. of more than 4000 of its 100,000 workers, in fact, gave a strong hint of how widespread this concern has already become. The survey revealed that:

- One-fourth of Du Pont employees require some form of child care to enable them to work.

- Most workers with children in day care report difficulties finding adequate infant care, after-school and summer care, and care compatible with their work hours.

- From two-thirds to three-fourths of employees consider child-care centers near their place of work and extended sick leave for children's illnesses to be "very important" job determinants.

- More than 1 in 5 workers overall—and some 2 in 5 women executives—who use child care stay away from jobs that involve travel or relocation.

- One-fourth of the men and about one-half of the women have "considered seeking a job with another employer who might offer more flexibility at work or in family matters."

Who Will Care for Mom and Dad?   But child care is only the obvious partner in the onrush of dependent-care duties facing the new work force. Less frequently mentioned, but often more taxing, is the need to provide daily assistance and supervision for elderly parents and grandparents.

An article in the January 27, 1989, edition of *The Wall Street Journal* offers poignant evidence of this changing aspect of family responsibilities. It cites the tribulations of three otherwise ordinary families whose often desperate burden is having to care for one or more infirm relatives. Perhaps most heartbreaking is the story of Patricia and Laurence Brady of Mahopac, New York. In their home, the late-30s couple must look after a 93-year-old grandmother with congestive heart failure and other illnesses requiring constant attention, a 65-year-old mother afflicted with emphysema and clinical depression, and a paralyzed 4-year-old son. Mrs. Brady admits, "I am hanging on by my fingernails."

Unfortunately, reports *The Journal,* such arrangements are no longer the exceptions. According to one estimate, 2 out of every 5 workers over age 40 now provide in-home care to one or more parents. These totals undoubtedly will build as the population continues to age and as medical advances add to people's longevity without producing equal victories in the battle against infirmity.

Just as clearly, these elder-care responsibilities, like those for children's day care, will affect the flexibility and productivity of the future work force in ways far more pervasive than most employers appreciate. *Business Week* magazine reports that "a growing body of research links employees' concerns for the care of...elderly relatives with productivity losses from increased absences, tardiness, and stress on the job—and such time-wasters as excessive use of the phone."

A study by the Employee Benefit Research Institute discovered that between 12 and 30 percent of all workers—predominantly women— have resigned their jobs for just this reason. Even of those who don't quit, some one-quarter either reduce their work hours, convert to part-time status, or take extended leaves of absence.

To date, most companies do not appear to have kept pace with this need. As Assistant Secretary of Labor Roberts T. Jones wrote in mid-1988, "many of our workplace policies were designed when men worked and women stayed at home....Because these policies do not, for the most part, address continuing family responsibilities, they may act as disincentives to women to enter the work force." The Du Pont poll rather pointedly suggests, in fact, that workers who do not receive what they want from employers in terms of dependent-care assistance and on-the-job flexibility may move to a company that better meets these concerns.

One corporate executive, who has been watching this problem for several years, is even more blunt: "The new workers will not be shy about asking for changes," he says, "and if we don't provide them, they will vote with their feet and go elsewhere.... The Depression doesn't scare them like it did their parents. They want a balance between jobs and family, and they'll move around until they find it."

6. Members of Minority Groups Will Account for a Much Larger Share of New Work Force Entrants

It's becoming more than a little ironic to talk about the participation of minority group members in the next decade's work force. Between now and the end of the century, the traditional American minorities, especially blacks and Hispanics, will be less of a minority in the workplace than ever before.

Together, members of these groups will represent almost one-third (29 percent) of all new entrants into the labor force—nearly *twice* the share of work force growth accounted for by the traditionally majority white males. That's their largest proportion of new worker cohorts in the country's history and double their current representation in the work force.

About one-third of these new minority employees will be black, raising their numbers in the labor force from 12.4 million in 1985 to 16.3 million by the year 2000. That's an annual growth rate of 1.8 percent, nearly double the white labor force growth rate of 1 percent. Among Hispanics, the rate of increase will be even faster, with the number of workers rising from 7.7 million in 1985 to 14.1 million in 2000. That represents an annual growth rate of 4.1 percent, more than 4 times the white rate.

The main reason blacks and Hispanics will form such a large contingent of the new work force is that their populations are growing so fast, both through births and (especially for Hispanics) immigration. For instance, between the years 1970 and 1984, the black population increased by 15.8 percent, compared with an 8.3 percent growth rate for whites, and this trend is expected to continue through the end of the century. Recent Census Bureau calculations also show that the Hispanic population in the United States has been growing 5 times as fast as the non-Hispanic population, another trend that is expected to persist for some time.

Help for the Disadvantaged. With these numbers, however, come some severe problems that companies will have to address. Most minority job applicants are well-educated and well-trained. Despite impressive gains in educational attainment in recent years, however, many minority workers continue to suffer from severe economic or social disadvantages that may hinder them in moving into many of the next decade's new jobs. Among the most serious problems:

- An increasing share of minority youth are born into poverty, often growing up in home environments where, in the critical first 5 years of life, there is inadequate attention to and resources for learning.

- Schools often may not compensate for these slow starts. Minority children are more heavily concentrated in troubled inner-city schools that often provide poor quality education. Moreover, minority high school dropout rates continue to be in the steep double digits, as high as 40 or 50 percent in some urban areas.

- Many inner-city minority kids grow up in neighborhoods where activities such as crime and drug dealing abound, and these activities are often more attractive and profitable than education and work. As one inner-city gang member told *Business Week,* "Fast-food places aren't paying enough, not for what they want you to do." But, the magazine's report concluded, the "lucrative alternatives—drug dealing, pimping, and theft—have no shortage of recruits...."

- Even among high school graduates, the increases in the number of minority youths entering college have stalled in recent years.

The news is not entirely negative, of course, as minority workers are succeeding in the job market as never before. One recent Bureau of Labor Statistics report, for instance, found that "across all broad categories, job growth in the 1980s has been more rapid for minority workers—blacks and persons of Hispanic origin—than for whites. Much of the employment increase since 1983, especially among minority workers, has been concentrated in managerial and professional specialty occupations."

Still, these bright spots cannot erase the difficulties business will have to confront. Even with worker shortages, many barriers to work will remain—barriers that employers will have to help job applicants overcome—if they want to turn disadvantaged minority group members into members of their work force.

7. More Immigrants Will Enter the Work Force Than at Any Time in the Past 70 Years

As the destination of choice for those seeking economic opportunity or political refuge, the United States has always been a nation of immigrants. This is as true in the late twentieth century as it was in the early

1900s, when millions of European refugees crossed the ocean to begin new lives. A 1986 report on the state of American society by an international group of scholars summed up the situation this way: "America's biggest import is people."

These trends continue, but their character is sharply changing. Europeans dominated the immigration rolls for more than half a century, turning New York's Ellis Island into a transatlantic symbol of opportunity and open shores. Even during the 1960s, when some 3.2 million immigrants legally entered the country, 40 percent were from Europe. Recent immigrants, however, have been overwhelmingly non-European; since the mid-1970s, more than 85 percent have come from either Latin America or Asia. The last time a European country was even in the top five as a source of immigrants was 1973.

The absolute numbers are changing too. All told, between the years 1970 and 1980, the foreign-born population of the United States increased by about 4.5 million. But this is only a small prelude to what lies in store. Through the year 2000, legal immigration should add about 9.5 million persons to the population and some 4 million to the labor force.

If illegal immigration also continues at the recent rates of about 750,000 people a year (a strong possibility despite the new immigration law), more than 16.1 million foreign-born persons will join the United States population and 6.8 million will join the work force. That means that legal immigrants alone will account for nearly one-quarter of all new workers—and immigrants altogether almost *half* of all new workers if illegal entrants are added in.

The Impact of Immigration.   Following the patterns of settlement established during the last decade, the effects of immigration will be felt most acutely in a few distinct parts of the country. Between the years 1970 and 1980, the number of foreign-born persons taking up residence in the cities of the South rose by 120 percent, and in the West by 97 percent. By contrast, in the North and Midwest these totals increased by only about 10 percent. In fact, three states—California, Texas, and New York—accounted for *one-half* of all new foreign-born residents, and fully 1 in 5 settled in the Los Angeles area. These geographic distributions should change little in the 1990s.

Nor will all immigrants affect employers in identical ways. Current immigrants represent a wide range of social and educational backgrounds. As many as 22 percent of the adults who entered the United States in the 1970s were college graduates, compared with only 16 percent of adults native to America; yet 25 percent of the immigrants had fewer than five years of schooling, versus a mere 3 percent for the native-born. Other problems also may confront employers faced with the option of hiring either new immigrants or nobody at all:

- Many of the entrants from Latin America and Asia come from the poorest areas of these regions and so may carry with them the social and economic disadvantages that hold back many minority group members already in the United States.

- A large number of young immigrants are not well prepared to learn English, a requirement for most jobs and certainly for advancement to better jobs. As of 1980, a U.S. Census Bureau survey revealed that 1 out of 10 families spoke a language other than English at home, and that percentage has undoubtedly increased since then.

- This lack of familiarity with English takes its toll on literacy. One estimate indicates that of United States residents whose native language is not English, almost one-half are functionally illiterate.

These problems notwithstanding, most immigrants appear to share a strong determination to improve their lives, and it is not uncommon to see new residents holding down two or three low-paying jobs at once. "No matter how hard it is," says a Cambodian refugee who works at two janitorial jobs, "it's not hard for me. I worked in a communist labor camp from morning until it was so dark you couldn't see the ground anymore."

The owner of a custodial service in Reston, Virginia, began hiring Central and South American immigrants when she couldn't find teenagers to fill the jobs. "Before, people quit for the same reasons you or I would quit: the work is boring, demeaning, and all those things you don't want in a job." But she notes that most of the people she hires now are trying desperately to better themselves. "I know many of them are thinking, 'I don't want to be a janitor for the rest of my life.' But this is a start."

The Corporate Response.   Among those looking for such a start may lie one of American business' greatest hopes for beating the worker shortage. For instance:

- In an industry in which 300,000 positions nationwide are unfilled, hospitals have started actively seeking out 20,000 foreign-born nurses to place in empty job slots.

- A Hyatt Hotel in Connecticut is investing thousands of dollars in training promising dishwashers to speak English as a second language because it can't find enough English-speaking workers to do the job.

- Southland Corp., the parent company of the 7-11 convenience store chain, is considering setting up similar arrangements with local community colleges for its English-deficient employees.

- And some companies can't wait. A language-training firm in Boston has had to drastically cut back its help to area businesses because so many worker-strapped firms have been willing to take on immigrant job applicants *regardless* of whether they can speak any English.

Stories like these are apt to become commonplace over the next decade as employers begin to translate their help-wanted signs into Spanish, Korean, Arabic, and Vietnamese. But more than a few foreign words will be required. Companies will have to be ready to make some fundamental changes in the way they hire workers, train them, and integrate them into the workplace. Successful corporate strategies built on an immigrant work force will have to be just as diversified as the people they are meant to serve.

8. Worker Skill Levels Will Fall Short of Those Demanded by New Jobs

Jeffrey Kovach tells a story that reveals more than it should about the quality of the next decade's work force. A businessman was visiting the downtown Burger King where he regularly ate lunch. But the lines this day were long and slow even by normal noontime standards. It wasn't until he reached the counter that he discovered the culprit: broken cash registers, the "deskilled" kind with pictures of food instead of prices, had forced the young cashiers to take orders and total bills on old-fashioned pencil-and-paper order pads.

The businessman ordered his usual—a Whopper with cheese, large fries, a cherry pie, and a medium Coke—and then watched as the young clerk "began scribbling indecipherable figures" on the pad, "pausing every so often to check, then double-check the prices" on the big board behind her. At last came her verdict: "A dollar fifty," she said convincingly.

"What a deal," the customer thought as he quickly paid up. "Buy one Whopper, get everything else free."

Misadventures like this—an increasingly frequent occurrence in businesses from fast-food to finance—might be funny on a Saturday night sitcom. But at the heart of the American economy, they're striking fear into executives whose main concerns not too many years ago were only fickle consumers and upstart Japanese competitors. Confesses the former president of one of the nation's top financial services firms: "I lie awake at night wondering where I'm going to find well-qualified employees for the future."

Indeed, the skills crisis and the literacy gap could not come at a worse time. Not only is there a growing shortage of workers, but the jobs that will be available will demand a much broader range of capabilities than they have in the past. Whereas the great bulk of entry-level jobs in the years immediately after World War II required only a fourth-grade reading level, most of those today demand an eighth-grade reading level as a bare minimum—and usually can't be done well without an eleventh- or twelfth-grade capacity. Nor is even a high school diploma enough; many firms look for two years of college just to let an applicant in the door.

Consider how even some of the simplest jobs are changing:

- Assembly line work used to be rote, monotonous, and almost completely without challenge. Now, workers in many manufacturing plants are being forced to learn statistical process control, a method of tracking inventory and output that is beyond the reach of those without a solid grasp of mathematics. Factory employees "need to think sequentially," notes the former operations manager at New Jersey's Wheaton Plastics, a firm that has sharply cut production costs with the new techniques. "Before the advanced technology," he says, "they didn't need to think as much."

- Insurance companies used to hire high school dropouts to process insurance claims, another rote task. Now, with computerization eliminating most of the routine aspects of the job, claims adjusters must have good communications skills, make judgment calls on unique claims issues, and be able to marshal information from a wide range of sources.

- Even Federal Express couriers are no longer mere messengers, but delivery managers. They must be able to operate the company's new computerized tracking system and often make spur-of-the-moment decisions on the most efficient ways to complete their rounds, chores that require higher-order basic skills. School dropouts and others who lack these faculties simply don't last.

These changes are being replicated in industry after industry and job after job. But for all that's happened so far, much is yet to come. Today, workers in almost 1 out of every 5 jobs still can get by with less than a high school education; in the next decade, they will be able to do so in only 1 of 7 jobs. The least educated workers will be eligible for only about 1 in 25 new jobs, dramatically fewer than the 1 in 11 they can qualify for today. And while only a little more than 1 in 4 jobs now require a college degree, that number will rise to nearly 1 in 3 during the 1990s.

And not just math and reading skills are involved. The Congressional Office of Technology Assessment has identified a number of less tangible skills that will become increasingly important for success in the decentralized, team-production, people-oriented jobs of the future:

1. A capacity for judgment and evaluation.
2. The ability to spot problems.
3. Social skills, including working well with others and the ability to communicate clearly about job tasks.
4. The ability to think abstractly.
5. A capacity for understanding and employing innovative concepts.

For inadequately trained workers and the employers looking to hire them, the implications of these changes are enough to cause many lost nights of sleep. All told, according to the U.S. Census Bureau, only 1 million new jobs will come about in the lowest skill and laborer categories, while more than 6 million will be created for those with executive, professional, and technical talents. And even most of the lower-skilled jobs that *are* produced will require workers who at least can read and understand written instructions, add and subtract, and express themselves clearly.

Where Are the "Work-Ready" Workers?   Will tomorrow's workers be up to the test? Not if current trends are any indication. Even now, complains Dr. James D. Howell, chief economist of the Bank of Boston, "work-ready high school graduates just don't exist." Not to mention nongraduates. Says William H. Kohlberg, president of the National Alliance of Business, during the next 10 to 15 years, a growing contingent of young adults will have been so poorly educated and trained that they will lack the skills "to obtain even their first entry-level job."

As much as businesses will be hurt by these developments, the workers themselves may fare even worse. If people are not qualified for tomorrow's new jobs, they may not find rewarding employment—the kind that trains them, motivates them, and lifts them out of poverty— no matter how severe the labor shortage becomes. The result, in the words of syndicated columnist Doug Bandow, author of *Human Resources and Defense Manpower*, would be an "increasingly competitive race for economic advancement in which half a generation of kids are left stranded at the starting line."

If that sounds like an exaggeration, you haven't been reading the papers lately.

- As many as 900,000 high school students drop out of school each year. That means between 25 and 30 percent of the kids who start school don't make it to graduation. By contrast, the dropout rate in Japan is a paltry 5 percent.

- Barely one-half of those who *do* graduate go on to college—and fewer still finish all four years.

- Anywhere from 17 million to 27 million American adults are functionally illiterate—meaning they read below an eighth-grade level—accounting for some 10 to 15 percent of the adult population. Another 45 million are only marginally literate. All told, says Jonathan Kozol, author of *Illiterate America,* we're adding 2.5 million functional illiterates to the work force each year. In contrast, adult illiteracy rates in Great Britain, West Germany, Canada, France, Japan, and Korea are no higher than 3 percent.

- American youngsters' capabilities in mathematics are even more deficient. The "Mathematics Report Card" issued by the National Assessment of Educational Progress reveals that nearly one-half of the 17-year-olds in the United States cannot solve *junior high* math problems, more than one-quarter can't perform *elementary school* math work, and less than one-tenth (only 6 percent) can solve problems that require algebra or several steps of reasoning. Compared to the rest of the industrialized world, these achievement levels are positively dismal. In one global algebra test, United States students scored fourteenth out of the 15 countries' students who were tested. A more recent survey showed American 13-years-olds finishing dead last in math and science. Against high schoolers from Japan, American students test two to three years behind in these subjects.

- The skills shortfalls aren't limited to book learning either. A Department of Labor survey noted that the talents new workers lacked most often included oral communication, flexibility and adaptability, problem solving, self-direction and initiative, and positive attitudes and work habits. These deficiencies are so severe, says Education Secretary Lauro F. Cavazos, that as many as one-half of the students entering the job market will not be able to benefit from on-the-job training.

- Nor are skills deficits confined to the young. According to one estimate, 25 million current workers of all ages will need to have their skills upgraded to remain productive employees during the next decade. That's more than one-fifth of the labor force and includes up to 40 percent of the workers displaced from their jobs because of industrial restructuring, a process that's bound to intensify in the 1990s.

"If Trends Like These Persist..."

Frightening stuff. But these are the parameters of tomorrow's work force. In some respects, they may have been easy to ignore so far, if for no other reason than the fact that employers have not had to dig very deeply into the queue to find ample numbers of workers for the job. Education Secretary Cavazos concedes that, even after a decade of attention to the defects in the United States educational system, the country still "has not recognized the severity of the problem."

But no longer; the coming worker shortages will take care of that. Even when new workers can be found, large majorities will have "skills deficiencies" red-stamped across their résumés. Before matters get worse, farsighted employers will have taken the steps necessary to bring their job applicants' skills up to par—and will have taken the lead in ensuring that the capabilities of America's youth never fall this far again.

There is, of course, an alternative: simply wait and let matters continue as they are. But it's certainly not the wisest solution. As Jule M. Sugarman, former director of Operation Head Start, recently told the Joint Economic Committee of the United States Congress, "There isn't going to *be* a work force, a productive work force, in this country" if trends like these persist.

3

The Work Force Revolution

In 1989, Stan Stephens had a problem. He needed people. *Lots* of people. Try 12,000.

Stephens is not an ordinary employer, though. In fact, he's not an employer at all, but a politician. A pleasant, plainspoken man, he is the governor of Montana, and he spent the year looking for new citizens.

The 1990 census was coming, and Montana was faced with the humiliation of being reduced to a single congressional district. Over the previous decade, Montana's population had increased, but more slowly than in most other states, making it possible that the state could lose one of its two seats in Congress. The fact that, if the redistricting axe did fall, Montana's would be the most populous congressional district in the country was hardly any consolation.

To avoid this prospect, several prominent Montanans began making public appeals to residents of other states, inviting them to move to Montana. If they would just come out here, Governor Stephens insisted, "they would fall in love with this place in a minute." Some state legislators (not entirely in jest) even suggested that "this would be a perfect time for Montana families to have more children."

In 1989, the state's people shortage was mainly a political problem, although there were scattered labor shortfalls even here in the small-town wilderness of the Northwest. But Stephens and his fellow Montanans were learning a powerful demographic lesson that transcends politics, and it is one that's bound to shock their unprepared counterparts in corporate America during the 1990s: *People are power.*

In an economy in which labor surpluses have been as bountiful as new markets, it has been easy for many businesses to forget this fact.

33

But it is one that, as Stan Stephens would gladly remind them, they had better start remembering—and fast.

Rx: The Management Revolution

If this emphasis on "the power of people" seems an odd message for business, it's easy to see why. In the modern age, the corporate competition appears to be governed by so much more than the people who comprise the company work force: global marketing strategies, leveraged buyouts, debt-to-equity ratios, international subsidiaries, the latest-generation technology. Pick up any copy of *Business Week, Fortune,* or the *Financial Times,* and the warnings will be right there. If you're not on top in all of these areas, say the trend watchers, not much else matters.

By now, in fact, such warnings about the staying power of American firms may have even grown a bit old hat. But with the burgeoning trade deficit, the shakedowns in the auto and electronics industries, and the rusting out of the Rust Belt, they seem no less urgent. To turn this situation around, a small army of politicians and academics has exhorted American companies to rush headlong into adopting the Japanese corporate model of discipline, cooperation, and work for work's sake. Others, most recently *Atlantic Monthly* editor Jim Fallows, have argued that we need only be "more like us" and stress traditional American values.

But no matter. The message is clear: if U.S. corporations are to continue prospering, they must change the way they operate, and quickly.

Tom Peters, one of the nation's foremost advocates of managerial change and restructuring, goes furthest of all in his proposed course for corporate revival. A revolution must take place, he declares, one that "challenges everything we thought we knew about managing, and often challenges over a hundred years of American tradition." Companies must begin to "love change," he says. They must become decentralized, they must become flexible, and they must learn to "thrive on chaos."

Peters is surely right. In the wake of ever more vigorous competitors from overseas, and the downsized, flattened-out corporations and start-up ventures at home, the company that stands still will not last long. As Peters cautions, "the rate of change demanded [by this management revolution] will be unfailingly new—and frightening." And so, too, must be the corporate response.

Study any management guide's list of recommendations—from self-management teams to structural reorganization, from "intrepreneuring" to incentive rewards—and this theme will emerge in big, bold letters. Companies, managers are told, must become agents of adaptability and change. The new credo is this simple: *The company that succeeds in an era of change will be the one that adapts more rapidly and effectively than its competitors.*

The Management Revolution Falls Short

No doubt this capacity to adapt will be critical to a firm's ability to maintain, carve out, or expand market share in the 1990s. *But will it be enough?*

The answer, almost certainly, is no. Corporate restructuring, flexibility, and organizational innovations are designed to meet a number of important objectives:

- Speed the pace of internal technological development.
- Create products and ideas for filling new market niches.
- Respond to or preempt competitors' marketing strategies.
- Move quickly to take advantage of new trade opportunities.
- Reduce overhead, lower production and distribution costs, and increase efficiency.
- Motivate employees to work harder and better.

As wide-ranging as these objectives are, they have one feature in common: they assume that the resources—for innovation, for production, for marketing—are already in place. They are strategies for managing existing resources better rather than for acquiring new ones.

That's hardly a trivial matter, of course, since these strategies *can* give firms a tremendous competitive advantage. For instance, the same set of machines in a factory can be organized into a production process that is either more efficient, like some team-production assembly lines, or less efficient, like some assembly lines in which each worker performs the same repetitive task for eight hours a day. A firm that chooses the more efficient arrangement for its production facilities obviously will have a significant edge in creating a better product, in a shorter time, and at a lower price.

But this may not always be such an easy option. Consider the same firm, and assume that its high production costs and slow turnaround time are due, not to faulty organization, but to a die-cutting machine that produces only eight usable parts an hour. In this case, *no* rearrangement of the assembly line will boost production to 16 or 24 parts an hour. The firm's adaptability and flexibility—its management's love for change—will be irrelevant to its achieving a competitive advantage.

To increase its productivity, the company has only one choice: it will have to invest in a new, more capable machine.

Although less often recognized, the same principle applies to people as well. Clearly, companies can use new and improved management styles to get the most out of their current work forces. Most employees perform better, and more diligently, if they feel they are respected, are listened to, and have a say in the company's operations. Hence the library of popular volumes over the past decade on how to better manage people for productivity—from the folksy *One-Minute Manager* to the 45-point, step-by-step recommendations of *Thriving on Chaos*.

Still, general management improvements are not always enough. No matter how inspiring the manager, workers cannot be motivated beyond their capacities. A job that requires complex, statistical calculations, for instance, cannot be carried out by an employee who can barely add and subtract, regardless of how well motivated he or she might be. Or if 30 workers are needed for a production shift, even the most creative manager will have trouble getting the job done if no more than 10 workers sign up.

Unlike a company that is suffering from equipment problems, however, a labor-short firm cannot merely "buy" the new workers it needs. In the past, when labor surpluses were abundant, help-wanted ads usually did prove sufficient for filling in gaps in the company work force, and so it may have seemed that "purchasing" new employees was as easy a matter as purchasing new equipment.

But when the workers are not there, as often will be the case in the 1990s, *they simply are not there*; "suppliers" of human capital cannot create more workers merely by opening up a new production line. A firm's only option at that time, when the moment of shortage has arrived, may be to dramatically raise wages. While this might pull in a few more workers, especially from other companies, the costs to a firm's competitive position could be severe, even ruinous—as the computer industry giants of Massachusetts' Route 128 have found out.

This is where the management revolution, for all its potential, falls short. While designed to make the best use of a company's resources, such strategies are only half the answer. They offer little guidance for situations in which the critical resources—*people* resources, in particular—are not in place. Yet in the competition of the 1990s, acquiring these people resources may be firms' most urgent need of all.

An Equal Partner: The Work Force Revolution

Thus, for the management revolution to work, it will need some help. Its equal partner must be a *work force revolution,* one that, to paraphrase Tom Peters, challenges everything we thought we knew about finding, training, and keeping good workers. Employers no longer will be able to design new plans for improving the *management* of their workers without devoting equal time to developing new ways of *finding* those workers. They will have to relearn the lesson that their political counterparts know so well: *People are power.*

As with the management revolution, this work force revolution brings with it some very practical implications. Companies must begin to think as carefully about production *inputs* as they do about production processes, markets, and consumers, and as carefully about *human* inputs as they do financial and material ones. Put in corporate parlance, they must begin to develop *strategic work force plans* right alongside their strategic business plans as a means of *securing* workers as well as using them.

It is simply a matter of survival. Already, companies without a strategic business plan do not last long amid the turmoil of the marketplace. In the future, the same will be true of firms—even those with a good business plan—that do not have a top-notch strategic work force plan at their disposal as well.

The Technology Fix

The worker shortage is a new experience for American business. Aside from the temporary fuel shortages of the 1970s, modern-day American firms have not experienced a general shortfall of production inputs except in wartime. Even when spot shortages have occurred, they usually have been resolved by higher prices, such as the rise in oil prices in the mid-1970s or in the cost of capital in the late 1970s. But while wage hikes, which almost certainly will occur, will draw some new workers into the work force, they will not be able to bring in trained workers that do not exist.

This is where the work force challenge differs fundamentally from more traditional management challenges. In the management realm, firms have learned that, in order to increase their market share at a time of rapid technological change and increasing competition, they must do many of the same things they have been doing all along—innovating, cutting costs, finding new markets. Only now, they must do them better and faster.

Acquiring new workers will be a much different challenge. Traditionally, companies have taken a largely passive approach to work force development, relying on schools and job-training centers to produce qualified applicants. Except at mass-hiring times (like the opening of a new plant), companies have tended to wait until job openings occurred before deciding how to fill them. And they have let prospective workers come to them, at most advertising positions in help-wanted sections, with employment services, or at school-based job fairs.

But even doing more of the same, only better and faster, won't be enough when it comes to dealing with a shrinking labor force. Employers will have to adopt entirely new ways of thinking about worker recruitment, training, and retention; they will have to transform work force planning from a *passive*, ad hoc exercise to an *active*, systematic one.

As with the management revolution, the territory will be unfailingly new and frightening. It will place a wholly novel demand on corporate operations: a demand to handle workers, like customers, as if they were scarce and easily lost assets.

Suddenly, people will be important too.

Will the Robots Take Over?

As always, there seem to be numerous shortcuts to save companies the trouble of having to change. The most common suggestion in the wake of the coming labor shortages is that firms should rely more heavily on advanced technology—computers, machines, and robots— to replace the vanishing workers. It is no small irony that what has long been viewed as the inevitable plague of industrial society—the triumph of machines over men—is now seen by some as its salvation. And there *will* be more robots and machines, no mistake about it. The Congressional Office of Technology Assessment projects that by 1992 some 134,000 robots will be at work in the United States, up from about 15,000 today.

Yet, as veteran labor force analyst Sar A. Levitan has remarked, "robots may be getting smarter, but they are hardly likely to replace humans at work in the foreseeable future." In total, he predicts, they will account for no more than "a tiny fraction of…the labor force by 1997. For every 'working' robot, there will still be more than 400 people in the labor force."

Indeed, spurts in technology are more likely to *increase* companies' need for workers than to reduce it. The U.S. Bureau of Labor Statistics has found that capital investment generally leads to higher, not lower, employment levels. A study in neighboring Canada came to the same conclusion: Of the 85 occupational groups reviewed, technological change raised the demand for workers in all but half a dozen.

There are a number of reasons why technology increases the demand for workers:

- Technology makes work possible that otherwise would have been too costly or time-consuming and so extends the range of tasks many companies can undertake.

- New technologies create collateral jobs, not only in producing, servicing, and using the technology itself but also in providing goods and services to support the new technology (as booms in computer furniture manufacturing and data-entry services have accompanied the office-computer explosion).

- Firms that adopt new technologies are able to increase their productivity, remain competitive, and expand their market share—resulting in a broader production base that, in itself, makes more workers necessary.

The United States has been experiencing just these developments in recent years. Between the years 1980 and 1985, despite stiff foreign competition, employment either rebounded or stayed strong in such sectors as motor vehicle manufacturing and telecommunications, industrial groups that rapidly automated and in which output per worker rose five times faster than the national average. By contrast, employment fell most sharply in sectors that automated least and whose declining productivity caused them to lose ground to more efficient European and Asian competitors.

Elsewhere, the same patterns have emerged, even where the adoption of supposedly job-killing technology has been proceeding most rapidly:

- Over the last two decades, investments in computers and telecommunications equipment have allowed the financial services industry to boost productivity by an average of some 3 percent a year. During that time, the industry's total number of jobs has more than doubled, to 6.8 million.

- In accounting, the occupation perhaps most endangered by the transition to electronic data processing, there were still more hand bookkeepers in the United States in 1980 than all workers in computer-affiliated jobs combined.

- And in the computer industry itself, the heart of the automation blitz—where machines are learning, literally, to design and manufacture themselves—the number of jobs rose by more than 50 percent during the first half of the 1980s, far out-pacing already bullish projections.

What is taking place in these individual industries is apt to occur throughout the economy. Despite the rapid creation and dispersion of new technologies, the number of jobs in the United States is expected to rise over the period 1985 to 2000 by between 15 million and 33 million, an increase in total employment of as much as one-third. Naturally, a prolonged recession could change that forecast, but the basic point remains: In an economy characterized by steady growth and technological advance, the number of workers needed will increase, not decrease.

Technology, rather than lifting the country out of the worker shortage, will only deepen it.

The New Competitive Advantage

Sometimes, technology does eliminate jobs. But when it does, it tends to destroy those involving the least skill or the most repetitive tasks: mail-sorting, forms-filling, rote assembly line work. Although some lower-skilled jobs proliferate in a service-oriented economy (the number of fast-food workers has doubled since 1970, for instance), the job mix generally tilts toward higher-skill requirements and will continue to do so throughout the rest of the century. Hudson Institute's Arnold Packer, one of the nation's leading experts on future job skills, has calculated that the *average* skill level of workers will have to rise by some 38 percent over the 1990s to keep pace with technological advance.

For example, jobs that once required only an ability to write compound and complex sentences will, in the next decade, demand essay and report writing. Jobs that once involved only the ability to read simple magazines and atlases will, in the future, require an ability to read and understand journals and complex manuals. And these are just the *average* requirements. Many jobs, even in the lower-level positions, will demand much higher qualifications.

But there is more to this development than higher skills; a different *type* of skills will be involved. It is often said, accurately enough, that technology makes workers more productive by allowing them to turn out more of a product or service in a given unit of time. One person might spend days weaving a single blanket, for instance, but that same person, using a weaving machine, might produce several blankets a day. Likewise for auto makers, chip makers, even drafters and cartoon animators. New or enhanced technology not only saves labor, it saves *thoughtless* labor. A fully automated assembly line allows an auto worker to spend less time inserting part A into part B and more time on quality control; a computer-assisted drafting program allows an architect to devote more energy to creating a new townhouse design and less to redrawing tubs and toilets.

Technology, in other words, squeezes the nonthinking tasks out of a worker's job. Technology places a premium on intelligence, understanding, creative thinking, the ability to see relationships or formulate abstract concepts, the ability to communicate and work with others—indeed, any activity involved with the development, sharing, or use of information. That is why the high tech era is so often referred to as the "information age." It is an era in which workers have to *do* less, and *think* more.

From Brute Force to Intellectual Dexterity

As technology eliminates more of the "brute force" aspects of human labor, the nonthinking components of labor will become less important. What remains will be the *thinking* aspects. The quality and effectiveness with which these thinking tasks are carried out will be an increasingly potent ingredient in corporate productivity, and will be the main basis on which companies will compete in the future. In short, *as technology becomes more prominent and manual labor less prominent in production, the source of competitive advantage in the marketplace will increasingly become the nonmanual component of labor, the intellectual dexterity of the work force.*

This is an economic phenomenon without precedent. For centuries, economies have been organized into a virtual caste system, in which the intellectual elite invested their brainpower in the production process and those on the production line their brawn and backbone. Even where sheer physical labor was not involved, as in banks, retail outlets, and other services, the duties of the front-line staff usually were more mechanical than creative. While this pattern has broken down somewhat with the emergence of white-collar service firms—financial consultants, marketing agencies, large hospitals, and research centers—in most entry- or lower-level jobs, intellectual and creative capacities beyond a certain minimum have not been important assets. These talents have added little, if anything, to a firm's capability to produce.

That situation is changing dramatically. As Chapter 2 indicated, a whole catalog of once routine entry-level jobs are being transformed by technology into positions where additional intellectual and creative capabilities make a difference in the employee's—and hence the company's—productivity. In the 1990s, even many supposedly low-skilled jobs will demand greater or lesser degrees of higher level skills. Not only that, but with other countries chipping away at the United States' historical technological advantage, the greater capabilities of its work force may be the main factor allowing a firm to set itself apart from the competition.

It's this simple: If technology and the best management techniques are widely dispersed, and if the sheer physical capabilities of the work force make less difference in the cost equation, what other way will there be for companies to compete on a day-to-day basis? Only one: the excellence, cost-efficiency, and creativity that come into play at every step of the production process, from concept to final delivery. And these are qualities that will come only from the capabilities and dedication of the workers themselves.

This is what we mean when we say that workers are America's *new competitive advantage*. In an economy in which added capabilities count at all levels, the firms that can marshal the most talent and skills among *all* their workers will be the ones that can consistently turn out the best product or service most quickly and at the lowest price. As Joseph Duffey has written, "we must recognize that...[while the United States] cannot match the wage rates of Taiwan or Mexico, it *can* potentially match anyone in its ability to provide an educated, creative work force."

Crafting this competitive advantage, by securing the right number and quality of workers, is the most pressing challenge American businesses will face in the 1990s. How to go about it—by explicitly addressing the needs and drawing on the capabilities of the new work force—is the subject of the remainder of this book.

The Arrival of 20/20 Management

"We are in the economic fight of our lives" with foreign competitors, says Representative Lee H. Hamilton, chairman of the Joint Economic Committee of the United States Congress. And he is right. Firms all across the country are finding themselves battered by fierce international *and* domestic competition. And they are discovering that they need a work force that is literate in basic areas such as reading, writing, and mathematics if they are to survive.

But not just basic skills. As Marc S. Tucker, chairman of the National Center on Education and the Economy in Rochester, New York, insists, "Over the long term, basic skills only give you the right to compete against the Third World for Third World wages."

Indeed, the United States already is trying to remain a First World economic power with only Third World performance standards, as the educational comparisons in Chapter 2 make uncomfortably clear. And turning this situation around will be neither easy nor automatic. "None of the transitions will take place by chance," warns former Assistant Secretary of Labor Roger D. Semerad. "They will require the most sophisticated strategic planning and resolute implementation to educate, train, retrain, and, more important, to instill hope and the necessary work ethic."

They will demand, in short, what Semerad calls "20/20 Management"—the ability of everyone, "from executives and managers to entrepreneurs and investors, to see into future labor markets, to carefully project the firm's needs for workers, and to understand what it will take to meet them."

Companies have long applied 20/20 Management to the product side of their operations. No firm would dream of going into business without trying to estimate the potential market for its goods or services, the cost of production and distribution, and the availability of raw materials and parts. Most major corporations, and some smaller firms as well, have entire departments devoted to projecting future economic conditions, technological developments, and the state of the competition, and to turning this knowledge to the company's advantage. Because all companies are vying for essentially the same customers, only firms with insight into these customers' wants and needs, and with the foresight to know how best to meet those needs, will be able to capture and hold onto a significant share of the market.

In the future, companies will have to apply 20/20 Management to the labor market with the same vigor as they now do to the product market. As they have long competed for customers, firms increasingly will have to begin competing for workers. And, just as with customers, those firms that are best able to foresee and meet their potential workers' needs will have the most to gain. "The companies that respond successfully," says Felice Schwartz, president of Catalyst, Inc., a business consulting group, "will be rewarded with stable, productive employees."

Or, as Louis V. Gerstner, chairman of RJR Nabisco, puts it: "How are we going to find, attract, motivate and retain well-qualified people as the labor pool shrinks in size and average skill levels decline? How will we compete in a labor market in which there's a rapidly widening disparity between the number of well-educated people who are required and the number of qualified, or even qualifiable, people who are available? The answer is we're going to have to attack this market with the same dedication we do any other. We're going to have to market our company well. We're going to have to understand our customers well. We're going to have to provide a better employment alternative than the competition. That means higher quality and more features that the customers—in this case our employees—want. In short, we have to be the best place for people to work if we want to be the best at what we do."

That is the credo of the work force revolution. In an economic world in which people, more and more, *really* are the source of power in the marketplace, it is a slogan that should be posted on every executive's, every manager's, every entrepreneur's door. Taking the notion to heart, in fact, is the essential first step to making 20/20 Management work. With a little creativity and determination, this credo can be applied to *all* members of the new work force—women, especially women with children; minority group members and the economically disadvantaged; immigrants; persons with disabilities; and older workers and retirees—the very people who will make the difference in the 1990s between full production runs and folding up shop.

The next few chapters, reports from the front lines of successful companies throughout the country, will tell you how it can be done.

4
Women and Work

In Margaret Atwood's acclaimed satire *The Handmaid's Tale,* the future has become a nightmare. The United States (now the Republic of Gilead) has reacted to a declining birthrate by "reverting to, and going beyond, the repressive intolerance of the original Puritans." Women are silenced, deprived of almost all of their rights, treated as little more than chattel. They are not expected to work, except at domestic chores; they are expected only to have babies.

So much for fiction. As a tract against sexism, Atwood's novel stings. But as a description of where the future is headed—as a compass pointing toward the "logical conclusions" of "certain tendencies now in existence," in the dust jacket's words—the book, only a few years old, is already a generation out of date.

As John Naisbitt and Patricia Aburdene write in *Reinventing the Corporation:* "Despite a lot of media publicity, we have not yet grasped the truth about working women: We are moving to a time when virtually all women will work at paying jobs."

Indeed, by the year 2000, nearly half of American workers will be women. Most of these women will be mothers, even mothers of small children. Many will be single mothers. Gone forever will be the days when marriage and motherhood automatically closed the door on a woman's professional aspirations. Married or unmarried, with or without children, American women are in the work force to stay.

And yet this still seems like news to many businesses. While the influx of women into the labor market has been going on for years, much of corporate America has not adjusted to this most fundamental of demographic trends. Women are no longer just peak-season fill-ins. They are no longer only to be found at cash registers, reception desks, and typewriters. They are the *core* of the future work force. As futurist Marvin

Cetron predicts, during the 1990s, "the only job a woman *won't* have is that of a Catholic priest."

Womanpower and the Future of Business

One reason women have become integral to all parts of the work force is that the lines between "men's work" and "women's work" are rapidly blurring. By 1986, 45 percent of full-time accountants and auditors in the United States were women, as were 40 percent of computer programmers, 29 percent of managers and administrators, and 15 percent of lawyers. And these are just the early signs of changes to come. By the late 1980s, women accounted for nearly half of students receiving degrees in accounting and business, and 4 out of 10 receiving degrees in law and computer science.

What does this growing prominence of women in the work force mean for business, particularly established, male-run businesses? For the smart ones—the employers who work as hard to recruit women and earn their loyalty as they do to recruit men—it means a larger talent pool to choose from. It means that critical jobs will continue to be filled, allowing companies to grow and prosper even at a time of serious worker shortages. And it means that experienced workers will stay on the job rather than taking their talents and skills elsewhere.

Still, launching a campaign to recruit, hire, and retain female employees is by no means an easy task. It involves a lot more than simply placing women's names on the payroll. While many capable and astute female employees have found ways to move ahead in male-dominated business settings, thousands of others' ambitions have been stifled, not because they lacked intelligence or drive, but because of circumstances related to their gender. To overcome these problems, employers are finding they need to improve the working environment for women in five key areas.

Pay Women in the Same Job the Same as Men

Despite moving more rapidly into professional fields, women overall remain concentrated in large numbers in traditionally female jobs (clerical work, elementary school teaching, nursing, housekeeping, and the like) all paying less than traditionally male occupations. In fact, women fill these traditionally female jobs in nearly the same proportions as they did in the 1960s. The average woman working full time still earns only

70 cents to the average male worker's dollar, and the persistence of female- or male-dominated occupations helps maintain this wage gap.

Yet even in jobs routinely held by both men and women, especially management positions, women's salaries fall short of men's. A 1987 Census Bureau study found that women in executive, administrative, and managerial occupations were receiving only about 60 percent of men's average salaries in the same occupations. In a Gallup survey taken a few years earlier, 70 percent of the 722 female executives polled felt they had been paid less than a man of equal ability. Pay differences are usually attributed to seniority, merit, or productivity, since the federal Equal Pay Act of 1963 forbids wage discrimination based on gender. However, these factors do not explain all of the wage disparity.

Break the "Glass Ceiling"

The situation is all too familiar. A female manager's career, spanning more than a decade, is marked by success. At every rung on the corporate ladder, she has earned respect and praise from both peers and supervisors. But when a top position opens up, she is passed over for a less experienced man who has been with the company only five years. And matters get worse. For years, she receives only lateral "promotions." Fed up, she ultimately leaves the company and starts her own business.

Top corporate executives often cannot understand these defections. Yet many successful businesswomen are learning that, after years of advancement, an invisible barrier prevents them from moving into the top managerial positions, where they would have genuine influence over company policy. A 1986 *Wall Street Journal* article on corporate women aptly termed this obstruction the "glass ceiling." And despite individual success stories, the numbers suggest that the "glass ceiling" persists throughout corporate America:

- Fewer than 2 percent of officers in the Fortune 500 companies are women.
- Fully 97 percent of a group of 800 newly promoted corporate chairmen, presidents, and vice presidents surveyed in 1987 by the University of Michigan were men. The study also revealed that the percentage of female managers being promoted to vice president was decreasing.
- In one poll, fewer than half of the male executives questioned said they would be comfortable working for a woman.

What could be the reason behind this apparent bias against women managers? Some male managers say they expect that women will give their professional duties short shrift if they conflict with family responsibilities. Others, particularly older men accustomed to a more gender-divided workplace, admit they do not feel comfortable with female colleagues. Many believe women who are "too feminine" cannot be tough enough for business; yet they resent women who "behave like men." Understandable or not, such excuses are just that—*excuses*.

As television producer Kim Friedman has remarked about her field: "It's a tough business to get your first shot in, man or woman, but if you are a man, once you get that shot, you're in the club and you're protected. For a woman, each thing you do, you have to prove yourself all over again—and you are never fully accepted in the club."

Help Meet Childbearing and Dependent-Care Needs

The days of overt bias against pregnant women in the workplace are largely past. But women who become pregnant while employed still pay a heavy price. Their carefully mapped out career plans may be thrown off track as they fight to maintain a balance between two very different worlds. Some mothers who choose to stay home during the first months or years of their children's lives (sometimes at great financial sacrifice to the family) find they have no job to return to or, if they do, that they are out of the running for promotions. Many women who do return to the office full time shortly after giving birth feel guilty about leaving their babies, and they have the added stress of trying to find an affordable child-care provider that accepts infants.

A 1984 survey by *The Wall Street Journal* suggests that it is especially difficult for these women to climb the corporate ladder. Of women who had reached corporate vice president or above, 52 percent had no children, while only 7 percent of men at the same professional level were childless. The previous year, *Fortune* magazine surveyed Harvard Business School's female graduates of 1973, many of whom had attained important corporate positions; 54 percent of them were childless.

Moreover, while men have gradually taken over more of the traditional parental and household responsibilities, women, even women who work full time, still spend more time than men caring for children or elderly dependents.

- Researchers from the Boston University School of Social Work found that working women were six times more likely to stay home with a sick child than were men.

- Even female managers at the corporate vice president level say they are responsible for a disproportionate share of work in the home.

- Women bear more responsibility for elderly dependents. According to a survey of Travelers Insurance Company employees, they are primary care givers twice as often as men.

Enhance Geographic Mobility

Anyone married to a military or foreign service officer expects to be uprooted from home, friends, and job every two to three years. Spouses of corporate managers in major companies often find themselves in the same position. Certainly, female officers or executives are as likely to be transferred as their male counterparts, and there are men willing to quit their jobs to advance a wife's career. But in most cases, it is the woman who sacrifices her job or career to accommodate her husband's, making it more difficult for women with families to pursue promotions involving relocation.

The staffing manager for a large bank maintains that this situation has held back some exceptional female tellers from advancing into loan officer or management positions. "People, especially women, want and need to work where they live," says the manager. "Bank branches are relatively small, so if a teller wants a promotion, she may have to move to another branch where there is an opening. But unfortunately, as much as the working world has changed in recent years, women are still not the 'mobile' ones in a family. If a man gets a promotion, his wife usually gives up her job to move with him. It seldom works the other way around."

Stamp Out Sexual Harassment

Although there are laws designed to protect both men and women from unwanted sexual advances in the workplace, a number of surveys show that sexual harassment remains common in the business world. In most though not all cases, the victims are female clerical workers who work for male supervisors. Because complaining about these advances can be embarrassing and risky to these women's careers, the harassment often remains a secret.

Such harassment, whether reported or unreported, can seriously undercut a woman's chances for promotion, not to mention her self-esteem. Management-backed employee grievance mechanisms are one way to attack the problem, but the issue's sensitivity still may discourage victims from pursuing formal complaints.

Employers as Problem Solvers

Knowing that these barriers could discourage women from seeking or remaining in jobs at a time when they are most needed, a new class of worker-oriented employers have taken up the mantle of problem solver. They are acting to eliminate obstacles to women's career advancement, making such steps a routine feature of programs designed to:

- Attract more women applicants.
- Make the best possible use of their talents.
- Promote them so they are not tempted to leave in search of better opportunities and working conditions.

There's good reason for these moves. Today's young female workers expect more from their employers than just a paycheck and an occasional pat on the back. And tomorrow's female college and business school graduates will be even less amenable than their predecessors to accepting dead-end associate positions while their male classmates move into the fast-track management jobs. With other successful women as role models, young women have no trouble seeing themselves as executives. But unlike their role models, they will be less willing to forfeit their personal lives for success in business.

Some firms are already responding aggressively to their female employees' demands to be recognized as equals and are establishing programs to turn equality into more than a handy corporate catchphrase. It's simply "the right thing to do," says Reuben Mark, chairman and CEO of Colgate-Palmolive, which provides a complete package of work and family benefits for its 27,000 employees. "It's also one of the mechanisms to attract and motivate high-quality people."

Unfortunately, many other companies have adopted a wait-and-see attitude toward these matters. They concede that certain issues of strong concern to working women (child care, in particular) will have to be dealt with soon, but preferably on someone else's watch. "We try to be receptive, flexible with respect to our employees' needs," says one corporate recruiter. "I sense that such arrangements will become company policy when the men start asking for them too. And that will take a while."

But businesses that wait for their male employees to speak up will be too late. Sensitivity to the needs of working women, especially those with families to care for, is no longer just a matter of legality, corporate social consciousness, or even simple fairness. It is a competitive necessity for employers wishing to attract and keep good workers—male *and* female.

Looking for a Few
Good Women

The area first to feel the effects of the worker shortage is almost always recruitment. With too few workers of any kind walking through the door, enlightened corporate planners, recruiters, and entrepreneurs are learning that attracting and retaining the best workers means recruiting women of all ages, family situations, and racial and ethnic backgrounds just as aggressively as they used to recruit white men in the past.

Recruiting by Reputation

The firms that are most successfully expanding the ranks of female employees actively call attention to company policies that appeal to working women, hold up their top women as examples, and encourage satisfied employees to promote the company among female job seekers.

One employer that uses these techniques effectively is the Gannett Company, owner of more than 100 publications and a dozen radio and television stations. Calling itself "The Opportunity Company for Women," Gannett aggressively recruits on college campuses, including women's colleges, and at national conventions and industry-association meetings. "Our best recruiters are Gannett employees," says Madelyn Jennings, Gannett's senior vice president for personnel and administration. "They know it's part of their job, and they refer people they think would do well here."

Gannett also uses the "Opportunity Company" theme in magazine advertisements and in a color brochure highlighting more than a dozen women in cities and towns throughout the country who are happy with the progress of their careers at Gannett. One woman says: "My first job with Gannett was as a secretary. Today, I am vice president and advertising director for...a publication with more than 12 million circulation. I have worked for other companies, but I came back to Gannett because it is a company on the move and a great place for people who want to move with it."

Similarly, Johnson & Johnson's (J&J) reputation as a company of high principles has been a potent force in its success in recruiting women. "J&J's best recruiting tool," says equal employment opportunity (EEO) manager Marion HochbergSmith, "is its integrity."

Clearly, being known as a company that treats women well is a plus for any employer's recruiting efforts. But even deserving employers will not reap these benefits without active public relations efforts. Whether through formal media campaigns or simple word-of-mouth, successful recruiters make their firm's strong points known to prospective female employees in whatever ways they can.

Recruiting Into Traditionally Male Occupations

Some of the best public relations campaigns start early. Many companies now reach out to potential female employees years before interviewing them for a job. By speaking with female high school and even elementary students, employers spark young women's interest in occupations traditionally dominated by men, including engineering, medicine, and other scientific and technical careers. Because academic preparation for many of these careers begins as early as high school, these companies know it is important to reach these prospective employees when they are still young.

Likewise, employers who hire in such male-dominated occupations as machinery repair or the building trades know they must encourage young women as well as young men to seek the appropriate training. While sponsoring firms realize there is no guarantee the students will ever work for them directly, they know that, by being the first employers to to show an interest in these women's futures, they will have an edge when hiring time comes.

An outstanding example of this long-range approach to developing a specialized work force is the 3M Company's Visiting Technical Women (VTW) program. The program, inaugurated in 1978, gives Minneapolis—St. Paul area students an "opportunity to meet and interact with women who enjoy their technical careers." The VTW program recruits women in a wide variety of technical occupations to visit local elementary, junior high, and senior high schools and to attend career fairs and special programs in colleges and vocational schools.

The 3M employees, explains a company brochure, "show students how science knowledge is applied every day in industry and that one doesn't have to be a genius to have a successful technical career." Program representatives also give students information about the educational preparation they will need for technical positions and information about financial aid and work-study programs in technical fields. To add a personal note, many women describe their own experiences on the job and tell how they have succeeded in combining career and family.

Former program spokeswoman Christa Lane-Larsen told the federal Task Force on Women, Minorities, and the Handicapped that "responses [from the community] are always favorable" and pointed out that "some teachers have noted that more young women are enrolling in science and math classes throughout the high school years." The 3M company hopes to expand this program to the company's manufacturing sites, usually located in small, rural towns. Already, the firm has helped several other locally based employers to develop similar programs, and has produced a how-to booklet for interested organizations.

On a smaller scale, female employees at California Institute of Technology's Jet Propulsion Laboratory (JPL) participate, as members of the Society of Women Engineers, in a speakers program directed at high school girls. JPL also routinely sends speakers into grammar schools to talk with students and help them prepare for science fairs. This kind of communitywide approach has worked especially well for companies that do not have a large enough staff to sponsor full-scale programs.

Recruiting the Returning Woman

Women who have temporarily dropped out of the work force to raise children or to accommodate a husband's career can be a valuable source of new workers for companies that help these women make the transition back to part- or full-time employment.

A large percentage of returning women say they would rejoin the work force immediately if they could afford decent child care. In a 1982 Census Bureau study, for instance, about one-quarter of all nonworking mothers of preschoolers indicated that lack of "reasonably priced child care" was the main reason they were not looking for employment. Another 13 percent said they would work more hours if they could find affordable substitute care. If just half these women returned to work, estimates Columbia University economist David E. Bloom, the labor force would gain 850,000 job seekers. Clearly, companies that help their employees with child care have a good opportunity, right now, to attract some of these women into their ranks.

Moreover, in their nonprofessional roles, many returning women have acquired marketable skills that make them attractive job candidates. For example:

- Raising a family develops nurturing talents that may be transferable to various health-care or counseling occupations.

- Running a household can involve accounting and financial management, negotiations with contractors, diplomacy, mechanical repair, and food preparation.

- Membership in volunteer organizations can provide valuable leadership and organizational experience.

To recruit these women, some companies place displays in their stores or circulars in their billings sent to customers. Mervyn's, a discount department store chain based in California, scouts out potential new employees by inserting leaflets in customers' shopping bags. "We are looking for people who are proud of their accomplishments in life," the advertisement reads. "Many of our people have done things like this: Managed a household, raised children, volunteered for civic affairs, organized clubs, groups or teams, decorated or remodeled their residences, or retired from other jobs."

Yet, while some women may place their established careers on hold, the pace of technological progress does not slow down. As a result, even well-educated women are bound to feel a little like Rip Van Winkle after a few years outside the workplace. Persuading these women to return, then, often requires assistance to update their knowledge of technology, training for positions that did not exist when they left the work force, or even subsidized refresher courses that cover recent developments in their professions.

One exceptional strategy for drawing experienced women back into the work force comes from California-based Hewlett-Packard, which launched an experimental policy in a country not known for progressive attitudes toward working women. "In Japan, women are expected to quit work when they marry and have children," explains worldwide equal opportunity specialist Bob Ingram. "So the managers in our Japanese location are making a special effort to keep in close contact with female employees who have taken several years off to raise their families."

Hewlett-Packard keeps its former employees informed about company activities and permits them to take computer terminals home. The firm also sends the new mothers business and professional publications and invites them to participate in technical seminars. By keeping the women "in the loop," Hewlett-Packard hopes they will want to return to work at their first opportunity.

The Procter & Gamble Company is another employer that has successfully used training to attract a number of returning women to the company. By gearing its programs to persons who have never worked with computers, Procter & Gamble bridges a technology gap that may otherwise discourage women from applying to work for the firm.

Military wives in particular are an often-overlooked source of returning women. Because these women tend to relocate with their husbands every few years, employers understandably view them as a high turnover group. Still, they can be a critical source of employees, especially in the short term.

One business that has many military families as customers, USAA Property and Casualty Insurance Company, decided that military wives' knowledge of protocol made them ideal candidates to handle telephone claims from USAA's clients, many of whom are military officers. Recruiting efforts by the company's Washington, D.C., area claims office resulted in two full units staffed predominantly by military wives. "Their knowledge of military etiquette made them perfect for the job," explains personnel and training manager Jacky Yeates. "These employees treated our clients with the respect they are accustomed to. And there was a great sense of camaraderie among our claims staff, since they had so much in common."

Helping Work and Family Work Together

In 1897, American woman's rights pioneer Charlotte Perkins Gilman poignantly described a dilemma that persists, to a certain extent, even today: "We have so arranged life," she wrote, "that a man may have a house, a family, love, companionship, domesticity, and fatherhood and yet remain an active citizen.... We have so arranged life, on the other hand, that a woman must choose; she must either live alone,... with her work in the world for sole consolation, or give up world service for the joys of love, motherhood, and domestic service."

But women aren't the only ones concerned about career-family conflicts. According to the 1988 Du Pont Company survey of more than 4000 of its employees that was cited in Chapter 2, about one-quarter of the firm's 65 percent male work force—and about one-half the women—said they had already considered seeking employment with another company that offers workers more flexibility to meet their family responsibilities. With 90 percent of its employees from dual-career households, many of which are planning to start families in the next three years, Du Pont knows it has a strong interest in keeping new parents as committed employees.

So how should companies respond? Where should they draw the line between home and the workplace? Is it even appropriate for business to become involved in child care, counseling, or other family matters? Maurice Wright, community relations officer for Shawmut National Bank in Boston, thinks it is. "The family comes to work with the employee," he says. "If we forget that, we'll have difficulty recruiting and keeping good workers."

Lynwood Battle of Procter & Gamble agrees: "At one time, it was considered paternalism for a company to become closely involved in providing for the needs of its workers' families. It had a negative connotation. It's not so much that way anymore; people expect certain benefits.

And we're seeing clearly that providing for those needs is in the company's interest."

Maternity, Parental, and Family Leave

Until the 1970s, many people considered childbearing exclusively a women's issue, not only for the obvious, physiological reasons, but because pregnancy (or even its possibility) had far more detrimental effects on female than male employees. Many women were kept out of well-paying, responsible jobs and, in some cases, even were fired. Women fought hard to overcome this discrimination, arguing that pregnancy was a temporary condition that in no way reduced their ability to be capable, reliable employees.

In 1978, Congress agreed and passed a law that forbids employers from firing or refusing to hire a woman because she is pregnant. The law also requires employers offering disability leave to include pregnancy and childbirth in their definition of disability and directs that women be allowed to return to work after giving birth. Although the law does not demand that employers provide maternity leave (time off beyond the disability period), those that do so must offer men the same benefits: hence the development of *parental* leave.

California and a few other states already have enacted legislation requiring employers to provide a minimum parental leave. Congress has considered, but not approved, similar legislation. Advocates of mandated leave say that, as it now stands, only women married to well-to-do husbands can afford to risk their jobs to be with their newborn children. But opponents worry that mandated parental leave may lead some employers to subtly discriminate against all women of childbearing age. Others contend that eliminating the jobs through automation could be more economical than providing such potentially expensive government-imposed benefits.

These issues may not be resolved any time soon. Still, even without a mandated leave law, many companies are finding they must look seriously at such policies in order to compete for good workers:

- Already, some 40 percent of larger American companies provide maternity/parental leave (in addition to paid disability leave) with full job guarantees.
- Many offer three to six months' leave, some even longer, upon the birth or adoption of a child; a few help new parents with related expenses.
- Some employers have broadened their definition of parental leave to

family leave, which permits care of ill or disabled family members. Company benefits may continue throughout the leave period, but employees usually receive no salary during this time.

Clearly, medium-sized and larger companies can offer family leave benefits much more easily than smaller ones. A substantial employee base helps make absences more tolerable because employees with training in interchangeable skills can fill in while new parents are out. Worker-oriented companies also know they have a good chance of recouping their investment in family leave. They may have devoted a great deal of time and resources to their employee's training and other benefits, and they know chances are good that she (or he) will repay the company with loyalty.

In 1977, Procter & Gamble introduced a parental leave policy that allowed either parent (or both parents, by splitting the time) to take up to six months off at the birth or adoption of a child. In early 1988, the company liberalized its policy in response to widespread employee requests, extending parental leave from six months to a year, with an option to work part-time during the leave period.

Procter & Gamble's decision to expand its parental leave policy was motivated, in large part, by its desire to retain experienced female employees and save money at the same time. Industrial relations manager Neil Barnett explains: "Before the change, we were losing some of our key people: talented women who thought it was worth giving up their job to spend a year with their babies, or even to work part-time during that first year. We found that when they were ready to come back, we were rehiring many of these women as contractors. From the standpoint of expenses, paperwork, etc., it seemed to make more sense just to keep them on."

Procter & Gamble is not alone. For example:

- New mothers employed by IBM may take up to 52 weeks of fully paid medical leave (in a two year period) to recover from childbirth. Six- to eight-week leaves are the norm; extra time is available to cover potential complications. The company also gives new parents, natural or adoptive, the opportunity to take up to three full years of unpaid personal leave with an option to work for the company part-time during that period. Throughout the leave, employees continue to receive their full benefits, and when they return to work at the leave's conclusion, the company guarantees they will be reinstated in the job they left, or in a comparable position.

- American Telephone and Telegraph Company recently reached an agreement with its unions to extend unpaid leave for parents of newborns from six months to a year. The company offers a similar option to employees caring for ill family members.

- At Campbell Soup Company, either spouse may take up to three months unpaid leave to care for a newborn or newly adopted child, as well as for sick children and ill or elderly family members. Employees who take advantage of this policy do not lose their benefits during their leave and are guaranteed the same or a similar job upon their return.

- HBO/Time, Inc., recently extended its standard 8 to 12 weeks of job-guaranteed paid disability leave to a maximum of 26 weeks. The company also offers an additional three months of unpaid leave for new parents.

Generous family leave policies like these, while attractive to employees and workable for larger employers, are tougher for smaller businesses to implement. Very small companies, which are unlikely to hire more full-time workers than they can keep busy, may not be able to get along without a valued employee for a few months to a year.

Still, it is not difficult for most firms to offer part-time work or at least conditional job guarantees to a new mother when she is ready to return to work. Continuing to pay benefits for a limited time may be less expensive than recruiting and training a new full-time employee.

Flexible Work Schedules

Flexible work scheduling is an inexpensive yet effective way to help employees meet their family responsibilities without compromising job performance. Flexibility can be as simple as allowing employees to choose between starting work at 8:30 or 9 a.m., or as sophisticated as letting employees allocate their own share of personal leave days among vacation, illness, and personal business. Flexible scheduling may involve part-time hours as well, or two persons sharing the same full-time job.

A generation ago, deviation from the 9-to-5, Monday-through-Friday, 50-week year was uncommon. But a 1987 Bureau of Labor Statistics survey found that 3 out of 5 American companies were offering some form of flexible work scheduling. Once viewing it with skepticism, employers have found that this kind of flexibility usually raises, not lowers, worker productivity and reduces business costs associated with tardiness, absenteeism, and high turnover.

Flextime.   Flextime, the best-known form of flexible work scheduling, came into wide use in the United States after having been tested in European businesses for more than a decade. With flextime, workers generally may choose their daily arrival, departure, and lunch hours, given certain guidelines. Employees work an eight-hour day and usually must be in the office during specified core hours. Employees may either be required to maintain their "flex-schedule" on a daily basis, or be allowed to vary those times according to personal circumstances, providing they work the required eight hours.

However flextime is implemented, employers find that even small scheduling adjustments allow workers to meet their family responsibilities more easily, cut down on commuting time, and minimize the stress associated with both. Office managers also report that staggered arrival and departure hours reduce distractions and wasted time that are common at the beginning and ending of a day when all employees arrive and leave at the same time, and increase productivity by allowing workers to tailor their workdays to their natural cycles of alertness and drowsiness.

This type of scheduling works well in both large and small office settings. Flextime may not be appropriate for every job—a receptionist in a small office, for example, or assembly line workers in a small factory where all workers must be present at once—but in most cases, only minor variations in the workplace routine are necessary.

All told, some 10 million workers in the private sector now participate in flexible time arrangements. And the federal government's six-year experiment with flextime worked so well that the scheduling plan was made permanent in 1985. An estimated 500,000 employees at 41 federal agencies now take advantage of the program.

One of the first major United States companies to institute flextime was Northwestern Mutual Life Insurance, whose policy has been in force since 1973. Most employees arrive between 7 and 9 a.m. and leave between 3 and 5 p.m. One employee remarked that the variable working hours are a "real boon to the working mother." Another told the company magazine: "I love it. I get home in time to pick up my son from school."

Two companies that have successfully implemented flextime in a manufacturing setting are Control Data Corp. and Hewlett-Packard. Both tried the new scheduling policies in one or two plants on an experimental basis before putting them permanently into effect, companywide.

Control Data Corp. allows its assembly line workers to select their own arrival times, subject to clearly defined core hours, and end their workday eight hours later. First-line supervisors are responsible for coordinating workers' schedules. While workers enjoy considerable flexibility in a number of Control Data's production facilities, schedules at most manufacturing locations are carefully monitored to prevent operating units from overlapping unnecessarily between shifts. Though flextime is not mandatory in any of Control Data's divisions, the corporate leadership now encourages all its subsidiaries to adopt it.

Hewlett-Packard takes a different approach to flextime, which affects more than 22,000 of its employees, almost 90 percent of these in manufacturing jobs. Hewlett-Packard's flextime has no formal mechanism for monitoring hours; all employees—whether in office or manufacturing jobs—work on the honor system. Flexible scheduling allows programmers and others whose performance does not depend entirely on the presence of other workers to control their own work pace. But plant personnel also have adjusted well to the system.

The company first tried staggered work hours at its West German locations and later introduced the concept as a summer experiment in its Waltham, Massachusetts, facility. Workers were given the choice of arriving any time between 6:30 and 8:30 a.m. and leaving, after eight hours of work, between 3 and 5 p.m. Plant management, operating on a three-shift, 24-hour schedule, allowed evening- and night-shift workers similar flexibility and maintained continuity between the three shifts with buffers of work-in-process inventories.

Since factory jobs typically require an entire team to be present at once, Hewlett-Packard restructured certain jobs, enlarging their scope to allow employees to work independently for portions of the day. First-line supervisors received special training to help them adjust to these changes.

Hewlett-Packard's Art Young, corporate benefits manager, believes that flexible scheduling improves morale by demonstrating the company's confidence in its employees: "Flextime was a breakthrough in how we view our people. It requires a great deal of trust. That is a small thing, but it says so much about the value you place on your employees."

Compressed Workweek.   Another scheduling approach that has been successful in retail stores and some offices and factories is the compressed workweek, which provides for full-time, 40-hour-week employment in fewer than five days. Under this system, rather than being on the job for five, eight-hour shifts, employees might work four, ten-hour shifts, affording them a free day for personal business that normally might require them to take time off work. There is growing evidence that the compressed schedule reduces absences, tardiness, and other expenses related to a five-day workweek.

The Washington, D.C., area claims office of USAA Property and Casualty Insurance Company has used a four-day workweek since the 1970s. Personnel officers report that it has been a strong recruiting tool, particularly in times of low unemployment, and that it is especially appealing to mothers who must work full time. Offices are closed on the standard weekend; employees have a rotating day off each week: Wednesday, Thursday, or Friday.

Seasonal Flexibility. Other employers have developed a schedule of rotating certain employees in and out of jobs on a seasonal basis. Some businesses, especially those in tourist areas, require a larger work force during school holidays than during the rest of the year, and use seasonal scheduling for that purpose. Others, such as traditional factories that involve a number of repetitive functions, often circulate trained workers through a variety of jobs, bringing in additional help as the demand increases. Seasonal hours are also a way of attracting a larger or replacement work force in order to free other workers to discharge their family responsibilities.

Susan Ensey of McKesson Industries gives one example of how this concept can work. Managers at McKesson's Worcester, Massachusetts, plant were having trouble recruiting factory workers a few years ago. They solved their worker shortage by allowing mothers of school-age children to work during the school year, then recruiting high school students to fill those jobs during the summer. USAA is looking at a similar arrangement for its telephone claim handlers.

Flexible Personal Leave. Giving employees flexibility in scheduling paid time off has been another attractive recruiting and retention tool, as well as a hedge against excessive absenteeism for personal business.

One innovative approach is Hewlett-Packard's Flexible Time Off program, which could save money for businesses that would like to offer—but cannot afford—a liberal, paid sick leave policy. In 1982, encouraged by its success with flexible daily schedules, Hewlett-Packard responded to employee suggestions to offer a combined vacation and sick leave package. Before the new policy went into effect, employees were allocated up to 25 days each year for vacation, plus 10 days of sick leave. Unused sick leave could be carried over from year to year and, after 20 years, redeemed for up to 50 percent of its cash value.

Under the new plan, employees receive the same number of annual vacation days (based on years of service), but in place of the ten annual sick leave days, which relatively few employees used, the company gives each employee a five-day block of flexible leave to cover short-term illness, personal business (including child care), or vacations. Employees still are permitted to carry over unused leave from year to year and, regardless of their years of service, may cash in on accumulated days when leaving the company.

Remaking Jobs to Fit the Worker

An even more dramatic form of job flexibility is the creation of alternative job arrangements, in which companies literally tailor the job to the needs of individual workers.

At-Home Work. At-home work is an idea that has been on the horizon for decades. Futurists of the 1960s and 1970s depicted offices that extended from downtown to the distant suburbs, with workers seldom leaving their homes, joined to their coworkers solely by computer terminals and telephones. In some respects, that vision already has come true. In 1988, the Bureau of Labor Statistics counted more than 25 million Americans—up from 18 million in 1985—working at home either part- or full-time. And that number will rise to 40 million by the year 2000, projects Thomas Miller, director of New York-based LINK Resources' 1988 National Work-At-Home Survey.

Still, telecommuting has been relatively slow to take hold in the corporate world, though there are signs this is changing too. Certain industries, including cottage handicrafts, translation services, free-lance journalism, direct sales, and telephone marketing, have for years routinely hired people to work in their homes. More recently, businesses have started using telecommuters for transcribing, computer programming, technical writing, and other jobs requiring minimal supervision.

Studies by LINK Resources and others suggest that most home workers are well-educated, highly-motivated workers. More than one-half are college graduates; 1 in 5 has a postgraduate degree. Although a number of telecommuters still work in offices part-time, others prefer to work at home exclusively, even if it means starting small businesses or consulting firms of their own. Employers hoping to avoid losing such ambitious workers may find part-time work-at-home programs a valuable incentive for keeping them productive and on the payroll.

For workers whose family responsibilities do not coincide with the traditional workday, telecommuting permits full-time employment at the most convenient hours. For some new mothers, this option might make the difference between continuing to work and dropping out of the work force altogether. In fact, women, particularly young women with children, were the fastest growing category of home workers in 1988, according to the LINK survey.

Despite the success large numbers of companies are having with home workers, some employers are hesitant to try this approach, fearing that, without close supervision, workers will be not be productive.

But other firms report that telecommuters are more, not less, productive than office employees performing the same jobs.

This has been true for Blue Cross/Blue Shield's South Carolina offices. Telecommuting began as an experiment in 1978, when a manager took claims reports home to key into a computer. A few years later, the office hired 14 local "cottage keyers" to key and code claims reports. The company was surprised to find that, for paid hours, these workers were about 25 percent more productive than their office counterparts and had zero turnover for the first five years. Considered part-time employees, these workers are not eligible for the same benefits as those who work full-time, but, paid by the claim, they sometimes wind up with a higher overall income than hourly or salaried claims processors.

A few companies actually employ more telecommuters than office staff. One of these is F International, a small data processing company that is virtually 100 percent home-based. Unlike other companies mentioned here, F International started out, 20 years ago, as a telecommuting company and has only recently begun relying more upon on-site work. Ninety-six percent of the firm's overseas work force (and 84 percent of its United States work force) are women, most of them with family responsibilities and most of them part-time.

Another company that has built its success on telecommuters is the American Service Bureau, headquartered in Des Plaines, Illinois, which contracts with several hundred telecommuters to collect and process medical data for the insurance industry. Telecommuting staffers, working within a franchiselike structure, interview insurance applicants, collect medical histories, and fill out reports. The company provides training and full benefits. Workers earn according to what they produce; an employee in a busy territory reportedly can earn up to $60,000 a year.

One firm that has succeeded with a largely home-based staff of skilled computer programmers and technical writers is the Learning Company. The small, northern California computer firm contracts with telecommuters to produce educational software and manuals, paying them by the job. The Gallup and Harris polling organizations also regularly hire home workers across the nation for telephone work.

Telecommuting is even suitable for some managers, according to officials of Pacific Telesis, which began a telecommuting program for managerial employees in April 1985. By the end of the first year, nearly 80 programmers, analysts, engineers, marketing planners, project managers, external affairs managers, and forecasters were working at remote sites or at their homes throughout California. The advent of relatively inexpensive laptop computers and facsimile machines makes this arrangement increasingly realistic, even for small firms.

Part-Time Work. For men and women with pressing family responsibilities, working part-time—that is, less than the standard 40-hour week—is another attractive option. As far back as 1977, more than two-thirds of mothers of young children said they would prefer to work shorter hours, even if it meant lower pay, in order to spend more time with their families. A decade later, part-time arrangements were even more in demand. Bureau of Labor Statistics data show, for instance, that between the years 1970 and 1986, the number of people employed by temporary-help firms, most of whom worked part-time, rose by more than 400 percent, from 184,000 to 760,000.

Switching from full- to part-time scheduling has a number of advantages. It can allow employers to maintain professional contact with employees who do not wish to continue working full-time, particularly new mothers. "Part-time employment is the single greatest inducement to getting women back on the job expeditiously," says Felice Schwartz, founder of Catalyst, a New York advisory firm specializing in women's work force issues.

Many companies have applied the part-time concept in original ways that have helped them hold on to longtime employees they otherwise might have lost:

- The Boston law firm of Foley, Hoag & Eliot permits its attorneys to ease back into their jobs following maternity or parental leave, usually on a three- to four-day-a-week schedule.

- Several women in high-level technical jobs at Bank of America's San Francisco headquarters switched to a three-day workweek following the birth of children.

- Honeywell, Inc., in one of its Massachusetts plants, places interested female employees on a "mothers' shift." These employees work hours that coincide with the time their children are in school, and high school and college students fill the women's jobs during the summer months.

"The permanent part-time approach isn't just for large offices," contends L. E. Sansum, head of a busy medical practice in Long Beach, California. The office recently hired a young mother to work part-time, during school hours, processing insurance paperwork. The new employee's duties do not require her to consult directly with patients or to keep the same hours as the nurses and appointment staff. "Twenty hours a week is enough time to complete her assignments," says Sansum, "and the arrangement seems to work out well for all of us."

Job Sharing. Job sharing is a more formalized permanent part-time arrangement that is used widely in government offices (particularly at the state and local level) but that has been slower to catch on in the private sector. Yet the idea is gaining more acceptance as news spreads about successful employee pairs.

Introduced in the late 1960s as a way to provide career-level opportunities for persons unable to work a 40-hour week, the concept has been employed effectively in a wide range of occupations, including receptionist, legislative aide, executive secretary, probation officer, computer programmer, medical technologist, personnel specialist, and even college president. Employers generally have adopted such arrangements only in direct response to prospective job sharers, however. To date, very few companies have made job sharing a regular part of their hiring plans.

Depending upon the duties involved, job sharing can involve splitting one position (usually clerical or blue-collar) with the two workers doing the same job but sharing few, if any, overlapping duties. The pair's main responsibility is to ensure the job is covered at all times, coordinating their schedules so that one worker is present if the other must be absent or is on vacation.

One of the first factories to institutionalize job sharing was The Rolscreen Company, a 2000-employee door and window manufacturing firm in Pella, Iowa. In 1977, two factory workers, sisters-in-law in their late twenties with young children, approached management with the idea of splitting a job. The improvement in the two employees' absentee and performance ratings inspired the company to extend the option to any job that could be adapted. Today, more than 50 pairs of employees, mostly line workers, share jobs. The personnel department keeps a list of employees interested in job sharing, but prefers that sharers find their own partners. While job-sharing employees, as individuals, generally work fewer than 40 hours a week, the company continues to provide them the same health and dental benefits they received as full-time employees.

Genuine job sharing, as opposed to job splitting, involves positions that ordinarily are available only to full-time workers. Such jobs cannot be easily broken down into small, stand-alone tasks and usually include some supervisory duties. These employees take a team approach to their shared job, communicating often with one another by phone and weekly in face-to-face meetings.

In late 1977, TRW Vidar, a small business within giant TRW's telecommunications empire, had its first encounter with job sharing when two mothers-to-be in the personnel department approached their supervisor about taking on, as a team, the demanding position of personnel representative. The supervisor turned them down but agreed to let both women continue working part-time in their original jobs. When it later became evident that the personnel representative position was too complicated for such an informal arrangement, the supervisor let the women share the job.

By 1983, each woman was working 2½ days a week, with a half-hour overlap on Wednesdays. The salaries were adjusted to account for one partner's more extensive experience, and, even though they were technically part-time employees, the two women received full company benefits. "They bring to the job a full-time commitment, not a part-time attitude," said Bill Connolly, TRW Vidar's manager of recruitment and staffing. "After all their years of experience...to think that one would have had to go away, that we weren't willing to change a little bit, would have been sad. I'm proud to have [this] example of teamwork."

Job sharing can work even in highly skilled professional positions. For example, two sisters working as anesthesiologists at a Kaiser Medical Center in Oakland, California, share their practice, each working three days a week and taking responsibility for each other's children during their time off. Even the redoubtable Harvard Medical School has experimented with shared residencies to allow students with families to extend their intensive, on-the-job training over a period of three years. Still, residency schedules are rigorous: job-sharing student doctors put in between 35 and 60 hours a week.

Who Will Watch the Children?

For mothers who work full-time—and even many who use these innovative part-time arrangements—there remains a troubling question that even the best flexible policies can't answer: When parents are at work, who will watch the children? Indeed, the child-care issue has moved, almost overnight, to the forefront of the national political agenda. More than 100 child-care bills have been introduced in Congress. Former U.S. Labor Secretary Ann McLaughlin made child care her top priority, and her successor, Elizabeth Dole, has continued this effort.

With rising numbers of working parents, this interest is not surprising, and neither is the demand by individual families for high-quality child care. Waiting lists of 100 children or more are common in the best metropolitan-area facilities. For some women, particularly single mothers with low-paying jobs, finding care that is affordable is the biggest challenge. But with a large portion of the day-care demand coming from moderate- to upper-income families, quality and choice, as much as affordability, remain prime concerns.

In *Fortune*'s 1987 survey of working parents, for example, a majority said they felt their children were not receiving enough time and attention in day care. "There just aren't that many good quality programs around," concedes the University of Virginia's Deborah Phillips, coauthor of a just-completed study by the National Academy of Sciences.

Seeing their own workers' needs for day care, a number of companies have begun offering child-care assistance as an employee benefit. These companies do one or more of the following:

- Directly subsidize child-care expenses, sometimes in lieu of other fringe benefits.
- Work to expand the supply of child care in the community.
- Sponsor day-care facilities on company premises.
- Provide referral services.

Employers that have become actively involved in providing or locating child care report lower worker turnover, higher productivity, and a boost in company morale. Many are finding that day-care benefits are a valuable recruiting tool. National surveys also show that many companies believe they are saving money by responding to their employees' needs for child care.

But while demand is high for such benefits, only a small minority of American businesses—about 25,000, or 2 percent, of establishments with ten employees or more—currently sponsor on- or near-site day-care centers for their workers' children. Another 35,000 companies provide financial assistance that can be used specifically for child care. Some companies choose to reimburse their workers, based on financial need, for a portion of their child-care expenses. More commonly, however, employers providing child-care benefits do not restrict them to lower-earning workers.

Child-Care Vouchers. One popular approach to helping out with child care is the use of vouchers. These reimbursable day-care coupons allow companies to meet their employees' child-care needs while maintaining some control over the facilities chosen. The company, contracting with a high-quality, usually licensed, child-care provider, pays a portion of each enrollee's tuition directly to the provider.

In situations where most of the affected employees live or work in the same area, a firm sometimes selects one or two specific providers ahead of time and issues vouchers for employees to redeem at those care facilities. Companies with employees at more dispersed locations also can issue vouchers, but trying to limit parents to specific providers in these instances is usually impractical.

Polaroid Corp., whose work force is scattered throughout Massachusetts and seven other states, uses vouchers to directly subsidize child-care expenses for employees earning less than $30,000 a year. The company signs a standard contract with any licensed provider the employee chooses, then pays a portion of the annual bill—between 20 and 80 percent, depending on the worker's financial circumstances—on a quarterly basis. The program has been in operation since 1971. According to Polaroid management, it has increased productivity by "freeing employees to work to their fullest potential."

Direct Reimbursement. An alternative to vouchers is direct reimbursement of child-care expenses, often as part of a flexible benefits package. Under flexible or "cafeteria" benefit plans, an employer lets workers choose from among a variety of benefits, up to a specified dollar limit. Cafeteria plans typically offer basic medical insurance and other optional benefits, such as extra vacation days, life insurance, college tuition assistance or child care. Such plans appeal to dual-earner families because workers can choose benefits that complement, rather than overlap, those their spouses receive from other employers. From the employer's standpoint, cafeteria benefit plans allow them to offer a wide array of benefits (even expensive items like child care) at a reasonable overall cost.

Procter & Gamble is one company that makes a child-care option available as part of its flexible benefits program. Employees may use their full credit—worth 2 to 4 percent of their annual salary, based on time with the company—for this option.

In special cases, an employer may opt to reimburse parents for child care as it would any other business expense. One such company is Johnson & Johnson. The firm reimburses employees' child-care expenses during its annual out-of-town meeting, which the company requires both the employee and his or her spouse to attend. And when American Can Company employees are sent on out-of-town assignments or must work long hours on short notice, the company allows them to submit extra child-care expenses for reimbursement.

On-Site Care. A limited number of companies have found on- or near-site child care facilities to be an effective way to alleviate working parents' on-the-job stress. Because nearby facilities allow parents to maintain some contact with their children throughout the day, "the line between work and family is not so brutal," as one child-care professional puts it. Providing this benefit also ensures that employers lose the services of key female employees for shorter periods of time, since on-site child care—especially a center that accepts infants—gives new mothers an incentive to return to their jobs at the earliest possible time.

One popular on-site program is Campbell Soup Company's top-of-the-line day-care center at the firm's Camden, New Jersey, corporate headquarters. Campbell contracts with a local child-care specialist to operate the center. With the company subsidizing half the cost, employees pay weekly fees ranging from $70 for infants six weeks and older to $46 for kindergarten children. The well-received program, which combines supervision with education, can serve 123 children at a time and usually has a waiting list, especially for infant care.

After the center opened, gains in the company's recruitment, retention, and productivity made a believer out of Campbell's CEO, Gordon McGovern. Having initially considered the center a "nice but insignificant" step, he quickly recognized its value as a recruiting aid: "We started hiring people we couldn't hire before, because they were able to bring their children to the center."

Similarly, hosiery manufacturer Neuville Industries, Inc., attributes its outstanding recruiting success directly to the on-site child-care center at its Hildebran, North Carolina, plant. The plant opened in 1979, a time of low unemployment in the region that sparked an intense competition for production workers among area factories. Nonetheless, Neuville received four applications for every opening. Fully 95 percent of the applicants said they had been attracted by the plant's child-care center. Since then, while its competitors have experienced 80 to 100 percent annual turnover rates, the Neuville plant reports employee losses at least two-thirds lower.

The popular child-care program has been expanded twice since its inception. The company's yearly investment has ranged from $22,000 initially to about $43,000 after its second expansion, but the expenditures are offset, a company spokeswoman says, by more than twice that amount in savings generated by reduced absenteeism, turnover, and payroll taxes.

The American Savings and Loan Association also has benefited greatly from on-site care. In 1983, the company purchased and renovated a church building for a child-care facility near its downtown Stockton, California, headquarters. The Little Mavericks School of Learning now serves about 160 children between the ages of 2 and 13. Parents using the facility pay their monthly fee through a payroll deduction of $185 to $260 a month, while American Savings subsidizes the center's operating expenses. The firm uses the renovated building for other extracurricular activities as well, such as parenting classes for employees.

The California Institute of Technology (CalTech) takes a similar approach. Using leased space in a partially empty public elementary school building, the institution contracts with a nonprofit firm to operate the near-site Child Education Center for employees of the Jet Propulsion Laboratory (JPL), one of CalTech's operating divisions. JPL's Women's Council, having learned through an employee survey of the widespread interest in company-supported day care, was the driving force behind CalTech's decision to provide a $31,000 interest-free start-up loan for the center.

Open both to laboratory employees and the community at large, the center specializes in caring for children below age five, and even accepts infants as young as two months, an unusual service for such facilities. The laboratory provides liability and workers' compensation insurance and helps offset other facility expenses; employees receive a 10 percent discount on tuition.

Employees and their spouses also participate in the center's maintenance and fund-raising. Parents are expected to volunteer 24 hours a year, and some also serve on the board. Codirector Eric Nelson says almost all parents he interviews, even those who do not choose to bring in their children, tell him the center's close-to-work location is one of its most attractive aspects. It is not unusual to find 200 children of employees on the center's waiting list.

Even the male-dominated construction industry is beginning to realize the importance of day care. B.E.&K., Inc., an industrial construction firm based in Birmingham, Alabama, started 1990 by opening BEKare, which *The New York Times* describes as "arguably the nation's most novel corporate day-care experiment." The center is composed of five 40-foot-long trailers hooked together, and is "open when the workers are working, closed when they're not—and it will pack up and drive off when the project is complete."

B.E.&K., whose labor force is 11 percent female, knew on-site day care was a necessity when absenteeism started to climb. "We had to remove the concerns the women had about their children," says Theodore C. Kennedy, B.E.&K.'s chairman. The program has already paid off in bringing in new workers. "I would have started a lot earlier," notes one female supervisor, "if there had been day care."

Opening a company child-care center can be an expensive undertaking, however, and is, therefore, more common among middle- to larger-sized firms. But some smaller employers—both small companies and branch offices of larger companies—have overcome this hurdle by joining with other employers in the same downtown or suburban business center.

The Tyson's Corner Play & Learn Children's Center in northern Virginia, one of four such establishments in the Washington, D.C., metropolitan area, is one example of how businesses in a common geographic area can work together to meet their employees' child-care needs. In return for tax benefits and reserved child-care slots for their employees, 22 local employers jointly contributed more than $100,000 ($1500 for each reserved space) toward the costs of establishing this independently run facility. Their efforts prove that company size is not an insuperable barrier to providing high-quality day care for working parents.

Referral Services.   Child-care referral services are another option both small and large employers often rely upon. Unlike on- or near-site day care, this service seldom requires a large investment of money or facilities. Moreover, such programs are flexible and can meet a wide variety of child-care needs.

Resource and referral services usually center around a local agency that becomes a clearinghouse for information about day-care options. Often, the referral services maintain a computer data base that can be searched by location, size, cost, hours, children's ages, or other considerations. Using the data base, agency counselors track down child-care providers compatible with employees' needs and preferences, and the employees contact the providers directly.

Where active local resource centers already exist, the job is easy; employers simply contract with them for this service. Where no suitable independent referral service exists, companies have started their own resource networks or have made day-care referrals a regular part of their employee assistance program.

Some companies also use this approach to help expand child-care services in the community. The most dramatic initiative of this type has been IBM's nationwide Child Care Referral Service. The first such network in this country, the referral program has assisted more than 25,000 IBM parents, free of charge, and helped expand the supply of child-care providers in local communities throughout the United States.

IBM began the referral program in 1984, both as a way to help its own employees and to improve the availability and quality of care that was available. The company hired Work/Family Directions, a consultant in Watertown, Massachusetts, to develop a network of 250 community-based resource and referral organizations to serve IBM parents in local areas.

IBM's former director of dependent care programs, Jack Carter, says the program has been successful because "it helps meet the diverse child-care needs of IBM parents. Each organization in the network is able to target its recruitment and development activities in response to specific community needs."

For example, Carter explains: "In Atlanta, there was a great demand for suburban day-care centers but not enough available. The local child-care resource and referral organization saw that suburban churches could be a potential source of child-care centers, so IBM funded a conference for churches interested in establishing nondenominational child-care centers. Those that decided to go ahead with a center received technical assistance as well." These efforts led to three new church-based centers, with spaces for approximately 230 children; six more are in various stages of development.

With additional funds from IBM and other sources, organizations in the resource and referral network have helped recruit or develop about 43,000 new care providers since the program began. More than 33,000 of these are home-based family day-care providers. The company also has funded training for 20,000 child-care providers in such areas as child development, safety, nutrition, and business management.

For firms that find the initial investment for a referral center to be prohibitive, a relatively inexpensive alternative is to affiliate with an existing service. For instance:

- Boston's Shawmut Bank contracts with the Child Care Resource Center, an independent, nonprofit organization that maintains an up-to-date listing of 3000 registered or licensed child-care providers in eastern Massachusetts. Shawmut then offers this service to its employees without charge.

- Both U.S. Bancorp and Pacific Northwest Bell, located in the states of Oregon and Washington, respectively, contract with the Northwest Family Network to provide their employees information about day-care centers and other family-related services.

- McKesson Industries in San Francisco uses a local child-care referral service for its employees.

Training and Licensing. Other firms work together to develop child-care services, an avenue available to large and small companies alike. In 1986, the New York-based American Express Company, through its American Express Foundation, recruited eight major employers and a national foundation in New York City to help fund a citywide expansion of these services. Combined, the nine donors contributed $395,000 to the Neighborhood Child Care Initiatives Project.

The program helped launch four new neighborhood child-care networks and expand two existing ones. Community-organization sponsors aided new providers in becoming licensed, while American Express contracted with Child Care, Inc., to provide the new resource centers with recruiting materials, training workshops, and other support services.

Sometimes the initiative extends to an entire state. Since 1985, California's BankAmerica Foundation has organized and run a program that is a collaborative effort between the public and private sector. To date, it has recruited, trained, and licensed more than 1200 new providers and created more than 5000 new child-care slots. Led by Bank of America, a 33-member consortium of private companies and public agencies provided money to California's state resource and referral agencies expressly to increase the supply of quality child care in the state.

Care for Sick Children. Even with accessible, affordable day care in general, many working parents face child-care problems all over again when their children become ill. On regular school days, relatives and neighbors, baby sitters, or after-school sports programs can supervise school-aged children until their parents come home from work. But when a child has to miss school because of sickness, the parent (most often the mother) normally misses a day of work as well. The same is true for children in day care, since these centers rarely accommodate youngsters with contagious illnesses. Inevitably, working parents' attendance and productivity fall.

Flexible scheduling is one way some companies help working parents meet these responsibilities without taking away from their time on the job. Another solution to the sick-child dilemma has been to provide or help employees find near-site day care for sick children.

Hospitals or clinics with partially empty wards are sometimes willing to cooperate with local employers in establishing sick-child facilities. One company that has had success with this concept is the Transamerica Life Insurance Company, which established a 15-bed sickroom for its employees' children at the California Medical Center, just four blocks from the firm's Los Angeles office. Parents pay only $5 to $10 a day, depending on how long the child stays and on whether siblings checks in together, and their employer picks up the remainder of the $45 daily cost—about one-third the cost of hiring a temporary clerical employee. Before initiating this service, the company estimated it lost between $150,000 and $180,000 a year due to employee absenteeism to care for sick children.

A more costly alternative (useful in special cases and for the most difficult-to-replace employees) is home-based care for sick children. The 3M Company operates a pilot program that sends health-care workers from Tender Care for Kids, an affiliate of several major Twin Cities hospitals, into parents' homes to care for children with chicken pox, the flu, or other illnesses. The company pays for a portion of the $9.50-per-hour fee, with the exact amount tailored to the worker's ability to pay.

While there are still relatively few programs like Tender Care that sit for mildly ill children of working parents, employers sometimes can attempt to identify the existing services in their areas by checking with local child-care resource and referral organizations. Where necessary, companies can fund their own studies. IBM took this approach, contracting, once again, with Work/Family Directions to research programs that care for sick children. The results of the study are presented in a booklet, entitled *A Little Bit Under the Weather,* which IBM has distributed to child-care professionals, the American Academy of Pediatrics, and various state and local government agencies.

The Other Day-Care Crisis

As America's work force ages, more and more employees, whether as spouses, siblings, or adult children, will face the responsibility of caring for elderly relatives. For many families, the recent drift toward delayed childbearing will impose a double burden of caring for young children and elderly parents at the same time.

For instance, the Travelers, a nationwide insurance and financial services firm based in Hartford, Connecticut, found in a survey of more than 1400 employees aged 30 or older that 20 percent were already providing some form of care to elderly relatives or friends. Eight percent said they spent at least 35 hours a weeks caring for elderly persons. Such numbers are bound to increase. By the year 2000, predicts Michael Creedon of the National Council on Aging, almost half the nation's employees "will be providing child care, elder care, or both."

As Chapter 2 noted, these obligations often force employees to reduce their work hours or even quit their jobs altogether. Like the quandary parents of small children face, these responsibilities are an added source of stress, both emotional and financial, to working people.

Since elder care is a relatively new issue for business, corporate initiatives to address the needs of employees with elderly dependents are much less widespread than programs in other family-related areas. But with the 65-and-older population projected to grow by more than 4 million between the years 1988 and 2000, the adequacy of *elder* care will become as critical a factor in workers' productivity and job attendance during the next decade as child care is today. And more businesses are recognizing this. *The Washington Post* reports, for example, that over the last two years, about 100 companies have adopted some type of elder-care assistance for employees.

Extending Employee Benefits to Elderly Dependents. Even though many retired persons have a number of resources to draw on for medical expenses and other services, younger family members often have to assume responsibility for some of these costs. Long-term nursing care is probably the largest potential financial burden elderly persons and their families face (although insurance plans to cover these costs are starting to appear on the market). To help relieve these burdens, some far-thinking employers are beginning to include elder care in their benefit programs.

One company that has opted to help employees and their families in this way is Procter & Gamble, which makes a long-term care insurance program available to the elderly parents of eligible employees. Workers and their parents pay for coverage at the company's group rate. The company reports that both workers and their older relatives are less anxious about long-term care since this plan became available.

While by no means an inexpensive option, elder care sometimes is incorporated into companies' cafeteria benefit plans. In any case, the cost of such insurance is almost always less than the cost of losing an experienced employee.

On-Site Elder Care. A generation ago, younger relatives, usually women, routinely cared for their elderly family members at home. But juggling such responsibilities amid a 40-hour workweek, as many families must do today, can be next to impossible. As one corporate personnel chief observed, "When people have concerns [about their elderly relatives], it's bound to affect their job....If the stress is relieved, it's bound to affect morale and...productivity."

Stride Rite, the Cambridge, Massachusetts, shoe manufacturer, has decided to help employees facing these concerns by creating a first-in-the-nation intergenerational day-care center. In this new facility, seniors receive whatever practical assistance they need during the day while enjoying the companionship of people their own age and youngsters from the firm's child-care program.

Stride Rite—in 1971, the first corporation in the country to establish an on-site child-care center as well—subsidizes the elder-care center's operating expenses. Employees pay a reduced rate of $85 a week. Families of nonemployees, also eligible to use the facility, pay the full cost of $140 a week.

The manufacturer and its partners, Wheelock College and Somerville/Cambridge Elder Services, were "determined that the center not have the look and especially not the antiseptic smell of an institution, and it does not." The aromas of chicken soup and pretzels "waft from the kitchen at noon," according to one report. Says Stride Rite chairman Arnold Hiatt, the center's originator, of the commingling of young and old: "Here we do not share the same names, but we have a chance to interact that is as old as the family of man."

Elder Referral Services. Company-supported referral programs for nursing care and other services are a less expensive but highly effective way of helping employees meet these difficult responsibilities. But since independent referral agencies are not as widely available for elderly services as they are for child care, a company may have to undertake its own regional survey, whether on its own or in conjunction with neighboring firms.

Taking the lead in employer-sponsored referral programs, IBM has established a nationwide resource network that can be a model for similar efforts by large companies, business consortia, or other community-based groups. The company's Elder Care Referral Service, established in February 1988, lists some 175 community-based organizations that provide such services in local areas. IBM employees, retirees, and spouses can call an experienced geriatric counselor in the area where their older relative lives. The counselor will discuss with them various near- and long-term alternatives, offer referrals to potential care providers, and supply them with consumer-education materials.

IBM took on this project after a company survey revealed that 30 percent of its employees had some responsibility for older relatives. "The wave of elder-care issues we thought was approaching is already here," explains former dependent-care program director Jack Carter, "and the common thread for employed care givers is a need for information and guidance." There are many providers out there, he says, but "the interrelationships among them are often difficult for the uninitiated to understand. What if an employee has a relative in a distant city who needs to be cared for? How can he or she, working alone, begin to find the best possible care for that person? It was obvious that a national network model was needed."

Interestingly, IBM's contractor, Work/Family Elder Directions, found that, because a great deal of expertise on geriatric care already exists across the nation, setting up a network of organizations with qualified counselors was far less complicated than IBM program managers had expected.

The Elder Care Referral Service is available free to any IBM employee, including overseas employees with elderly relatives living in the United States. In the program's first month, more than 2700 employees contacted the network for help, nearly twice the number contacting the company's child-care referral program in its initial month. Carter predicts that before long, many more companies will be providing similar services to employed care givers.

One firm that already has already stepped in to help employees meet their care-giving needs is the Travelers. Well known for its involvement in a number of innovative community programs for older Americans, the Travelers has committed itself to aiding its employees who face the pressures of caring for elderly family members on a daily basis.

A 1985 survey of Travelers employees revealed that 80 percent wanted more information about care giving. In response, the company called together more than 20 community agencies to provide facts and suggestions on home health care, financial assistance, and coping with stress. The care-giving fair was a success; some 700 employees and retirees attended.

The Travelers continues to offer regular lunchtime seminars on topics of interest to care givers and provides other educational resources, such as videotapes, library materials, and company newspaper articles. Corporate strategists believe that services of this kind can give them a competitive edge: "If our people don't spend as much time worrying about these at-home issues, we'll get more productivity and loyalty," asserts Harold E. Johnson, senior vice president of personnel and administration. "And the companies that don't do the things we're doing in this area won't have such a quality work force."

Counseling for Elder Care. As a smaller-scale solution to helping out with elder-care problems, many companies have directed their established corporate employee assistance programs to broaden their services to include service referrals for the elderly or care-giver support groups. Johnson & Johnson, for example, expanded its employee assistance program to accommodate employees seeking care for both children and elderly dependents. "Once we were looking only at day care," equal employment opportunity director, Marion HochbergSmith, told us. "But then we realized that today's parents have many more issues to deal with—supporting elderly relatives as well as children."

HochbergSmith, herself the mother of a young child and the daughter of elderly parents, recently was placed in the difficult position of having to find nursing care quickly while balancing a heavy work load at the office. An employee assistance coordinator gave her several leads to investigate. "Not only did I find what I was looking for," she reported, "but I found it with a minimum of stress and without having to take time off from work."

The Travelers' employee assistance program's counselors sponsor support groups for employees that regularly care for elderly family members. Said one support-group member: "We learn from each other, learn to cope....I don't feel all alone anymore. I never realized there were so many people in the same situation who feel the same way."

When Careers Conflict

Companies that have lost valuable workers due to conflicts with their spouses' occupations know that incompatible job locations and goals, or other adjustment problems, can be hard both on working couples and their employers. Some employers are wising up to ways that can reduce or soften such conflicts, thus improving their chances of retaining good workers.

Permitting or encouraging both spouses to work for the same company, for example, may help avoid split loyalties. Where both partners worked for the company before marriage, employers also can save money by consolidating two sets of family benefits. Such policies may help a firm retain not just one, but two valuable employees.

Du Pont is one company that enthusiastically supports dual-career couples. In fact, nearly 7000 of the 100,000 Du Pont employees in the United States are married to one another. There are 80 married couples, for instance, at Du Pont's plant in Cape Fear, North Carolina.

Earlier, we quoted a bank executive's observation that employees (figuratively) bring their families to work with them. Nowhere is this more true than in companies that regularly transfer their managers. Such moves mean that spouses and children are uprooted from their own jobs or activities and separated from friends or family.

Some employees (especially those in two-career families) may look for another job rather than accept a transfer, as Du Pont's recent worker poll, cited in Chapter 2, confirms. Employers that are sensitive to these conflicts will have an edge in recruiting and retaining men and women with families. Some, including General Electric and Procter & Gamble, already have modified their policies to require fewer transfers for up-and-coming managers.

Where transfers are necessary, companies that employ both a husband and wife may try to find the transferee's spouse a company job in the new location or, if no positions are open, help with his or her job search expenses. Several dozen big corporations take this approach, some even granting the transferee's spouse a leave of absence where necessary.

But transfers usually affect children as well, and the Baxter Healthcare Corp., headquartered in Deerfield, Illinois, decided to do something about it. A 1981 employee survey convinced the firm that its relocation policy needed to focus more closely on the family aspects of employee transfers. Although the company currently moves less than 5 percent of its personnel each year, those relocations are considered critical to the firm's growth, and Baxter has found that a heightened sensitivity to personal and family considerations has paid off in terms of worker satisfaction.

For the children of employees being transferred, the company prepares special kits, geared to different age groups, that "try to address relocation from the child's perspective, making an effort to emphasize the positive aspects of moving." Follow-up surveys show that the kits, which include such items as T-shirts, scrapbooks, coloring books, crayons, school bags, address books, key chains, and stationery, have helped youngsters adjust more quickly to their new surroundings.

Managing for Retention

Though family benefits and family-related programs make it easier for firms to recruit top-notch female employees, many companies are realizing they must do even more to build the kind of reputation that consistently brings in the best applicants and makes them want to stay. Usually, this requires special attention to enriching female employees' development, both personally and professionally.

Employees of either gender will perform better if they know they are respected and are treated fairly. Even a hint of discrimination can turn a harmonious working environment into one filled with suspicion and dissatisfaction. Most women, still far from having equal representation in corporate management, are particularly sensitive to these issues, and they will be watching for the company's actions to match its words.

The Most Important Step: Equal Pay

As we noted earlier, although pay differentials have shrunk over the last few years, women on average still earn less than men. It is sometimes difficult to tell whether these differences are justified by variations in experience and productivity or whether subtle discrimination is involved. But to develop a reputation for fairness, several employers are acting *before* actual disputes arise—at a minimum, adopting formal policies on the equal-pay issue, even where they are not required by law to do so.

In very large companies, it is difficult, if not impossible, for top management to be aware of individual employees' progress. To reduce this problem, IBM has put in place a set of programs to assure equality in administering salaries. Every IBM employee's pay is determined by performance appraisal rather than by seniority. As an additional check, each woman's (or minority-group member's) salary is compared with a peer group of employees performing the same job in the same appraisal category. If the woman's (or minority-group member's) salary is more than 3 percent below others in the same group, the company's compensation staff reviews the individual's situation for equity.

The company also has a long-standing open-door policy for resolving work-related disputes. Any IBM employee has the right to raise his or her concerns with any manager and at any level, even the company's chairman, if desired. Don Devey, manager of equal opportunity programs, credits the policy with greatly reducing the incidence of discrimination claims, since most employee concerns can be resolved internally.

Sensitivity Education

Another technique for improving the working environment for women involves education: for women, to learn how to be effective within a predominantly male company structure; and, for men, to become more sensitive to women's concerns, both on- and off-the-job. Offerings may include seminars for women on negotiation and office politics or joint sessions, such as Du Pont's "Women and Men Working as Colleagues." Such programs help employers reaffirm the value they place on coworkers regardless of gender.

One highly regarded initiative geared to female employees is the Du

Pont Company's Personal Safety Program, introduced in 1985 "in acknowledgment of the increasingly greater number of women in nontraditional jobs in the company." The educational program was designed to help Du Pont employees deal responsibly with problems like sexual harassment, physical assault, spouse battering, child and elder abuse, and, especially, rape.

Trained employee volunteers called facilitators conduct workshops in each department and at every plant site. Rape prevention workshops, available to female employees, employees' wives, and adult female dependents, teach assertive behavior, preventive safety strategies, and self-defense techniques. Another workshop, open to men, is intended to shatter myths and sensitize managers to the needs of rape victims and battered women.

"Managers have noted a new assertiveness and new sense of power exhibited by women who have taken part in the program," declares a company publication. "There is better sharing and communication between men and women in the organization." Program director Mary Lou Arey believes the policy will aid the company's efforts to attract women: "We want to keep and attract women. And we're trying to say, 'You are important to us.'"

Sensitivity-training pioneer Merck & Company, as well as other employers that offer affirmative action training, often include sessions designed to sensitize men to women's concerns. Said one young man about his reaction to one such seminar: "In the event a position I want is offered to a woman, I'll know it's because she was better qualified, and I'll just have to try harder next time." That kind of understanding helps the company itself as much as it does the female employees.

Professional Development and Upward Mobility

Talented workers, men and women alike, seem to thrive in companies that value creativity and initiative. Female employees who do not find appropriate opportunities in traditional corporate settings often decide to join smaller, more progressive firms. Many even choose to go into business for themselves, as confirmed by the recent dramatic increase in the number of women-owned small businesses: a 48 percent jump in sole proprietorships between 1980 and 1985, compared with a 32 percent increase for such businesses owned by men.

"We've all had good opportunities to work for larger, more established companies," says Raisa Scriabine Smith, founder of TKG International, a public affairs and marketing firm based in Washington, D.C. "But why struggle along in someone else's corporate structure when you can start your own firm—and be a lot more professionally satisfied in the process?"

Working Within the System. Not surprisingly, women who remain within the system often fare best in rapidly growing businesses and in decentralized corporations, both of which rely on innovative, entrepreneurial managers. For example, to achieve maximum profits, Citicorp operates within what former Chairman Walter Wriston called a "meritocracy," a system of rewarding people according to their performance, not their seniority. Competition for promotions is tight in this "company of overachievers." Yet because the corporation is so decentralized, one young manager says, "there are lots of small organizations [within] Citibank, so you feel you can rise to the top of something." Another employee, a young black woman, agrees. "There's lots of horizontal doors here as opposed to just vertical ones. This institution has flexibility. It's easy to move around."

Management at Nordstrom, Inc., the Seattle-based department store chain, is not afraid of delegating decision-making authority to sales persons, the majority of whom are women. Enthusiastic young female managers are routinely put in charge of new stores. And in another recently decentralized company, Campbell Soup, the concept of an "independent business unit" has allowed many women to rise to plant manager and assistant plant manager positions.

Rewarding Managers for Extra Effort. Another way many companies accelerate the door-opening process for women is through aggressive corporate policies that reward managers for making special efforts to recruit, hire, and promote capable women. Successful corporations also regularly evaluate each department's performance in this area, identifying practices that unfairly discriminate against women or bar their further progress.

The Gannett Company, which proudly calls attention to its female managers, launched its Partners in Progress initiative in 1979 to "assure that the makeup of Gannett's people force—more than 36,000 employees—will ultimately be as diverse as the communities it services." The initiative includes a system for setting goals and measuring every manager's success in finding, hiring, developing, and promoting women and minorities. Managers' bonuses are tied in part to their progress in these areas. This step, says Madelyn Jennings, senior vice president for personnel and administration, represents the most successful aspect of the program: "When their pocketbook reflects their progress, it's amazing how much improvement can be made."

Gannett's management makes no secret of its confidence in Partners as a recruiting tool: "To gain the edge in a highly competitive market for talented women and minorities, we communicated openly about our commitment, our programs, and our opportunities to our employees, to the industry, and to the public. Partners in Progress built Gannett's reputation as an industry leader in progressive hiring and promotion of women and minorities, further honing our competitive edge." "You have to believe in it," says recently retired Chairman Al Neuharth, "then practice what you preach."

Redefining Jobs for Greater Responsibility. But employers need not limit their career development efforts to women already on the road to management. Many start by improving and expanding workers' skills at the entry level. One way they do this is by redefining lower-level jobs to include greater responsibility. This approach often increases workers' job satisfaction, increases their interest in seeking further training, and raises retention rates. Businesses also find that restructuring lower-level jobs increases company productivity by reducing the need for an additional layer of workers.

This approach has worked well in the banking industry, which recently has been having trouble filling teller positions, and in other businesses, such as insurance, that tend to keep clerical functions separate from account responsibility. For example, as many routine clerical operations have become automated, several banks have begun to restructure traditional tellers' jobs to include more challenging duties. "The added responsibility allows these entry-level workers to plug into the advancement chain," one bank executive told us. Northwestern Mutual Life Insurance Company also has redefined its clerical staff positions to include new tasks.

Formal Education and Training. Formal education is another way in which companies are preparing employees in lower-level jobs to take on additional responsibilities, and helping employees obtain that education could be especially valuable for companies that promote exclusively through the ranks. Training courses in such job-related skills as word processing, computer programming, and written or oral communication also can help improve employees' performance in their current jobs.

Tuition reimbursement for job-related courses is fairly common in medium-sized to larger companies. Johnson & Johnson is one company that provides this benefit. "By taking advantage of our tuition reimbursement program, several motivated J&J employees have worked their way into promotions," one corporate official reports. Hewlett-Packard takes a broader approach than most companies to continuing education, reimbursing employees' expenses for almost any educational program, whether or not it is directly job related.

Pacific Telesis, through its Telesis Management Institute, sees higher education as "an important means for moving women and other 'targeted groups' ahead and redirecting them to jobs as they exist," according to Constance Beutel, who runs the institute's self-directed education program. Pacific Telesis, which also reimburses employees' tuition for bachelor's and MBA programs, recently began sponsoring a two-year degree program in business and technology for its adult employees.

To fit in with a full-time work schedule, course work is accelerated and, whenever possible, taught on company premises. Groups of employees voluntarily assemble themselves to go through a course of study together. The program is available to any employee, regardless of age, position, or length of time with the company and leads to diverse and stimulating groups that otherwise might never be formed.

Networking.   Ensuring that women can succeed within a company may also involve putting them in touch with other women who have already made their way up the corporate ladder. For years, men working in business or government organizations have used informal, voluntary networks of counseling and advice to younger men whom they considered worthy of career advancement. The older or more experienced men, often referred to as mentors, help their younger colleagues learn the company ropes, introduce them to top management, give them challenging or visible assignments, and serve as their advocates within the company.

Women's greater difficulty in finding mentors no doubt has contributed to their comparatively slow ascent into top management positions. In one recent survey, 44 percent of the managers questioned agreed that women have a harder time than white men in finding someone to nurture their professional growth. Moreover, when women do have a mentor, the person very often is an older man, a situation that can contribute to damaging office gossip about both parties. For similar reasons, many women find it difficult to build informal relationships with their male peers.

One way to combat this problem is for companies to help female employees form self-help groups or mentoring networks, or to formally institute mentoring and career-counseling programs for them. Such efforts, particularly in medium-sized and larger companies, help ensure that capable women know and can pursue their advancement opportunities in the same way men can.

Like many corporations, Johnson & Johnson and its subsidiary companies "mentor" promising female and minority employees on a case-by-case basis by purposely giving them additional responsibilities and special opportunities to prove themselves. But some of Johnson & Johnson's smaller subsidiaries, reports its corporate equal opportunity manager, have more formal mentoring programs that "aggressively seek out bright female or minority employees and deliberately match them with someone further up the ladder." Half a dozen subsidiaries already have obtained positive results.

Many firms find that their top female executives are role models for other women, both inside and outside the company. For example, the success and personality of accounting firm Coopers & Lybrand's first female partner has helped attract a number of top female candidates to the firm, and she has continued to play an active role in informal mentoring.

Companies that hope to retain female employees throughout their careers encourage them to look at their jobs as a place to grow. Procter & Gamble is one of many companies that use the annual performance review process to discuss an employee's long-term career goals, as well as his or her accomplishments and areas for improvement. The company also recently established a corporate career-counselor position to help nonmanagement workers develop personal and professional growth plans for themselves and to help those aspiring to management to make that move.

Open posting, or publicizing, of all company job openings, ranging from clerical to top management positions, is another technique that allows employees to play a more active role in their own career development. Women, in particular, benefit from open posting by becoming more familiar with the qualifications for desired positions and deliberately acquiring those skills through intermediate career steps and supplemental training. "It keeps people motivated to have this information and be able to pursue those opportunities," says one corporate equal opportunity director. And motivation is the first step toward advancement.

Equal Opportunity: Just the Beginning

With women's increasing participation in the work force in recent years, many businesses have begun to reorient their efforts to attract and retain new employees in ways that take their female employees' special concerns into consideration. Some employers have seen this trend coming for a long time and have made policies to recruit women and address family-related needs a standard part of their corporate procedures. Those that have done so report higher employee retention rates, fewer absences, less tardiness, higher morale, and higher productivity.

But these efforts are just the beginning. Much more remains to be done to take account of female employees' demanding roles as mother, daughter, wife, *and* worker.

And much more *will* be done—you can depend on that—by the government, by professional associations, and by forward-thinking competitors. Equal employment opportunity for women is no longer just a part of the agenda of the women's movement. It is central to the strategic posture of every company that is thinking seriously about work force planning for the 1990s.

As the Labor Department's Marilia Robbins puts it, "Firms that don't take female employees' concerns to heart risk losing half their potential job applicants. That's a little like running a footrace with one leg in a cast. It makes it darned hard to compete."

5
Unemployment Rolls to Payrolls

The story of Jaime Escalante is an American fable by now. The subject of magazine articles, a book subtitled *The Best Teacher in America,* and the Hollywood film *Stand and Deliver,* Escalante is the East Los Angeles businessman turned teacher who proved that inner-city kids can make their way through even the toughest course material—and do so as well as any more privileged youngster. All they need is *ganas,* the desire to succeed.

Escalante's remarkable accomplishments are a matter of public record. His Hispanic students at Garfield High School are the archetype of disadvantage. Many are from broken homes. They are burdened with domestic and work responsibilities that often overwhelm their time for study, peers who ridicule their attempts to better themselves, and unsupportive parents who insist they not waste their energy on high school fantasies.

And they suffer from years of intellectual neglect. When the first regiment of students entered Escalante's math class, most could barely add and subtract, much less understand abstract concepts like sets and negative numbers.

But whereas many teachers would settle for showing them how to use calculators, Escalante taught them calculus, the most difficult math course a high school usually offers. More daring still, he prepared them to take the advanced college placement calculus test, which fewer than 2 percent of students nationwide attempt.

In his first year, 18 of Escalante's crew sat for the test, and all 18 passed—many with perfect scores. It was a feat unmatched by any school in the country, and it *keeps* happening year after year. The number of students passing the test is already five times higher than at the start. The testing service at first refused to believe that an entire class of ghetto kids could perform so well. But they did—and do—barriers notwithstanding. *Ganas.*

Cut to Washington, D.C., same time, a continent away. An energetic, mid-thirties black man sits astride a wooden stool at the edge of the crowded sidewalk outside one the city's best-known hotels. But he's not begging for spare change; he's not even idling while waiting for his next assistance check. He is working, earning money, shining shoes. An entrepreneur, the shoe-shine stand is his own business. The proprietor's name is Ego Brown.

But Ego Brown, the subject of an extensive media coverage and a controversial (and ultimately successful) court case, is not content to make a living just for himself. He aggressively recruits homeless men to enter his shoe-shine business. He gives them a shoe-shine stand, a shower, and a new suit of clothes and sets them up to work on profitable street corners in the heart of the city. Through these efforts, several disadvantaged men, who without Ego's help would not have a job, managed to find a way to support themselves.

At least for a while—until the city government intervened. Invoking a long-forgotten Jim Crow-era law still on the books, the government banished the bootblacks from the city streets. At the same time, other vendors—from popcorn peddlers to hawkers offering photographs with life-size cardboard cutouts of the President—remained in abundance.

A travesty? Without question. Yet when the Center for Civil Rights, the D.C.-based arm of the Landmark Legal Foundation, stood to challenge the law, it met with fierce government resistance and a vigorous defense of the bootblack prohibition—from the same city politicians who fill their noontime speeches with appeals for equal opportunity and nondiscrimination.

In the end, all the attention and arguments that have followed these cases come down to just two men—Jaime Escalante and Ego Brown—linked by a determination to see their less fortunate counterparts succeed in life. But these men are nothing special, really. Ask them and they will tell you: they are as ordinary as the man or woman down the street. In fact, their very ordinariness, set up alongside their success, is proof that inner-city men and women, no matter how great their disadvantage, can make good on the opportunity of a good job and the start on a self-sufficient life.

The reward cannot come without effort, of course. Like the kids of Garfield High School, those who want to succeed have to put away the nighttime cruising, the midnight drug deals, and the sometimes consuming self-doubt. But employers who look closely will find there is a reservoir of talent in all disadvantaged communities. These talents may be underdeveloped; they may be hidden by pride; they may be squeezed dry by those who tell the underprivileged they are too poor or too put upon to do more than ask for help from someone else. But the talents are there.

Companies determined to beat the coming worker shortages cannot allow these talents to remain hidden any longer. In the future, bringing economically disadvantaged men and women from the unemployment rolls to the payroll will become as vital a part of the competition for good workers as every other aspect of training and recruitment efforts—in some ways, as the shortages spread, even more so.

Believing in Success

Who are the economically disadvantaged? They commonly live in urban areas, are often dependent on public assistance, and are usually poorly educated and inactive in the labor market. Though the group is disproportionately comprised of minority-group members, it is an oversimplification to view their work problems solely in terms of race or ethnicity. Rather, what these people share is their *isolation*—physical, economic, or social—from the mainstream of American life.

To successfully draw upon this potentially important source of new workers, employers must find ways to eliminate the barriers separating people, whatever their color or ethnic background, from opportunities to work. Doing so could not be more important. As the *Workforce 2000* study has documented, although nonwhites account for only about 14 percent of today's labor force, they will constitute 42 percent of potential labor force entrants over the next decade.

But just as the need to more fully integrate minority group members and the economically disadvantaged into the work force becomes more urgent, the task of doing so grows more difficult. Despite the combined impact of equal opportunity laws and tight labor market, factors that ordinarily would make it easier for growing numbers of minority persons to enter the mainstream, a considerable proportion remain outside working-class society. The National Academy of Sciences' recent report, *A Common Destiny*, for instance, found that, while many disadvantaged blacks have moved up economically over the last decade, many others have fallen further behind.

Statistics highlight this paradox. The unemployment rate is twice as high among blacks, for example, as it is among whites. The number of black men even looking for work also continues to decline. By 1989, 26 percent of black males over age 20 had dropped out of the labor force altogether, more than double the 1950s nonparticipation level.

And these problems could worsen in the coming years. Blacks and Hispanics are disproportionately represented in occupations that will lose the greatest numbers of jobs over the next decade, and they are concentrated in the cities while jobs are moving to the suburbs. "If the policies and employment patterns of the present continue," William Johnston and Arnold Packer conclude in *Workforce 2000*, "it is likely that...blacks and Hispanics will have a *smaller* fraction of the jobs by the year 2000 than they have today."

The price of this failure will not be borne alone by those individuals who remain outside the work force, however. Companies that do not find, motivate, recruit, and train these minority and economically disadvantaged workers will face a range of even more costly alternatives. As *Workforce 2000* predicts, such companies will be forced to "bid up the wages of the relatively smaller numbers of white labor force entrants, seek to substitute capital for labor in many service occupations, or move job sites" to other areas of the country or the world where skilled labor is more abundant.

An increasing share of employers is discovering that the preferable course is to build up the talents of workers currently outside the economic mainstream. These firms are seeking to employ more blacks, Hispanics, and other disadvantaged minority group members, not merely as a matter of social conscience or legal mandates, but because they need more good workers as well. As companies take these steps, they are learning—often to their surprise—that such people's main disadvantage in life may be only this: that no one else ever really believed in them, and believed they could succeed.

Building Human Capital

Why aren't these people already part of the work force? There are two basic sets of problems:

- Problems of *employability*. People who are theoretically available for work often lack some of the basic skills that make them useful to employers.

- Problems of *recruitment*. For one reason or another, willing workers with useful skills are not stepping into the jobs that exist.

Unfortunately, many companies still view these as someone else's problems to solve. Employers traditionally have depended upon public schools to produce employable workers, high school graduates who possess the basic skills necessary to perform entry-level work. And they often have relied on the prospective workers themselves to track down the available jobs, frequently doing little more than advertising with mainstream employment services and newspapers.

Such reliance today is ill-advised. As Chapter 2 emphasized, in the 1990s, minimum requirements even for entry-level positions will involve far more than rudimentary reading, writing, and arithmetic. Yet although the need for higher-level basic skills is rising, the supply of skills produced by the public schools is declining. Companies themselves will be left to make up much of the difference if they hope to turn these potential workers into *employable* workers.

This challenge cuts across racial and ethnic lines, and so will require nonracial solutions. Even if it weren't prohibited by law, few companies today could afford to discriminate on the basis of race—simply because there aren't enough qualified workers to arbitrarily turn anyone away. But employers must and do discriminate against those applicants with inadequate skills. One company official from labor-starved Boston summed up the situation this way: "A black kid with decent skills can find a job anywhere today. But a kid without adequate educational skills won't find a job whether he's white or black."

What these conditions require, to use former Labor Secretary William Brock's description, is a Manhattan Project-sized investment in "human capital"—that storehouse of individual skills and qualities that turns job applicants into good workers. It is becoming all the more clear that companies themselves must take the lead in making this investment because no other social institution is both willing and able to do the job in time—and to the scale required—to beat the impending shortages.

Bridging the Skills Gap

Training, the linchpin of work-related human capital development, is nothing new to American business. Regardless of the raw skills a worker brings to a company, firms have long dedicated themselves to refining these abilities and making them specific to the company's needs.

But since many of today's new employees bring fewer basic skills to work with them than ever before, employers must do more than merely refine those skills; often they must create them from the ground up if they are to tackle problems of employability. Hence, the concepts of recruitment and training must undergo a significant change in the 1990s. Employers will no longer be able to limit their search to *qualified* workers. They will need to seek out *qualifiable* workers—and then invest them with *both* basic and advanced skills before trying to integrate them into the firm's operations.

The need for this new approach cannot be overstated. The problem of hiring "a million new workers who can't read, write, or count," as Xerox Corp. Chairman and CEO David Kearns has warned, is not just a bit of boardroom hyperbole. As Linda Tufo, director of training for Boston's Shawmut Bank, points out, "Reading and writing are essential for even entry-level jobs. In our business, even one mistyped zero can be a megaerror—the difference between one hundred thousand and a million dollars."

For a growing number of businesses, basic skills training has become the key to averting these and other costly mistakes—and an essential part of building a more highly skilled work force for the coming decade.

Direct Basic-Skills Training

The surest way for companies to invest their work force with adequate basic skills is to provide the training themselves. In so doing, employers:

- Create a much larger supply of potential workers, complete with basic job skills, for their entry-level positions.
- Can control the quality of skills training.
- Can tailor the training to their specific needs.
- Have the opportunity to evaluate new employees before making them a part of the company's actual labor force.
- Can ensure that trainees gain the tools they need for career growth, thus expanding the labor pool for higher-level positions as well.

While providing this training directly can be expensive, companies taking this step have the chance to fulfill their work force needs without sacrificing worker quality or depending on lucky breaks in the labor market.

Aetna's Institute for Corporate Education. One of the most comprehensive corporate training programs is Aetna Life & Casualty's Institute for Corporate Education. Established in 1981, the institute trains 20,000 people a year, some at its state-of-the-art facility in Hartford, Connecticut, and others through satellite courses.

As long ago as the 1970s, the institute's founders recognized, in former Aetna Chairman John Filer's words, that, in the service industry, "the only resource that will distinguish us from other companies is our people." Bearing this in mind, the company began to systematically project the skills its future labor force would need. Realizing that it would not be alone in competing for skilled workers, the company took steps to ensure that it could satisfy its own labor needs, no matter how tight the market became.

The institute's programs range from supplemental education for Hartford public school students to advanced training for Aetna managers. But one of the institute's most important tasks is providing basic skills for entry-level workers. Central to this mission is the recently established Effective Business Skills School. The school expands the company's labor pool by providing basic reading, writing, and math for both low-skilled employees and unskilled applicants. The courses also are infused with the corporation's values and ethics.

Aetna spends about $750,000 annually to teach basic skills to 500 employees, a cost of $1500 a student. But corporate officers believe this cost is small compared to the benefit Aetna receives from having a larger number of qualified workers to draw upon at hiring time. Not only does the program help reduce direct recruitment expenses, but it also cuts down on productivity losses stemming from inadequate skill levels.

The Rise of Direct Training. Another company that has taken on the task of basic-skills training is Boston's Shawmut Bank. The bank's community relations officer, Maurice Wright, laments that "we're doing a lot of basic-skills retraining." But the company has no choice. "Basic-skills training is becoming mandatory in our business," he explains. "We have to take people where they are and develop them, give them the skills the company needs."

Accordingly, Shawmut has expanded its training beyond job-specific capabilities, such as data entry, to include such subjects as basic English, math, and reading comprehension. New employees also receive specific instruction in corporate citizenship, which stresses such skills as dealing with customers and answering telephones courteously. Wright emphasizes an integrated approach to skills training. "We can train you to use a word processor, but if you can't spell, what good does it do?" Such an approach benefits the employees, he adds. "Unless basic skills are integrated into employment training," says Wright, "trainees will find any job is a dead end."

Other companies are replicating these ideas on whatever scale they need and can afford. Many firms whose facilities are vacant nights and weekends have set up their own minischools. Since 1982, for instance, the General Motors Truck and Bus Group plant in Flint Township, Michigan, has offered its workers classes and one-on-one tutoring in a cluster of rooms overlooking the shop floor, leading to the award of 14 high school diplomas by 1988. General Motors' employees form the core of the teaching staff.

Basic-skills training is becoming indispensable even for many nontechnical entry-level jobs. As Chapter 1 noted, Domino's Pizza of Ann Arbor, Michigan, discovered in 1987 that its new bakers had trouble understanding its dough-making manuals, even though they had been written at an eighth-grade level, leading to unacceptable variations in the quality of pizza dough from store to store. As a result, the company launched a $50,000 reading program featuring lessons on cuisine chemistry.

A year later, the company replaced its five-inch-thick manual with an integrated-skills and literacy-training program. The program uses interactive videodiscs that combine pictures with text and includes a 700-word dictionary that helps prepare the trainee for the required written "dough certification" test. In this way, Domino's combines dough-preparation training with the literacy skills necessary to perform the job.

Some Training Rules of Thumb. The experiences of companies involved in direct basic-skills training suggest several rules of thumb:

- At least *consider* direct basic skills training as an option, since it is often a good investment, expands the pool of workers for entry-level jobs, and provides employees with the skills necessary to move on to better jobs.

- To make the most of this investment, forecast the skills entry-level workers will need in future years, and determine whether these skills will be available in adequate supply in the local labor force—bearing in mind that other companies will be competing for the same workers. If the available skills are inadequate, that is all the more reason to provide basic-skills training directly.

- Make sure basic-skills training is job-related. As Hudson Institute's Arnold Packer argues, too often the "wrong things are being taught to adults. It's not how to read a fifth-grade book that counts, it's the ability to read a computer screen or an invoice." Still, cautions Packer, training "should not be so narrow that the skill is not transportable from one job to another."

- Investigate whether existing facilities and training programs can be adapted to integrate basic-skills training. If so, such training may not require a large additional investment. Moreover, on-site training allows trainees to apply their skills most directly to the environment in which they will be working.

■ Where possible, use existing employees to provide the skills training, further minimizing costs.

■ Consider offering basic-skills training for existing employees to improve their chances for advancement.

The message from firms already committed to direct basic-skills training is clear: If you give *qualifiable* workers the skills they need now, you won't be short *qualified* workers in the future.

Cooperative Basic-Skills Training

Not every company has the resources to sponsor its own basic-skills training program, and not every company's needs justify such an effort. But virtually *every* business can benefit from training potential employees in some or all of these skills. Cooperation often can secure such benefits in cases where an in-house training program is unaffordable. Among the most common cooperative options:

■ Form basic-skills training consortia with companies that have similar needs.

■ Create training partnerships with labor unions.

■ Establish relationships with training facilities sponsored by civic groups, such as the National Urban League.

■ Create linkages with community colleges, technical institutes, or public work force services.

■ Encourage local business associations to create training centers.

Firms whose workers require similar technical skills are excellent candidates for cooperative basic-skills training arrangements. This is especially so for smaller companies who may be unable to fund sophisticated training courses on their own but who can pool resources with others having similar needs. As Johnson & Johnson's Marion HochbergSmith admonishes, "companies should think more about becoming creative in a collaborative way. We can still compete with one another, but if we can combine our resources, we'll create a pool of talent we can all tap."

The Consortium Approach. One successful collaborative training program is the Microelectronics Training Consortium in San Diego, California. Established nine years ago when a group of semiconductor manufacturers joined with the San Diego Private Industry Council, the center is an autonomous entity, though participating companies launched it by donating equipment and management assistance.

The consortium's efforts focus on developing practical skills in prospective workers from poor families and neighborhoods. Contract Manager Brenda Barrett explains that the center's main objective is "to integrate members of San Diego's economically disadvantaged population back into the economic mainstream." Enrollment in the center is limited to low-income persons who can demonstrate perceptual accuracy, manual dexterity, and the ability to read and follow written instructions. No high school diploma is required.

Over the short-term, the program is designed to produce entry-level technical workers for placement with participating companies. But the center's longer-term goal is much broader, says Barrett; it is designed "to provide skills that prepare participants for *careers*, not just jobs." Thus, in addition to teaching job-specific skills, the center's three-week program teaches work-orientation skills, including preparation of job applications, résumé-writing, and effective interviewing.

The center recruits students through newspaper advertisements and referrals from companies and graduates of the program. In 1986–87, 28 local firms participated in the program. The center trained 163 people that year and placed more than 90 percent of them in jobs.

Training tailored to a specific industry permits graduates to get a quick start in companies requiring highly technical skills in entry-level positions. But the same principles work for more general basic-skills training. The Greater Washington (D.C.) Board of Trade, for example, sponsors an ambitious training program designed to relieve the capital area's entry-level worker shortages, especially in retail sales. With funding from the District of Columbia Private Industry Council, the Board of Trade offers a seven-week training program to unemployed or economically disadvantaged persons that combines classroom work with apprenticeships.

For the first four weeks, the participants are taught basic job-search skills, such as interpersonal communications and self-motivation. Those who have not completed high school also receive counseling for the General Educational Development (GED) tests.

Following classroom instruction, students begin three weeks of "job shadowing." Under the guidance of participating firms' more experienced workers, they learn through watching what will be required of them once they enter the workplace full-time. "In those situations where the retailers like the associates' work, they hire them," explains Program Director Enrique Palacios. Those not immediately hired are given placement assistance and have an opportunity to meet with area company recruiters at a career fair that the Board of Trade sponsors.

The program leads to anything but dead-end jobs. Some associates placed by the board, says Palacios, have "moved into management roles in less than a year." Employers also may refer unqualified job applicants to the program for job-readiness training. The program has found favor with many D.C.-area employers. Retailer Woodward & Lothrop's Joe Culver, vice president for human resources, emphasizes that "with the area's current shortages of entry-level candidates, it's important for us to use all approaches to augmenting the available talent pool."

Finding Other Training Partners.   Employers and unions also are starting to work together to provide training. In New York City, for instance, local affiliates of the American Federation of State, County and Municipal Employees (AFSCME) have offered basic skills courses to their members since the 1960s. Today, some 15 percent of their 20,000 members enroll in fundamental literacy and math courses each year. Many other unions offer similar programs for their members.

Companies are also joining forces with community organizations to supply the economically disadvantaged with marketable job skills. In 1968, IBM teamed up with the Los Angeles office of the National Urban League to sponsor its first Job Training Center. Since then, IBM has set up 70 other centers nationwide, graduating more than 25,000 people. Working with other companies, IBM provides equipment, managerial advice, curricula, and, in some cases, classroom instructors to help each new center get off the ground. Local community organizations, including the Urban League, Opportunities Industrialization Center, and SER-Jobs for Progress, manage the centers, recruit students, arrange job placement, and raise operating funds.

The program charges no tuition and even provides transportation assistance where needed. Students are expected to dress and conduct themselves as if in an actual work setting. While the centers gear the specific skills training toward local labor needs, all of the centers provide instruction in word processing, typing, general office skills, mathematics, literacy, assertiveness, personal grooming, and business conduct.

According to Caleb Schutz, IBM's program manager for community programs, the program places 80 percent of the workers in wage-paying jobs. A 1986 survey of 274 companies who had hired center graduates reported encouraging results: 93 percent of the new workers remained on the job beyond the probationary period, and a significant proportion had been promoted. And that's not all. By 1987, Schutz says, the centers' graduates, no longer in the ranks of the unemployed, had earned a total of $50 million in taxable income.

Schools have been among the valuable collaborators for businesses interested in training. In suburban Washington, D.C., where 72 percent of high school graduates go on to college, local automobile dealers concerned about the drop in high school graduates pursuing automotive services careers have created five used-car minidealerships within the local public school system. Through the program, youths who choose not to go on to college develop the mechanical and administrative skills they will need for entry-level jobs with automobile dealerships.

Some 350 high school seniors and juniors now divide their time between classrooms and the minidealerships, where they are trained in reconditioning used cars for resale. The program, according to George Price, auto mechanics teacher at Marshall High School in Fairfax, Virginia, teaches "more than mechanical skills. We work with our students on *job-seeking* and *job-keeping* skills. That means showing a relationship between what they do here and what they will be doing after they graduate."

Local vocational foundations and participating dealerships donate equipment and cars for the program. In addition to basic mechanical skills, students are taught to use high tech diagnostic equipment and to apply classroom computer and math skills to the automobile business— capabilities easily transferred to other professions, should they decide to change careers later. As in other training programs, many graduates end up working for sponsoring firms, and a number of dealerships promise job offers to graduates. "Getting these kids into our dealerships and getting them productive is a big plus for us and a big plus for them," declares Jim Gordon of Herb Gordon Nissan in Silver Spring, Maryland.

Another company that has worked with public schools is Dow Chemical Company in Saginaw, Michigan. But Dow's relationship with the schools has a twist: the firm contracts directly with the local school system to provide potential job applicants with special training in English, math, and science. In 1987, the program trained 50 students in basic skills, and Dow hired 11 of them.

Even smaller firms successfully use this approach. When Bill Gregory, owner of Gregory Forest Products Sawmill in Glendale, Oregon, noticed that a forklift operator "took forever" to count loads of lumber, he realized the worker had a worse basic-skills problem than he had thought. So he paid nearby Umpqua Community College to provide math and English training to about 10 percent of his work force. As he told *Time* magazine, "We're spending millions of dollars to modernize the mill. It just didn't make sense to pay for that without providing training for basic skills as well."

Still other companies have hired outside consultants to train workers in specific job skills. After rejecting most of its job applicants because of poor basic skills, the Prudential Insurance Company, based in Newark, New Jersey, contracted with Control Data Corp. to provide potential employees with computer-assisted training in reading and math.

Prudential's director of equal opportunity programs, James Robertson, found that "for many of these people, it was their first shot ever at learning the minimum skills necessary for really meaningful jobs in today's employment market."

Turning the Hard-Core Unemployed Into Full-Time Workers. Programs like these aren't meant just to skim the cream, helping the most employable of the poor while ignoring the hard-core unemployed. Organizations in the labor-strapped Washington, D.C., area, for instance, have begun offering training directly to those segments of the disadvantaged population least likely to move into the work force through normal channels, including the homeless, the mentally ill, recovering addicts, long-time welfare mothers, and prison inmates. Says John Gerson, president of a suburban Maryland Chamber of Commerce, many of whose members had complained about homeless persons camping in front of their stores: "There was some talk about just busing these people somewhere else. But in a community where workers are the most valuable commodity, we could ill afford to let these people" languish.

Washington-area businesses are doing anything but that. In 1989, the Greater Washington Board of Trade started to move beyond its regular entry-level training efforts to help local firms recruit and train workers from among the area's most impoverished populations. Already, the group has identified 80 programs being operated by local governments, non-profit community organizations, and business associations that are available to provide assistance.

One of these is the Suburban Maryland Building Industry Association's training program for prison inmates, a companion to the group's program for the unskilled poor. To date, 500 people have graduated from the two programs combined, and the association's training center has succeeded in placing 95 percent of them in jobs in construction and related trades. Ed Roberts, the center's training director, contends that these people "are perfect for the industry. It's one of the last industries where you can really start at the bottom and work yourself up."

An even more ambitious project, sponsored by the Greater Washington Resource Center, began its pilot run in October 1989. The first of its kind in the country, the program is a comprehensive effort to link the poor directly with local employers. The center is asking participating companies to hire at least five women currently on the welfare rolls—to train them, counsel them, acclimate them to the work world, and generally do whatever is necessary to keep them employed. Even before the official kick-off, seven area firms had joined up, including American Security Bank, Giant Food, Gannett Company, and Fannie May Candies.

Another local employer, Potomac Electric Power Company, operates a similar program on its own, called Action to Rehabilitate Community Housing (ARCH). One-third of the program's clients are homeless people. Because many of these people's problems are so severe, far more than normal classroom training is required to turn them into dependable employees. ARCH instructors therefore help would-be workers find housing, select and take care of their clothing, find day care, and learn again what it means to be responsible. The intensive assistance pays off. According to the program director, Duane Gautier, more than 90 percent of graduates have remained on their new jobs for six months or longer.

One of them is Steve Wilson, a former homeless alcoholic who spent years wandering the streets in search of money for his next drink. Now he is a crew chief for the utility, earning $24,000 a year. He even talks of one day opening his own construction firm, a dream he harbored before falling victim to the bottle. "You might say I got sidetracked," he told *The Washington Post*. "But I'm thinking in that direction again."

"Job Practicing": A First Step Into Work

While many firms are banking on preemployment, classroom-oriented instruction to expand their labor supply, other companies are turning to direct, on-the-job techniques of developing basic skills, including internships, work-study programs, and apprenticeships. Such "job practicing" often proves to be a fast-track method for getting qualifiable workers in place, even if the applicants at first lack some of the skills necessary for full-time jobs.

Internships and work-study programs differ from each other only slightly. An internship is a temporary, often full-time position; work-study is part-time and integrated with classroom training that complements the work involved. Apprenticeships, by contrast, are direct lead-ins to permanent positions. Sometimes linked to classroom instruction as well, their main emphasis is providing on-the-job training. Although apprenticeships are most frequently associated with skilled-craft jobs, particularly in the construction industry, they are proving increasingly well suited to technically sophisticated jobs in many other fields.

All three job-practicing methods offer a number of advantages:

- They allow companies to recruit from a larger pool of workers, since the participants do not have to bring well-developed basic skills with them.

- They offer firms an opportunity to provide basic-skills training tailored to the specific needs of the company without paying initially high wages.

- They integrate training directly with work, which itself can be an effective training tool.

- They give the employer a chance to evaluate the worker before making a longer-range investment in training, payroll, and other benefits.

- They give companies a recruiting edge, allowing them to begin building up their future labor pool years in advance.

Job-practicing methods are particularly useful for bringing the economically disadvantaged into the work force. Even more important, internships and work-study programs give disadvantaged youngsters an incentive to stay in school until they graduate, since these on-the-job experiences link school studies so closely to future chances of employment and demonstrate that jobs *are* available for those who finish school.

Although job-practicing techniques are used most frequently in large companies, most small companies can easily adapt them to their own settings. With the cost of permanent, full-time employees continuing to rise, these interns often are a good bargain. Nor are companies that lack the funds or staff to establish formalized programs left out; in most communities, they can coordinate intern-recruiting efforts with local business associations or other civic groups.

Job-Practicing Innovations.   One such program is San Francisco's summer-jobs program, sponsored each year by the local Private Industry Council. In 1987, one of the participating companies, the Big Eight accounting firm Coopers & Lybrand, volunteered to manage the program. The firm enlisted a professional artist to design an eye-catching recruitment poster and publicized the program with human-interest news features describing the first work experiences of local CEOs. The company then worked with local businesses to build up a summer-jobs bank and created a skills inventory to match applicants' abilities with the companies' needs. Coopers & Lybrand launched the program with a full-day summer-jobs fair, which also featured information on basic work skills. Local high school guidance counselors helped out by prescreening applicants and preparing them for job interviews.

The program netted 1113 summer jobs, primarily for youngsters from the city's poorest areas. Coopers & Lybrand partner James T. Clarke, who chaired the summer-jobs initiative, is emphatic about the effort's continuing success. "This program accomplishes more than giving young people jobs," he says. "It prepares them for life."

Aetna Life & Casualty's work-study program is another good example of job practicing designed as a lead-in to long-term careers. As corporate staffing official Jack O'Neill explains, "for entry-level jobs, we're now looking for technical skills that high schools don't provide." Hence, the work-study training emphasizes keyboard operations, which are used in 70 percent of the company's positions. The company eventually hires two out of every five of its work-study students, making the program an effective entry-level training and recruitment tool.

Aetna also links work-study with a special program called Project Step-Up, geared toward 15-year olds who do not plan to go to college but whom their guidance counselors have identified as promising future workers. These students are enrolled in 15 hour-long sessions covering such subjects as computers, interviewing, and business ethics. Many later find positions through the company's work-study program. Project Step-Up helps keep these youths in school and gives them a leg up on their career plans while identifying potential future employees at an early age, a competitive advantage that Aetna finds crucial in the tight New England labor market.

The Pelican Bay Experiment. An especially adventurous job-practicing program is underway at Pelican Bay Products, a 20-plus worker unit of the Klamath Falls, Oregon, wood and construction products manufacturer, Jeld-Wen Corp. The brainchild of Jeld-Wen's President Richard Wendt, the program is designed to turn unemployed men and women, many with poor work histories, into productive employees while putting the Pelican Bay subdivision in the black financially.

Led by its affable general manager, Ed Cacka, veteran director of one of the company's $20 million manufacturing operations, Pelican Bay's half dozen experienced supervisors train, counsel, and monitor the progress of workers referred by the Klamath Lake Employment and Training Council, the local affiliate of the federal Job Training Partnership Act network. But Cacka's crew isn't trying to build lifetime Pelican Bay employees. Rather, they hope to graduate their trainees into other local jobs that pay more than the firm's own minimum wage positions.

The program is demanding in three important ways:

1. It puts new recruits to work at simple tasks within minutes of their arrival.
2. It sets explicit but achievable production goals at the start.
3. It raises these goals as soon as lower-level goals are reached.

Supervisors also regularly meet with workers, evaluating their performance and offering personal interest and concern to help build their self-esteem.

Where necessary, the company adjusts its production process to fit workers' capabilities. For example, when Pelican Bay realized one wood-assembly operation was too complicated for its unskilled labor force, the manager split the operation into three less complex parts and delegated the computations to a supervisor. Thanks to accommodations like these, the new workers perform as efficiently as the more highly skilled wood processors—and their dedication is even greater. When the shift bell sounds, not a single worker rushes to the exit; instead, they remain until the job and clean-up are finished.

Helping Schools Build New Workers

We have already mentioned how companies are enlisting schools to help meet their labor needs. But many firms are returning the favor by becoming directly involved in the educational process. This assistance is particularly helpful in poor areas like the inner cities, where funds are tight and the obstacles to obtaining a worthwhile education are sometimes insurmountable. But the companies also benefit because these efforts often give them exposure in areas where they might remain unknown, thus increasing their pool of potential workers.

One early innovator in local educational involvement was Aetna Life & Casualty. The firm dedicates weekends at its corporate training facility in Hartford, Connecticut, to a Saturday Academy, which brings in a cross section of public school seventh graders for nine weekends of instruction in computer literacy, math, science, and communications skills. The program is a collaborative effort between Aetna, which provides the program facility, and the Hartford Board of Education, which selects and transports the students.

The students come from diverse socioeconomic and ethnic backgrounds, allowing youngsters who normally wouldn't interact with each other the chance to do so. As Aetna Institute President Badi Foster explains, "if you continue to have kids coming out of segregated schools, you will have kids who are not equipped to operate in a culturally diverse environment." The academy's goal, says Foster, is to help make economically disadvantaged youngsters the future employees of *first resort* by investing them with basic technical skills, enthusiasm for learning, and the ability to work effectively with people of different backgrounds.

Hartford public school teachers and Aetna volunteers guide the children through group-learning activities, role playing, and field trips. One unique aspect of the program is that a parent must accompany each child. The parents serve as classroom aides and field trip chaperones or attend adult education classes. In this way, the parents develop a personal interest in their children's education.

Aetna's Foster attributes much of the program's success to careful cultivation of support from community organizations. The academy, he says, has enhanced the company's image in the community and has helped enlarge the future pool of skilled workers. Aetna is so pleased with the program that it may expand it to some of the cities in which it has field offices.

IBM contributes to public education in a different way. Concerned about the declining numbers of engineering students, particularly among blacks, IBM helps build teachers' knowledge and skills in engineering and the sciences. One summer program brings high school teachers to the University of Wisconsin for classroom training, followed by laboratory work at an IBM facility. In return for the company's help, the teachers' schools commit to improving their science curricula.

A number of firms have provided direct financial support for the schools as well. In 1987–88, Herb Schervish, owner of the Renaissance Center Burger King in Detroit, contributed $10,000 in tuition assistance to employees at Henry Ford Community College. The investment produced a high return for the labor-intensive franchise: while the store's usual turnover rate was an intolerable 240 percent overall, turnover among the college-enrolled employees fell by more than three-quarters, saving the business $62,000 in training and expenses for the year. In addition, worker productivity rose sharply, and absenteeism and tardiness declined. The tuition assistance thus not only was a cost-effective investment in human capital but also proved an excellent retention and productivity tool for entry-level jobs.

The New Business Role: An Education *Partner*. A growing contingent of companies is helping to bridge the skills gap and produce employable graduates by creating full-fledged partnerships with local school systems. Employers typically furnish instructors or equipment to help out in underfunded subject areas like physics and computer science. Or they may provide role models who help students set goals for themselves and plan for careers.

Some companies engage in these efforts on their own, while others pool their resources with interested firms. One exceptional joint venture is called The Fourth R: Workforce Readiness, a multicity initiative of the National Association of Business (NAB). The program is modeled on the path-breaking Boston Compact, in which Boston companies joined forces to help the public schools combat a 60 percent dropout rate.

The NAB program is tailored to specific local needs. In Louisville, Kentucky, for instance, the program targets at-risk students—low achievers, pregnant teenagers, and economically disadvantaged youth—giving them counseling, remedial instruction, job-skills training, and help in finding summer jobs or part-time work. After graduation, counselors assist the young people in finding full-time jobs or enrolling in higher education. The partnership already has shown signs of reducing the high school dropout rate even as it builds up the local work force.

The American Express Company's Academy of Finance.   Another innovative nationwide approach is the American Express Company's Academy of Finance, operated in cooperation with local school officials and teachers. A two-year program for high school juniors and seniors, the academy combines classroom instruction and on-the-job experience with the goal of preparing young people for careers in financial services.

In addition to their normal high school classes, students enrolled in the academy take two special courses each term (such as introductory finance, banking, economics, accounting, or computer science) as well as a college course on the principles of finance during their senior year. In the summer after their junior year, students work as paid interns at one of more than 100 participating financial services firms, giving most students their first exposure to real-world jobs in the financial services industry and also helping them to better understand their course work.

Overall, more than 1300 public high school students in 34 schools in 14 urban areas are enrolled in the academy program, and another 249 have already graduated. But these are only the most obvious marks of success. In addition, fully 98 percent of the youngsters who start the two-year program finish it, and, according to academy instructors, many students once at risk of dropping out have become motivated to stay in school.

Moreover, though students are selected for the program without regard to their college plans, so far 90 percent of the graduates have moved on to college, most majoring in finance, economics, or accounting. Many have gone on to careers in the financial-services industry, some to positions with the firms that offered them their first summer internships.

Other Partnerships That Work.   Partnerships between school systems and individual, locally based companies are typically less comprehensive but no less important in filling the gaps in America's public education system. San Francisco-based McKesson Industries, for example, has launched a prototype program at the city's Mission High School to improve retention and college attendance among Hispanic students. The company's Career Exploration Club encourages students to remain in school by sharing with them information about career opportunities, assisting in career planning, and helping students develop job-hunting skills and summer jobs. Parents often are invited to the club's workshops, both to extend the program's benefits to other family members and to build family support for the club's efforts.

McKesson plans to expand the program to middle school students, with high school participants acting as mentors, and to create an alumni network to assist students with job placement.

Across the continent, in Fairfax County, Virginia, the aerospace giant Honeywell, Inc., recently joined the ranks of firms establishing broad-based partnerships with public schools. Jerry O'Brien, Honeywell's director of implementation and support services, says that the company wanted to help bolster academic courses in the school system but at first didn't know how best to contribute. After a series of strategy sessions with education officials, the company decided to adopt three schools, one each at the elementary, middle, and high school level.

In the elementary school, Honeywell sponsors an early-morning tutorial program called Excel, designed to help students raise their skills to grade level. In the intermediate school, the company assists in planning science fairs, graphic arts programs, and other academically-oriented extra-curricular activities. And in the high school, Honeywell helps plan special events and provides guest speakers on such subjects as the space shuttle program. Honeywell also sponsors a mentor program to provide one-on-one support for students with low self-esteem, as well as a "shadow program" in which high school students spend a day at the company to see firsthand the skills used in high tech jobs.

Honeywell's O'Brien believes the program is as beneficial for the company as it is for the students. The employee volunteers are enthusiastic, he reports, because the contact with the students adds "a different dimension to their lives," allowing "people with fairly narrow technical specialties to interact with kids and make a positive contribution to their lives." What's more, "they may be tutoring a future Honeywell executive."

Similarly, IBM lends its employees to teach at schools that serve primarily black, Hispanic, Appalachian, Native American, and disabled youngsters. Since 1971, more than 700 IBM employees have supplemented schools' teaching staffs through the company's Faculty Loan Program. Typically, the IBM volunteers teach computer science, engineering, or business administration, while assisting with strategic planning, curriculum development, student counseling, and efforts to increase participation among minorities and economically disadvantaged students in engineering programs.

IBM pays the full salaries of their participating employees. Beyond the obvious short-term benefits of the arrangement, IBM Program Manager Dolly Christian says, the program yields long-term gains, since schools often make the curriculum innovations inspired by IBM's volunteer teachers a permanent part of their education programs.

Partnership Rules of Thumb. The experiences of the most successful public school partnerships suggest the following general principles for such efforts:

- Create an advisory board comprised of representatives from all the entities involved, both inside and outside the company (school authorities, parent-teacher associations, community organizations, and the like), to design the program and monitor its progress.

- Establish a close, formalized relationship with school authorities, clearly stating expectations for all parties involved in the partnership.

- Determine the most significant contribution the company can make in light of the school's needs and the company's expertise.

- Involve the company's personnel office to maximize the program's potential for producing future workers.

- Publicize the program widely within the company, and encourage staff participation.

William Zeigler, director of the Tenneco Automotive Training & Development Center in Ann Arbor, Michigan, says an effective school-company partnership is one in which the business "gets completely integrated in a school, and the school gets completely integrated in the business." Before long, he says, the business can come in and help with the school's problems, almost by second nature.

Strategic Philanthropy

Another group of companies is starting to influence the educational process through strategic corporate giving. Although indirect, the careful targeting of philanthropic dollars both expands educational opportunities for economically disadvantaged children and develops future employees for business.

Among the leaders in this field is the General Electric Foundation, which has made education funding a top priority. The foundation emphasizes help to minorities and economically disadvantaged persons who want to pursue careers in engineering. Phyllis McGrath, program manager for civil and cultural contributions, describes the foundation's efforts as "strategic philanthropy."

The foundation provides seed money for promising educational programs and often backs its awards with personal assistance from GE employees. In New York's Spanish Harlem, for example, GE has made a sizable three-year grant to the Manhattan Center, a new science magnet school. The foundation has designated 27 talented juniors at the school as "GE scholars," an honor that comes with financing for field trips, courses at Columbia University and Hunter College, help in preparing for the Scholastic Aptitude Test, and monthly advisory meetings with GE mentors. The foundation also awarded a grant to Eastern Montana State College to develop a preengineering program for Native American youth. Other programs are geared toward keeping high school students in school and helping dropouts enter the job market.

RJR Nabisco has gone even further with its Next Century Schools program, inaugurated in November 1989. The program provides three-year challenge grants to public schools across the nation. The $30 million effort is designed to foster innovative, even radical, risk-taking on the part of "enlightened principals, teachers, and parents" who are committed to dramatic improvements in student achievement. "The biggest risk in education," asserts RJR chairman Louis V. Gerstner, Jr., "is in not taking one."

Recruiting From an Isolated Work Force

In addition to skills deficiencies, the second major barrier separating people outside the economic mainstream from available jobs is isolation. *Physical isolation* keeps many inner-city residents from jobs in the suburbs, where many of the new jobs (particularly those requiring fewer skills) are located. *Social isolation,* while less tangible, can be equally crippling. Many economically disadvantaged individuals are out of touch with ordinary employment channels, such as word-of-mouth recruitment, newspapers, and placement offices. In tandem, physical and social isolation create a troublesome scenario: an increasing demand for labor and a large supply of potential workers that never manage to get together.

If companies are to successfully meet their future labor needs, they will have to bridge this logistical gulf. Firms must move beyond the easy recruitment styles many have grown accustomed to and go about actively looking for economically disadvantaged workers. This means expanding recruitment efforts:

- *Geographically,* to attract workers from areas not drawn upon previously.

- *Demographically,* to reach workers from different socioeconomic backgrounds.

- *Methodologically,* to employ innovative, more culturally sensitive techniques to which new workers may be more receptive.

- *Strategically,* to take steps now to meet labor shortages that may be months or years away.

This new type of recruitment isn't something that can wait. Companies that delay until the labor crunch is upon them may find themselves lagging hopelessly behind. As one recruitment official told us, "if you haven't recruited early, you're out of luck."

Bringing Jobs to Workers

One recruiting tradition that has gone the way of mimeograph copiers and mechanical adding machines is the corporate practice of relying solely on applicants to take the initiative in applying for jobs. Today, particularly at companies with large numbers of entry-level jobs, too few people walk through the door looking for work. Not only do many companies not have enough potential workers in the surrounding labor market to fill all their job openings, but many of the most readily available employees are isolated from the jobs and from information about those jobs.

To redress these problems, these firms are finding they have to actively reach out to both new and nontraditional workers, and a number of employers have developed innovative techniques for doing just that.

Giant Food, Inc., based in Washington, D.C., is one such employer. The capital area's leading grocery store chain, Giant began having trouble recruiting entry-level workers at its suburban stores in the mid-1980s. So the firm created an office on wheels, a rented Winnebago van that is draped in a Giant banner and parked in locations where potential new workers are mostly likely to see it, such as shopping centers and school parking lots. The van is a totally self-contained recruitment center, staffed by professional interviewers and equipped with applications, brochures, and other essential information. Barry Sher, Giant's vice president for public affairs, reports that the program is "extremely successful" in bringing in new employees, despite the region's tight labor market.

Louisville-based Kentucky Fried Chicken is another company searching for nontraditional workers. The firm's approach, according to Flo Barber, director of field human resources development, is, "if you won't come to us, we'll go to you." In addition to renting vans for recruitment, the company tailors its recruitment in ways carefully calculated to reach the intended audience. For instance, in order to identify and recruit economically disadvantaged workers who normally might be inaccessible if only conventional methods were used, the company places ads and miniapplications in mass-transit stations and vehicles and in product-promotion coupons that are delivered to selected residences in low-income neighborhoods. The technique, says Barber, has been an unequivocal success.

Another useful approach has been to create among minority and economically disadvantaged employees the same sort of word-of-mouth recruitment networks that exist among more traditional worker groups. Existing employees, often a good source of recruiters, provide a valuable entrée into previously hidden labor sources, such as inner-city residents. Larry Adams, executive vice president of the Carolina Lumber & Building Material Dealers Association, notes that it is becoming "common to find employers who reward employees with a finder's fee, such as a $100 bonus for an employee who recommends a friend who stays for six months."

Such efforts reflect a growing corporate realization that firms must strive as vigorously to win over potential workers as they historically have tried to obtain new customers: first, by identifying them and, second, by reaching out to them in the most persuasive ways possible. Company officials are learning that they must ask themselves: Who are our prospective workers? Where are they most likely to read or hear our ads? What messages will appeal to them? And, how can we make sure potential employees know we want them to work for us? As the old fund-raising axiom goes, you can't get someone to give if you don't ask—and ask in the right way.

Bringing Workers to Jobs

The flip-side of this awareness barrier is a transportation barrier. Even if would-be workers outside the mainstream find out about jobs, many can't reach them. Many inner-city residents, for instance, do not own cars, and suburban work sites often are not adequately served by subway or bus routes. While public transportation generally works to bring suburban workers to urban jobs, too often service in the opposite direction is insufficient.

One way some companies are avoiding this problem is by factoring worker availability into decisions about where to locate headquarters, plants, and service centers. Still, many firms continue to move to the suburbs without adequate thought as to where they will find their employees. An official of one company that transferred its operations from the inner city to the suburbs told us: "We wanted to get closer to our customers but found there weren't any workers there. So now we've got this facility out in the suburbs and have to bus employees in from the city to work there. It doesn't make any sense."

For many other firms, however, even perfect foresight is not enough. Because their locations have been fixed for years, their only alternative is to find creative ways to cope with worker shortages that emerged long after they set up shop. Polycast Technology Corp., a Connecticut firm, has taken up this task. The firm contracts with a private van company to provide round-the-clock transportation for factory workers and machine operators from the Bronx and other parts of New York City to its Stamford, Connecticut, plant. Although New York, with its abundant labor supply, is not far from Stamford, inadequate public transportation makes commuting difficult. As Polycast's employee advocate Philip Demas observes, because of the company's transportation program, "employees are very happy, and they're always on time."

Worker transportation programs are especially ripe for collaboration and entrepreneurship. In Atlanta, Temp Force, Inc., transports temporary workers to suburban companies that can't be reached by public transportation. "Due to job growth in the suburbs," explains Corporate Service Manager Dean Morgan, "there were more jobs than there were people. We provide a guarantee that the companies will get the people they need, and we'll get them there." From a base of two corporate clients in 1985, Temp Force now transports employees, ranging from clerical workers to telemarketing specialists to warehouse help, to nearly 40 companies. Declares Morgan: "It's a very effective tool, and it gives us a competitive edge."

Other companies are looking to labor-surplus parts of the country to fill their needs in labor-scarce regions. For example, when Kentucky Fried Chicken's stores in booming central Florida needed managers, they turned to the depressed Houston labor market for help. The company placed ads for managers in Houston newspapers, trained the new hires in Houston stores, and offered them jobs in Florida. As Kentucky Fried Chicken's Flo Barber reports, "things worked out well for everyone. Orlando got employees, and several of Houston's unemployed got gainful work with good career potential."

Looking to the Community

Business is not alone in its desire to reach out to those who are economically disadvantaged. A number of community and volunteer groups are helping employers identify and recruit potential workers from nontraditional labor markets. Firms committed to looking to the community need to develop what Shawmut Bank Community Relations Officer Maurice Wright calls "a grass roots approach to gathering information," finding out who might be seeking work, what skills they possess (or lack), and how to bring them into the company work force.

Public unemployment, workfare, and welfare rolls provide a good starting point. Yet public sector resources alone are insufficient for recruiting those outside the economic mainstream since, as Wright explains, "agencies don't always successfully track these people." He urges instead that business develop ongoing relationships with community organizations. Self-help groups for ethnic minorities can prove very effective in helping companies identify economically disadvantaged workers with high potential. Likewise, private training centers—including companies' own training programs—often provide firms with access to willing workers who might otherwise be unreachable.

But employers find they can help out, too. Aggressive recruiters try to:

- Create reliable skills inventories for open job slots.
- Provide training whenever it's needed for high-demand jobs.
- Offer meaningful jobs with possibilities for advancement.

As management consultant Alannah Steinbach, president of Executive Business Services in Anaheim, California, explains, "earning a reputation as a company interested in the well-being of the economically disadvantaged is step number one in recruiting from these groups."

Promoting From Within

Bringing workers inside the company's doors is only part of the challenge, as all employers sooner or later find out. Keeping them there is another matter. It is tempting to view employees from outside the economic mainstream as a solution only to one's entry-level needs. But such an approach is shortsighted. Entry-level workers are often the best candidates for higher-level positions; they're familiar with the company, managers know their capabilities, and training for these higher-level jobs often can be incorporated into the worker's current duties.

Even more important, the next decade's workers will have lots of choices. If entry-level employees are unimpressed with working conditions or their chances for advancement within a company, observes Robert Harloe, director of training for Dunkin' Donuts, they won't "have to take [it] because they can walk across the street and get another job." The problem, says Harloe, is that many employers "are focusing solely on recruitment, and that is only part of the answer."

Escaping from this bind requires an important change in approach: *Companies must begin to treat employees as the important people that they are.* Firms must start tailoring corporate policies to the needs and desires of their workers as well as the needs and desires of corporate management. Not that it will be easy. This way of thinking is "alien to managers," Harloe argues. "For so long, people were a dime a dozen. It's going to take a tremendous readjustment on [management's] part." He says he constantly hears managers saying, "I don't have time to interview; I don't have time to do an orientation; I don't have time to train." "My response," says Harloe, "is 'What *are* you doing, Mr. Manager?'

Those things are part and parcel of the management's job, and if you're not doing them, you're gonna pay the price."

The key point is that companies must work as hard to keep good employees as they did to recruit and train them initially. This is especially true for the economically disadvantaged workers for whom the investment in training may have been especially great. Training managers in retention techniques, as well as rewarding those with the best retention records, have been two of the most effective ways of communicating this message. Another has been to make employee retention efforts a central part of the manager's evaluation.

For the workers recruited into entry-level positions, the most critical requirement is to ensure that clear paths exist to high-level positions. Again, a new approach is necessary, one that views *every worker as a candidate for promotion*. This principle makes sense not only because it helps firms retain good workers but because the best way to prevent shortages in mid-level ranks is to train and promote entry-level employees. A cafeteria worker, for instance, can become a receptionist with a bit of basic-skills and interpersonal-relations training; a receptionist can become a word processor with a little computer training; a word processor can become a paralegal with some technical training; and so on. More importantly, knowing that opportunities exist for advancement can be a strong incentive for entry-level workers to stay with a company and to improve their skills on their own.

Training for Upward Mobility

One company that aggressively encourages training for upward mobility is Memphis-based Federal Express Corp., which offers more than 250 practical courses on such subjects as Effective Business Writing and Is Management for Me? The Aetna Institute for Corporate Education also provides a wide array of courses for employees at every level, including literacy training, to allow service workers to enter the company's mainstream. Efforts like these, says Sheila A. Dixon, president of the Monterey, California, worker-search firm Cypress Research, make the employer's commitment to upward advancement "crystal clear" and let employees know in advance that "they won't be confined to the entry-level forever."

One of the most well-developed worker-education programs to promote upward mobility was created by the Pacific Telesis Group in 1985. Telesis Management Institute's (TMI) self-directed education program, referred to in Chapter 4, affords employees of Pacific Telesis the chance to "engage your mind, empower your future, extend your education." Like many other companies, Pacific Telesis offers tuition reimbursement for degree programs related to its employees' jobs. But TMI goes further, making self-directed education programs possible by offering classes on company premises in collaboration with California colleges and universities.

Pacific Telesis views its emphasis on continuing education as an important part of its upward-mobility opportunities for minorities, but the effort also pays off by keeping all employees on top of technological trends. As TMI's Constance Beutel observes, "without extensive continuing education, we'll lose competitively to the Japanese. Employees and management both know education is important—they can see the handwriting on the terminal screen."

The Career Path

Taking these ideas further, some firms have begun to institutionalize upward mobility through career paths that ensure no job is a dead end. In developing career paths, employers identify realistic opportunities for lateral movement or upward mobility from *every* position in the company. Firms also counsel employees in developing career goals and taking the necessary steps to achieve them. They also make sure that information about promotion possibilities is available to all employees.

Though essentially cost-free, career paths have proven to be a powerful force for keeping workers on the job and filling higher-level vacancies. Federal Express, for example, posts more than 200 career-path job openings at all its facilities and gives existing employees first preference. The company fills 65 percent of its vacancies in this way and finds that this policy is an especially effective method for providing clear avenues to promotion for minority employees.

Affirmative Action: A Human-Capital Approach

When many managers consider how to recruit more minority workers, they often think in terms of affirmative action. In so doing, many come to view racial preferences, goals, and numerical quotas as something distinct and apart from—even hostile to—the mainstream recruitment and promotion process.

Such race-conscious approaches have sparked a great deal of debate over the years among politicians and personnel administrators alike. Yet whatever success they may have had in compensating for historical discrimination, these tactics will not be enough for reaching out to economically disadvantaged workers in the 1990s. Setting numerical goals based on race, for instance, will do nothing to overcome low skill levels or transportation barriers that prevent would-be employees from taking advantage of jobs that may go begging for want of workers of *any* race.

This does not mean that affirmative action should be abandoned. On the contrary, the programs and approaches described here *are* affirmative action in its highest sense. They empower minority individuals to take advantage of the whole range of opportunities available to them by increasing workers' qualifications rather than by reducing job requirements. This is the kind of affirmative action that will be most critical in the coming decade. *In the 1990s, affirmative action will be largely about human-capital development.*

A human-capital approach to affirmative action will provide the most help to those people who need it. Such an approach will ensure that companies can continue to increase worker quality and that minority applicants will continue to move into jobs in larger numbers. Most important, companies will engage in this type of affirmative action not because government tells them to but because the competitive climate demands it—a development that will win greater allegiance to *real* affirmative action efforts than any amount of federal rule-making could achieve.

As one company official told us: "In the past, we concentrated on numbers counting, and we did this because someone told us we had to. Now we aggressively recruit and promote minority workers because there's no other option but to develop a multicultural work force."

"Trickle-Up" Benefits

Many of the efforts described in this chapter cost money—some, a lot of money. After all, it's one thing for a dedicated Hispanic math teacher to redouble his student's commitment to learning or a determined black entrepreneur to open a street-corner shoe-shine stand. It's another thing for a company to devote tens of thousands of dollars to a training or recruitment program when that money just as easily could buy a new computer network or an advanced manufacturing system. Facing these possibilities, even the most forward-looking managers will not be able to escape this question: Does the return justify the investment?

The short answer is that there isn't any other choice. Even in an era of rising wages, the supply of workers will be severely limited unless companies can find ways to bring productive new workers into the labor force.

But the payoff in human-capital development is more immediate and tangible than that. IBM, for instance, calculated the costs and benefits of its Job Training Center program in 1985 and discovered the added production from each new worker was several times the training expense. Not only that, but evaluators found that the benefits reached far beyond the company's doors. After graduation, the trainees earned an average of $11,700 and paid $2200 in federal, state, and local taxes. So far, 4500 workers, earning a total of $43.3 million, have completed the program.

The result: everybody gained. The company acquired new workers, the government received new tax dollars, and a few thousand people who were previously outside the economic mainstream began earning their own living—some for the first time in their lives.

And yet the real reward is still to come—a head start in claiming a generation of productive, enthusiastic new workers. The examples in this chapter should prove this point many times over. But one needn't go as far as IBM or GE or Pelican Bay to sense what is happening. Just ask Jaime Escalante, or Ego Brown, or any of the thousands of new, once disadvantaged workers who have joined the labor force over the last few years.

They've been there, on the front lines, watching the transformation take place. They *know* the future works—if employers only take the time and energy to give it a chance.

6
Cultural Matchmaking

Ghulam Safi earns $18,000 a year as an insurance adjustor in Fairfax County, Virginia. This is not his first job in the United States. Since arriving here in 1982, he has sold sandwiches, washed dishes, listened to customer complaints, and even worked as a butler. Not a bad progression for someone with few job skills. But Safi is anything but unskilled. In his native Afghanistan, he held several demanding, high-prestige posts, including governor of a province.

Safi has no regrets about his seeming slip down the economic ladder. He is, instead, quite proud of the progress he has made in his adopted country. Taking lower-level employment, he says, is just the price of making a new start, especially when one speaks so little English, as he did when he arrived. "When I came here, despite my education and background.... I had to be a layman.... It's subsistence employment. It's a necessity....[But] what I like about the United States is, whatever you do, it's noble."

These words certainly ring true in a nation that has built much of its prosperity on the sweat and ingenuity of immigrants. But for many of them, unlike Ghulam Safi, the pace of assimilation has been painfully slow, and the price high. From the Irish immigrants crowded into slums in the Northeast to the Chinese railroad workers in the West, from the African slaves in the South to the migrant farm workers of modern-day California, millions of immigrants have found the road to the American social and economic mainstream blocked by an array of obstacles, both visible and invisible.

Strangers in a Strange Land

The main problem most immigrants face, even in the era of high tech, is not just a lack of education or technical skills. To be sure, as Chapter 2 noted, about one-quarter of those who arrived in this country during the 1970s had completed fewer than five years of school—but almost another quarter were college graduates. And while immigrants from Mexico generally have little education, those from the Pacific Rim, the Middle East, and a few other areas usually are well trained and educated—some even more so than adults native to the United States.

Still, many immigrants, regardless of their education or training, feel out of place in the American mainstream, not because they cannot master the mechanics of a particular job, but because they have difficulty performing the job in the context of the workplace. These people find themselves, in Harriet Tubman's classic phrase, as "strangers in a strange land." To add to the challenge of the day-to-day job responsibilities that every new worker experiences, the newcomers:

- May not speak or understand English.
- May find themselves left out of informal American hierarchies or social arrangements, especially in the workplace.
- May not be familiar with educational opportunities, job referral networks, or corporate hiring patterns.
- May have few friends or professional contacts outside their own ethnic community.

These invisible barriers can prevent otherwise highly capable people from entering or progressing through the ranks of the labor force—or discourage them from even trying.

And not just immigrants are affected. Many native-born youngsters living in the inner city grow up as socially isolated from American work culture as do people who came here from other countries. As University of Chicago sociologist William Julius Wilson laments, in many ghetto neighborhoods, "the chances are overwhelming that children will seldom interact on a sustained basis with people who are employed" and will be exposed instead to "joblessness as a way of life."

Without adequate role models, ghetto youngsters may fail to develop such necessary workplace traits as teamwork, the ability to compromise, acceptance of personal responsibility, and appropriate demeanor and dress. Thus, some employers may view them as poor job candidates, despite the technical skills they may possess.

For employers in the 1990s, the implications of this cultural mismatch are clear: effective recruitment will not be enough. Even good on-the-job training will not be enough. What will be needed, in addition, is cross-cultural matchmaking. Companies wishing to turn non-English-speaking immigrants and other culturally isolated persons into top-notch employees must be prepared to assist their transition into mainstream society and its often tumultuous, loosely structured economy. These efforts may be as far-reaching as intensive English language training or as simple as giving special attention to helping newcomers through the orientation process. But whatever steps are chosen, they will be linked by one overriding goal: to turn *job-ready* applicants into *workplace-ready* ones.

At the same time, employers must be willing to make *themselves* over when that is called for. Just as forward-looking firms are retooling their personnel policies to accommodate demographic trends toward dual-earner and single-parent families, they are starting to look at new ways to accommodate cultural diversity. Of course, some aspects of corporate culture are essential to productivity and quality, and these cannot be sacrificed. But by making a point to recognize new workers' cultural differences and adjusting company practices to accommodate these differences wherever possible, astute employers help ensure that these workers will feel accepted and valued from the start.

The Fourth Wave

The Urban Institute's Thomas Muller and Thomas J. Espenshade call it America's "Fourth Wave." While people from other countries have entered the United States continuously over the years, there have been three high-water marks of immigration and intramigration.

- In the mid- to late-1800s, peaking in the 1880s, a massive flow of people from the British Isles and what is now Germany settled in the northeastern United States, with Irish newcomers moving heavily into New York City and Boston.

- A more ethnically diverse mix of immigrants, mostly from eastern and southern Europe, arrived in the early 1900s and settled in the northeastern and midwestern states.

- Internally, rural black southerners traveled to northern cities in search of employment. This intramigration began around World War I and continued into the 1960s.

Now the United States is in the midst of its Fourth Wave of immigration, which commenced in the 1960s and continues to the current day. These immigrants come primarily from Latin America (especially Mexico) and Asia, though a sizable number still move here from other areas, including Europe, the Caribbean, and the Middle East. A large proportion of these newcomers settle in California, but many others make their way to New York City, Miami, Chicago, Houston, and Washington, D.C.

The members of this Fourth Wave are rapidly making their presence felt in the labor market—by their sheer numbers, if nothing else. Before the year 2000, another 9 to 16 million of them—4 to 7 million of working age—will join their ranks. Already:

- More than 30 percent of New York City's current residents are foreign-born.

- The proportion of foreign-born Los Angeles residents nearly equals New York City's at the peak of European immigration. At least 1 out of every 10 workers in Los Angeles County is a Mexican immigrant. About one-half of the skilled blue-collar and service employees who came to that area between 1970 and 1980 were recent immigrants from Mexico.

- English will be the *second* language for the majority of California's population by the year 2000. By the year 2020, more than one-half of that state's entry-level workers will be Hispanic.

- People of Hispanic origin, both new immigrants and their descendants, constitute an absolute majority of the populations of Miami, San Antonio, and El Paso.

Some of these immigrants have brought impressive skills and work habits to their new country. For them, unfamiliarity with the English language and American culture may be their greatest barrier to advancement. Others, mainly the poor and the uneducated, may come relatively empty-handed but with a strong desire for a better life. They face a more substantial hurdle: the lack of both cultural *and* basic job skills.

Those who are motivated and talented enough to do so on their own will pick up the language, cultural savvy, and technical skills they need to prosper in the American labor market. But the business sector, especially companies operating near large immigrant communities, cannot afford to wait a generation or two for these newcomers to become acclimated. They need workers *now*. Clearly, it is in these firms' interest to shorten the adjustment period for both educated and undereducated immigrants.

English as a New Language

Often the first step toward making foreign-born persons work-ready employees is to teach them English. Helping a highly skilled immigrant acquire good language skills immediately produces a qualified worker, and at a fraction of the cost of training an unskilled person. For immigrants with few marketable skills, basic English instruction is typically a prerequisite for other job-related training. Yet even here, many companies find the investment in language training pays off. The strong motivation to learn that many immigrants possess not only makes them eager and diligent students, but also increases the likelihood that they will repay the company's language training with hard work and loyalty.

Eliminating Language Barriers

A Philadelphia-based manufacturing firm has had trouble filling jobs, despite its no-layoff policy, good wages, and liberal benefits. The owner has recruited immigrant workers through ethnic churches, among other sources, but turnover remains high. One employee who has stayed is Aldoberto Perez, described as "a hard worker who says he dislikes standing around." But because his inability to speak English has prevented him from learning technical skills, Perez never has progressed beyond menial labor.

For many foreign-born workers like Aldoberto Perez, the English language is a wall standing in the way of their advancement. Language barriers may even be a strong disincentive to joining the work force. For example, one recent study estimates that, for married women, lack of fluency in English is responsible for more than *three-quarters* of the difference in work force participation between foreign-born Asians and native-born whites, and for *one-half* the difference between foreign-born Hispanics and native-born non-Hispanic whites.

Non-English-speakers are not the only potential employees who suffer because of poor workplace literacy. This problem also affects many native-born, English-speaking Americans who, somehow, never learned to read or write. For these functionally illiterate adults, as Natalie Merchant has described it, words and letters are just "lines and circles—a complete mystery." Unable to read job instructions, stockroom signs, and even safety warnings, these workers are often lost in the workplace. Because they cannot *understand* many jobs, they cannot *do* these jobs.

But the situation, while urgent, is far from hopeless. Through language and literacy training, path-breaking companies are already moving thousands of non-English speakers into the labor force.

Workplace English. Many American employers claim it is counterproductive to hire workers not fluent in English. "How can the benefits of teaching them the language ever compensate for the high costs of training?" is a common reaction. But for many jobs, English training geared to the specific job is all that is really needed—and costs much less than full-scale, academic language instruction.

Northeast Utilities, based in Hartford, Connecticut, has found this to be the case. The company worked with two local vocational-technical high schools to prepare Spanish-speaking persons to become meter readers. Subsidized by state and local social service agencies, the program includes five weeks of classroom training and a week-long on-the-job orientation. The utility has hired several new full-time and temporary employees as a result and reports that workers trained in this manner showed better-than-average productivity.

Similarly, several northern Virginia hotels are enrolling their immigrant employees in job-related English classes. In many cases, county agencies offer these courses right at the work site, and employers generally pay the workers' salaries throughout the training period. In the program's first few months, more than 400 kitchen, bar, and housekeeping workers, representing at least 40 different countries, finished the course. Participating firms say the program has reduced staff turnover and greatly enhanced employees' ability to communicate with supervisors and customers. Says Gerry Frank of Western Executive Inn, a hotel that once faced turnover rates as high as 90 percent: "The benefits are much bigger than whatever we spent."

One of the most effective workplace English programs in the country is the brainchild of Long Dinh, a Vietnamese refugee. Dinh is the founder of Amtek Systems, a small high tech firm based in Arlington, Virginia. Amtek had so much success teaching English to Southeast Asian immigrants in its own work force that it began training workers for other local high tech businesses as well.

The company recruits largely from county unemployment and welfare rolls. Trainees, who come from a variety of ethnic backgrounds, receive three months of concentrated instruction in computer and electronics terminology, basic components assembly, and job hunting. "Everything we do is hands-on," says Dinh. "After [workers] complete this training, they are ready for the jobs in every way." The program boasts a 96 percent placement rate. Indeed, immigrants now comprise 40 to 50 percent of the assembly line labor force among the area's high tech firms.

Knowing English is important even when foreign-born employees work only with other immigrants. Without some linguistic unity, a workplace can become an unproductive Tower of Babel. That was the situation faced by managers at the Digital Equipment Corp.'s Roxbury, Massachusetts, plant, where people from 16 countries who spoke 13 languages worked together in the same production unit. Company employees are expected to work as teams, but the language differences made this nearly impossible. So, in July 1988, the firm hired Boston-based consultant Fern Brown to bring her VOICES (Vocational Onsite Instruction in Cross-cultural and English Skills) program to foreign-born Digital Equipment workers. During the first summer, 39 employees completed English as a second language (ESL) courses.

VOICES groups are kept small (no more than ten students at a time) to allow instructors to tailor the lessons to each student's ability and job duties. The workers receive overtime pay for time spent in the two-hour, twice weekly classes. Donna Robertson, an employee development consultant to Digital, says managers tell her that program graduates are more enthusiastic about their jobs and are no longer afraid to take part in group planning and decision making.

Workplace English courses clearly expand the base of employable persons for entry-level positions and improve their on-the-job performance. At the same time, such training can help prepare existing employees to take on more responsibility. "Almost my entire dishwashing crew is Haitian," says Chuck Palid, human resource director at the Hyatt Hotel in Greenwich, Connecticut. "We're starting training in English as a second language as a way of making the promising dishwashers more promotable."

Where employers do not have formal programs, managers or workers fluent in English often help non-English speakers learn job-related terminology in a nonstructured fashion. For instance, employees at the Washington, D.C., branch of Rudi's, a Boston-based wholesale bakery, learn whatever English they will need by referring to a handwritten, five-page Spanish-English dictionary of bakery terms. Now, when a recipe calls for flour and sugar, they know to use *harina* and *azúcar*.

The Computer as Trainer. Interactive video technology is one of the most promising developments in workplace-English instruction. Now available as complete systems marketed by leading computer firms, interactive video programs teach foreign-born employees how to handle typical workplace problems—in English. Students watch movielike portrayals of actual on-the-job situations, then respond to questions by typing in or simply touching the correct answer on the computer screen. The self-paced nature of these programs and the electronic instructors' endless patience make learning with interactive video both rewarding and efficient.

One innovative interactive videodisc (IVD) program is SKILLPAC, created by the Hudson Institute's Dr. Arnold H. Packer and the Center for Applied Linguistics in Washington, D.C. Each SKILLPAC lesson gives students a chance to apply what they have learned to realistic problems. For example, one exercise for warehouse workers asks the student to compare photos of various supplies against an order form listing those items. If something is missing from the visual stock room, the student is asked how he or she would tell the supplier, in English, to provide the missing item. Another lesson displays pages from a maintenance manual and a pickup truck's maintenance log. The student's task is to calculate the truck's mileage since its last oil change and, based on that computation, find the proper recommendation in the manual.

Throughout the country, in a wide variety of fields, American businesses and employee organizations are putting this technology to work. In New York City, for instance, eight unions have joined to offer IVD literacy training to union members and their families. In Michigan, a collaborative program sponsored by Ford Motor Company and the United Auto Workers uses IVD programs for industrial mathematics. Domino's Pizza in Ann Arbor, Michigan, even uses this technology to teach people to make pizza dough.

This imaginative technology "empowers the student," says Hudson Institute's Packer, by "put[ting] learning into the context of the job the trainee is expected to do, not what a school administrator believes necessary."

Clearing Away Misunderstanding

What can be done for foreign-born employees who understand English well but have trouble making *themselves* understood? Heavy foreign accents can handicap even those with superior intelligence or technical ability. "A dialect or pronunciation problem can lead to misunderstanding that can lose your company thousands of dollars," admits Burke Stinson of AT&T, a company with many employees who are not native English speakers.

To stave off such problems in the short term, many managers have had to:

- Encourage native employees to be patient with workers just learning English.

- Direct both native- and foreign-born speakers to talk slowly and listen carefully to one another.

- Insist that native-born employees ask for clarification when something a foreign-born employee says is not understood.

- Follow up important conversations or meetings with written memos.

But some employers are taking a more formal approach. Accent-reduction programs are one effective way of permanently clearing away communication problems. A number of foreign-born professionals in the Detroit, Michigan, area, for instance, have taken advantage of training offered by the speech pathology unit at Beaumont Hospital in Royal Oak, Michigan. "I used to have to repeat myself a lot," says Richard Chancellor, who came to the United States from China. Chancellor (his Americanized name), a product-assurance engineer for Ford Motor Company, has to talk with many new people each time he visits one of the company's manufacturing plants. Correcting his English pronunciation has helped him do a better job. Another student, Paraguayan-born Dr. Maria Maas, says the course has enabled her to dictate letters and reports more easily.

From job-specific dictionaries to accent-reduction courses, teaching workers to communicate is far more than a passing fad. Just as wheel-chair ramps have made once off-limits work sites accessible to many people with disabilities, language-training programs are making the same workplaces just as accessible to those who have not yet mastered English.

Eliminating Unnecessary Language Requirements

Is it always necessary for employees to speak English on the job? Possibly not. Some positions, such as those involving strictly mathematical or drafting functions, may require little or no English. While foreign-born workers must learn the language to get ahead in most businesses, companies often can put these newcomers to work immediately and teach them English later. By taking a careful look at each job's duties, employers are beginning to separate tasks that demand English proficiency from those that do not.

At Aetna Life & Casualty, for instance, the personnel office scrutinizes each supervisor's request for a new employee. If a job description includes skills easily developed through existing corporate training programs, these skills are deemed nonessential entry requirements. As a result, several jobs at Aetna no longer demand English fluency, allowing the company to move foreign-born employees into the job and the workers to contribute to the company even before they complete ESL and literacy training.

Across the country, at California's Burke Industries, nearly 70 percent of the factory workers are Spanish-speaking immigrants, many of them former field laborers who came to the San Jose rubber-products firm for more stable employment. "Some of the workers in our plant don't speak *any* English," former affirmative action coordinator Leslie Whorff told us, "but it doesn't seem to be a problem. If they don't understand something, bi-lingual crew members are always on hand to help them out."

Another California employer, Bank of America, has had enormous success in hiring non-English-speaking Vietnamese immigrants as proof-machine operators, a high-pressure job that requires workers to rapidly compare the dollar amounts of deposited or cashed checks against the bank's records. While English was not a job requirement, the company needed some way to test applicants for proofing skills. Translating the written test into Vietnamese proved impractical, since not all applicants spoke the same dialect. So the company turned to its bilingual employees, who now administer the test orally. This informal approach has become the standard at more than 30 San Francisco-area proofing centers, a corporate manager told us.

The bottom line is: Where English fluency isn't necessary, eliminate it.

Workplace Acculturation

When a person moves from one state to another, the transition is almost always difficult, at least for awhile. Before one can feel comfortable in new surroundings, there are new friends to make, business relations to establish, road layouts to learn, and perhaps a few local customs or traditions to understand.

But if a state-to-state move can be disorienting, a move from one country to another can be a revolution in life-style—especially for those leaving vastly different customs, languages, and economic or political systems. This is, in fact, the situation that confronts many people from abroad (or even from American ghettos) as they enter the mainstream workplace for the first time.

Often, what comes across as poor preparation for work may be no more than the person's disorientation to the corporate life-style. Companies that are serious about recruiting from the nontraditional labor force are starting to realize this and are finding ways to make the transition smoother for the new worker.

Teaching the Corporate Culture

It's called acculturation, a fancy word for showing new workers the lay of the corporate landscape. As one analyst describes it: "*Training* is tell-ing a worker how to use the photocopier. *Orientation* is showing where the copier is located. And *acculturation* is explaining why there is a copying machine in the first place." In this sense, acculturation complements skills training by helping a new worker become familiar with the job's *context*.

Preemployment Exposure. The first steps toward acculturation often occur before new workers have even signed on with a company. These can take the form of internships, work-study programs, and other arrangements aimed at preparing immigrants and economically disadvantaged persons for the corporate life-style—the same techniques, as Chapter 5 discussed, that are often used to recruit and train minority and disadvantaged workers.

Two utility companies, New Jersey-based Public Service Electric & Gas Company (PSE&G) and the Carolina Power & Light Company, have played an active role in introducing disadvantaged minority youth to the corporate world. PSE&G's Inroads program encourages disadvantaged students to pursue careers in engineering and related fields. Equal opportunity manager Joseph Liedtke says the company wants to motivate such young people to "turn their heads and look at jobs they might not ordinarily seek."

PSE&G sends company officials into schools to talk with seventh- and eighth-grade students about the company and the jobs it offers. Students also receive invitations to tour nuclear power plants and other operations. The company's efforts, says Liedtke, are meant to "reach [students] early enough so they can steer their careers in [a relevant] direction" rather than signing up for a general curriculum in high school and college. PSE&G offers some students internships as well.

The utility also sponsors a Black Achievers Linkage Program, which pairs disadvantaged black high school students with successful black managers, who offer inspiration, career guidance, and personal assistance to their student protégés. The program gives students an opportunity to see these successful managers in action as well—often their first exposure to professional role models.

Similarly, Carolina Power & Light Company's Career Beginnings program is directed to high school juniors with demonstrated tenacity and drive, but who are considered at risk of dropping out of school due to financial, personal, or family problems. Carolina Power assigns employee mentors to individual students, and provides work-study arrangements to help young people learn about the company, develop good work habits, and plan for their future.

Mentoring. A second tool a growing number of companies are using to teach the corporate life-style is mentoring. Mentoring programs give newcomers to the workplace (especially those from other cultures) someone to turn to, without embarrassment, who has a genuine interest in their success. At the same time, experienced workers who become mentors learn to better understand people from different backgrounds.

One effective mentoring system is Amoco's Advisor Program. The Chicago-based oil-industry giant recruits employees who know the company well and get along well with colleagues to help recruits gain confidence in the work environment. Even before the new worker's first day on the job, an advisor will call him or her with information about benefits, relocation assistance, and other services. Advisors then work with the personnel department to ensure that their charges' employment paperwork and job orientation go smoothly. Eventually, the mentor's role matures from being a host to a friend and helper whom the new employee can call on when needed.

Corporate Recruiting Coordinator Zelda Hughes explains that the Amoco program was originally intended to help minorities and women assimilate into the corporate environment. Because these groups often lack the same access to networking relationships that white men have, she says, "this program has particular relevance in helping them become a part of the corporate culture." The program's success among women and minority group members has led Amoco to provide mentors for all new employees, regardless of gender or ethnic background.

In addition to formal mentoring, a number of firms are sponsoring support groups that help ethnic minority employees become familiar with corporate operations. For instance, employees at U.S. West and Pacific Northwest Bell, with management's backing, have organized such groups as the Black Employees' Telecommunications Association and Viento, an Hispanic employee group. These organizations have proved to be low-cost, yet effective ways of integrating culturally diverse groups into the work force.

Managing for Retention

Acquainting new employees with the workplace is only the beginning of acculturation. Even more important is making sure that the initial burst of corporate friendliness and cooperation remains as the new worker's novelty fades. Acculturation cannot be a one-shot effort, as orientation is, or frustrated workers, like weary visitors to a foreign country, may decide to pack their bags and go home.

This is exactly the problem that Boston's Shawmut Bank faced a few years ago. Alarmed to discover that many clerical employees were leaving the company before the end of their second year, managers discovered the root of the problem: well-intentioned but insufficiently sensitive management. The result was Shawmut's Managing for Retention policy, a program designed to help supervisors learn to "focus more on people and less on jobs," in the words of training director Linda Tufo. Seminars include instruction on coaching for productivity, motivating employees, and progressive discipline.

Managers at Shawmut say these efforts, combined with an expanded employee-orientation program, are helping workers to understand their importance to the company and are fostering good corporate citizenship among those new to the workplace. While employees of all backgrounds find the change helpful, the greatest beneficiaries are those from other cultures, who are now much less likely to leave because of simple confusion about the company's culture.

Managing a Culturally Diverse Work Force

In any culture, it takes time for newcomers to be fully accepted by those who came before. In the United States, racial and ethnic segregation— in some ways, voluntary, in others, imposed—for years consigned ethnic populations to separate neighborhoods and specific occupations. But in time—a very long time, in many cases—the lines between second-, third-, or later-generation immigrants softened, especially in the workplace, even as many culturally distinct practices and beliefs remained.

To a certain extent, affirmative action laws may have accelerated this assimilation process for native black Americans and for women, two groups that, by the 1960s, still were not accepted on an equal basis in the workplace. But the national consciousness that led the government, employers, and other institutions to fight unfair stereotyping also may have made some managers wary of policies that seek to recognize and appreciate cultural differences. For many of them, managing cultural diversity has meant nothing more than treating people of different ethnic backgrounds the same, with an emphasis on legally acceptable non-discrimination.

But acculturation, like good medicine, involves more than "doing no harm." To effectively manage diversity, the more farsighted employers understand that the workplace is changing from one in which success depends on employees' ability to conform to the dominant—that is, white male—culture to a workplace in which individual perspectives remain distinct, complementing and strengthening the company's goals. As some proponents of diversity management argue, the workplace has been transformed from a "melting pot" into a "salad bowl."

In the firms that best manage diversity, their commitment is also more than just a corporate policy statement that is written, read, and then forgotten. That commitment is integrated into company operations, from the nuts-and-bolts aspects of management to strategic recruitment plans. At its core is the fostering of good working relationships, day in and day out, among people with very different—even conflicting—outlooks on the world, and ensuring that all important information makes its way to people who may be just learning English.

All of these innovations are needed to make acculturation work. As Aetna's Badi Foster puts it: "It is one thing for a select group of executives or board members to develop awareness or insight into diversity. It is quite another for that insight to become a part of an organization's culture. People say, 'I get along with everyone,'" he explains. "But it's a much tougher problem than that."

In one high-profile example of corporate emphasis on better diversity management, a group of more than 30 national companies has joined forces to produce a videotaped program to help managers prepare for some of these challenges. The three-part series, called *Valuing Diversity,* highlights supervisory techniques that promote cooperation among workers of varied backgrounds and that enable each employee to be as satisfied and productive as possible. The videotapes use real-life situations to demonstrate how to prevent culturally rooted misunderstandings from causing conflicts or poor job performance. Program sponsors include AT&T, Bank of America, Apple Computer, Ford Motor Company, Hallmark, Pillsbury, and Avon.

Other employers have crafted their own diversity-management programs or brought in outside consultants to train managers. The most successful programs:

- Include experiential and participatory training that mirrors actual workplace situations and allows participants to role-play.
- Cast members of dominant ethnic groups in minority roles, and vice versa.
- Require participants to search for their own answers to problems so that the right answers are *their* answers.
- Include participants from different cultural backgrounds.
- Ensure that all supervisors go through similar training.

The Public Service Company of Colorado is one company that believes familiarity leads to appreciation of diverse cultures. The firm offers diversity training to its entire management team. It's not enough to "teach people how to parrot the correct answers" about their commitment to a diverse work force, maintains equal opportunity coordinator Betty Franklin Harrelson. "If they have the right values, the correct answers will come."

Fostering the right values, of course, is a daunting task. Public Service

Company of Colorado approaches it through a three-day workshop (conducted by a Denver-based consultant, Transformative Management) that encourages attendees to confront their prejudices and preconceptions about people different from themselves. The workshop then turns the tables on the managers with an exercise, developed by Peabody Award winner Jane Eliot, that forces those not normally the object of discriminatory perceptions to experience irrational discrimination firsthand. The exercise places "vice presidents and managers in the role of underdogs," says Harrelson, "often for the first time in their lives." As Linda Guilory of Transformative Management explains: "To begin to address the needs of a diverse staff, managers must first understand what it is like to be *different* in a work environment."

The Benefits of Diversity

How important is it, really, for employers to learn about cultural differences? Lennie Copeland, author of the *Valuing Diversity* film series, and other students of cross-cultural communication describe the kinds of insights managers can obtain by being prepared. For instance:

- People from Asian or Hispanic cultures may resist taking the initiative in a task, a reluctance that stems from a respect for authority and the feeling that beginning a task without specific instructions shows disrespect and defiance to their superiors.

- Asian employees also are likely to avoid a manager who regularly pats workers on the back or arm.

- Some foreign-born employees resist admitting they have not understood instructions because they do not want to embarrass themselves or their supervisors.

- Native American employees may feel humiliated if managers praise them loudly in front of their peers.

- A white manager may feel that a black subordinate is not paying attention to what he or she is saying, while a black manager and his or her white subordinate may both feel the other is being unnecessarily intrusive or aggressive. What is really going on, though, are two culturally distinct speaking and listening styles.

Successful diversity management not only reduces potential conflicts and misunderstandings, but it also seeks to capture the *benefits* of cultural diversity. American firms eager to expand their markets abroad, for instance, have found it profitable to draw upon the experience and insights of employees who grew up in other countries. The same is true for businesses hoping to market to immigrant populations in the United

States. "Our strength is our plurality," says Pacific Telesis' Constance Beutel. Apple Computer's Kevin Sullivan agrees: "When you are surrounded by sameness, you get only variations on the same."

Some companies have experienced this situation firsthand. A few years ago, Avon Products examined its public image, found it unsuited to the times, and set about developing a broader work force that included many different cultures and races—and men as well as women. Avon's Daisy Chin-Lor explains: "As a consumer-focused marketer, we needed to be responsive to diverse segments in our consumer base, and we realized that the company could be most responsive by having a diverse work force."

Los Angeles-area grocer Mark Roth, a native North Dakotan who does not speak Spanish, has turned his Mars Market into a bustling community center for area Hispanic families. Roth bought the store in the late 1960s, after the previous owner's refusal to adapt to the rapidly changing neighborhood nearly drove him out of business. Roth decided that, to be successful, his store needed to become a community fixture. So he hired local Spanish-speaking people to help him communicate with his customers and make the market look like it belonged in the community. Today, Mexican residents of El Monte, California, know that, at Mars Market, they will find freshly made *tortillas* and *salsa*, bright colors and *piñatas* decorating the aisles, Spanish-speaking clerks, and a store owner who has taken the time to learn about their culture—and clearly appreciates their business.

The Flexible Corporation

The Orem, Utah, software manufacturer WordPerfect Corp. makes the best-selling word processing package in the English language. In its latest version, the software performs not only advanced text processing but also some desktop publishing functions. The heart of the software is a few hundred thousand tightly packed, highly interrelated computer codes that took dozens of programmers years to perfect. Yet for all its complexity, the program can easily be converted for use in Spanish, French, German, Arabic, Korean, or any of a number of languages; all that is needed is a foreign language conversion module and four or five taps on the keyboard. In fact, it is almost as easy for every terminal in a company's computer network to "speak" a different language as it is for all of them to use English.

In the 1990s, productive firms will have to adapt to diverse cultures and languages in their workplaces just as WordPerfect adapts to the different languages of its users. Companies dedicated to bringing people from backgrounds as varying as Harlem and Haiti, or Vietnam and Vene-

zuela, into a workplace that not a generation ago was overwhelmingly
Middle-America—and doing so as quickly as possible—are learning this
lesson. And they are beginning to think of ways to help new workers fit
into the corporate culture with almost as much ease as a foreign-
speaking word processor loads a new language module into the computer.

Of course, people will always have more diverse needs and learning
abilities than machines or computer programs, and wise managers realize this. But the analogy is still apt. The better that workers mesh within
an organization, the more productive the organization will be. And the
more attuned management is to the special concerns of workers from
different backgrounds, the more eager these workers will be to help
their company succeed.

That is no small advantage at a time when the quality of one's work
force is competitive edge *numero uno* in the international marketplace—and when immigrants and the economically isolated are a more
valuable source of members of that work force than at any time in the
country's recent past.

7

Opening Doors to the Disabled

American history is filled with extraordinary people, individuals whose accomplishments are reason enough for their distinction: President Franklin Roosevelt, inventor Thomas Edison, Grand Canyon explorer John Wesley Powell, newspaper magnate Joseph Pulitzer, tuberculosis researcher Edward Livingston Trudeau, and Olympic runner Glen Cunningham, to name just a few. But what sets these achievers apart is not only their success, but that they succeeded in the face of seemingly overwhelming physical limitations.

Tens of thousands of their lesser-known brothers and sisters have pursued life and work with the same kind of determination. And when that determination is combined with a little enlightenment and commonsense accommodations on an employer's part, most physical limitations prove to be no barrier at all to productive, even exceptional, job performance.

Worker-oriented companies are finding ways to make disabilities even less of a barrier in the workplace than they have been in the past. For never has the marriage of interests between employee and employer been more important, nor its potential payoff greater. Hundreds of firms, faced with worker shortages on one hand and budget-breaking training costs on the other, already are discovering that the small investment needed to recruit and accommodate people with disabilities is just that—a sound *investment* in long-term work force quality.

Unfortunately, over the years, many people with disabilities have been needlessly isolated from mainstream jobs because they lacked access to normal classrooms and workplaces. But this situation is changing. Laws and technology are removing barriers to accessibility, and, today, it is not unusual to see disabled persons attending regular public schools, holding mainstream jobs, and even participating in competitive sports. Business establishments, ranging from supermarkets to concert halls, provide wheelchair entrances and marked parking spaces. And public-awareness campaigns are helping to reshape attitudes about what disabled persons can or cannot do.

Yet, of the estimated 13 million disabled Americans of working age (16 to 64 years old), only 37 percent work full- or part-time, leaving 63 percent—more than 8 million people—without jobs. When public-opinion researchers from Louis Harris and Associates spoke with members of the unemployed group, 2 out of 3 said they wanted to work.

But who *are* the disabled? They are a much more diverse group than many employers realize. "They range from functionally dependent quadriplegics to asthma sufferers," says one pair of social policy analysts. "They include persons who have never worked, those with limited skills and education, others who are afflicted with transitional problems as they adjust to their disabilities, but some who are fully employed and drawing good salaries."

The disabled community as a whole also is much larger and more pervasive than commonly believed. According to the 1980 census, 35.6 million persons—about 1 in 6 Americans—have disabilities. Moreover, as people age, they have a 1 in 4 chance of becoming disabled and an ever present, if small, chance of doing so, whatever their age. This is the reason why virtually every American family, regardless of its race, ethnic background, educational level, or income, has, or will have, some direct connection to the disabled community. As syndicated columnist George Will has remarked: "The most striking fact about the [disabled population]…is that it is the most inclusive. There is a sense in which we live in the antechamber of the handicapped community. I will never be black and I will never be a woman. I could be handicapped on the drive home tonight."

This sobering fact, in itself, is a compelling reason to open the personnel office doors to people with disabilities. More than any other part of the new work force, they are *all* of us.

Historical Barriers:
A Few Facts

While some individuals with disabilities have overcome imposing barriers to lead successful careers, the path to rewarding employment has been a rocky one for disabled Americans as a group. During the Second World War, for instance, American manufacturers recruited large numbers of women and disabled persons to keep production going while the able-bodied male population was fighting overseas. But when the war ended, many of these workers lost their jobs to returning soldiers. The wartime employment opportunities that had brought, for the first time, thousands of people with disabilities into the workplace had disappeared, practically overnight.

To encourage employers to rehire disabled persons for jobs they had held during the war, Congress, in August 1945, approved a resolution declaring National Employ the Handicapped Week. Then, in 1947, President Harry Truman signed an executive order establishing the President's Committee on Employment of People with Disabilities, an advisory body committed to expanding opportunities for disabled persons by disseminating information to businesses, promoting voluntary action, and encouraging cooperation among governmental agencies.

More than 25 years later, Congress passed the Rehabilitation Act of 1973, which set affirmative action hiring requirements for firms receiving federal grants or doing more than $2500 a year in business with the government. And by early 1990, Congress was close to approving a measure that would bring people with disabilities fully within the protections of the nation's civil rights laws.

But these federal initiatives, important as they are, have not changed the way many employers feel about hiring the disabled. Company decision makers are often unsure of these workers' abilities and uneasy about their limitations. And they worry about the costs of accommodating disabled employees in the office or factory.

Most high-level managers also have trouble accepting that people with disabilities *want* to work and are capable of doing a good job. A 1986 Harris poll, for instance, showed that only 1 in 10 top managers had a "strongly optimistic" attitude toward disabled people as a potential source of employees; they were more likely to consider racial or ethnic minority group members and the elderly as "excellent" sources of workers. "Although most believe that the disabled will be...reliable," writes George Washington University's Sar A. Levitan, "they fear involuntary absenteeism and turnover...[and] also...a lack of flexibility in job assignments and the difficulty of promoting."

These negative attitudes no doubt have contributed to disabled people's isolation, which, in turn, has prevented the majority of them from getting the necessary education and training to compete with mainstream job seekers. And until recently, mobility barriers kept these persons away from most office buildings and factories. Many disabilities also make standard office functions such as typing, filing, or answering the phone difficult, if not impossible. These factors, along with generally inadequate information about employment opportunities, have contributed to a crisis in self-confidence among large segments of the disabled community—a crisis that still keeps far too many readily employable persons out of the workplace, confined to hospitals, isolated group residences, or their own homes.

Looking Over the Overlooked

As the Harris poll suggests, people with disabilities often are overlooked at recruiting time. They shouldn't be. The disabled community is as critical to beating the worker shortage as women, minority group members, and older people are—in some ways, even more so. Many persons with disabilities are well-educated, and they are well suited to the economy's shift away from physically demanding factory jobs and toward service occupations.

According to firms who have hired them, people with disabilities, more often than not, are reliable, loyal, motivated, and safety-conscious employees. For instance:

- A recent survey of the hotel and restaurant industry concluded that hiring disabled workers could alleviate the problem of high turnover.

- A 1981 employee survey by the Du Pont Co. found that disabled workers' safety and performance records matched or surpassed those of their able-bodied colleagues.

- A 1987 Harris poll reported that an overwhelming majority of managers of disabled employees gave them a good or excellent rating on their overall job performance and that nearly all disabled employees did their jobs as well as or better than other employees in similar jobs.

- The Harris survey also found that 8 out of 10 department heads and line managers felt workers who had a disability were no harder to supervise than able-bodied employees.

Chuck Cuyjet, coordinator of a pilot training program for the Greater Washington (D.C.) Resource Center, sums up the situation best. At one time, he says, hiring "a person in a wheelchair was a totally foreign experience to most employers. It took years before they were willing to make the necessary adjustments. But once they found out these people could be productive, that was all they needed."

Recruiting Persons With Disabilities

From the human-resources standpoint, potential employees with disabilities fall into four main categories, each requiring different types of accommodations:

1. *Existing employees who become disabled through accident, illness, or drug and alcohol abuse.* To avoid losing valued workers in whom the company already has made a substantial investment, employers need to be sensitive to these situations as they develop, making accommodations, where necessary. "Unfortunately," confides one personnel manager, "it's usually [psychologically] easier for companies to deal with a handicapped person coming into the personnel office from outside the company than it is to deal with someone already working for the company who becomes disabled."

2. *Experienced workers from other companies whose disabling injuries or illnesses have necessitated a change in career.* People in these circumstances, having already spent many years in the work force, are likely to apply for new positions through the same channels nondisabled applicants use.

3. *People who became disabled early in life but mainstreamed themselves by voluntarily joining public schools, college degree programs, and training courses dominated by able-bodied participants.* These are the people with the courage to knock on employers' doors on their own, without needing any special introduction. They tend to be highly motivated, have a healthy self-confidence, and usually are as work-ready as able-bodied applicants.

4. *Finally, the large number of people with disabilities who have never held a job (or have only limited work experience) but who are enrolled in school or in training and rehabilitation programs.* Like members of other disadvantaged minority populations, these people may be less knowledgeable than most would-be workers about the job market and less likely to have developed a network of contacts that will lead them to jobs. Employers therefore will have to take the lead in finding and reaching out to these potential job applicants.

Aside from making an extra effort to retain employees who become disabled, how *does* an employer begin recruiting and hiring more people with disabilities? Is it enough to give those who come in independently the same consideration as able-bodied applicants? This is the obvious first step, but it probably will not be enough. Bringing disabled workers on board—in more than just token numbers—often demands assertive recruiting techniques, as a number of companies are finding out.

Recruiting From Rehabilitation Agencies

State, county, or private rehabilitation agencies help newly disabled persons relearn everyday tasks and, ultimately, return to the work force. A rehab center may train its clients in job-related skills or help them pursue additional training or education. Many offer job placement services, such as writing letters of reference, helping with résumé preparation, or educating prospective employers about specific disabilities. Others may arrange for transportation, sign language interpreters, or other special assistance for their clients during the application and interview process—continuing, if necessary, into the first weeks on the job.

While rehabilitation agencies are responsible first to persons who become disabled, they serve as a resource for the business community as well. But despite their efforts to provide this service, it is sometimes difficult to match rehab clients' training with a company's specific needs.

Some employers have minimized this problem simply by visiting rehabilitation facilities on a regular basis and making their needs known to program coordinators. One company that successfully uses this approach is Marriott Corp., whose regional human resource representatives and operations managers often exchange ideas with rehabilitation professionals about:

- The company's business objectives.
- The types of jobs available at the firm's hotels, restaurants, and contracted services.
- The skills those jobs require.

Marriott managers say they often invite counselors to visit potential job sites to learn, firsthand, how the businesses operate.

Another firm that has forged a useful partnership with an educational and training facility is Shawmut Bank in Boston, Massachusetts. In an effort to address the company's deficit of skilled clerical workers, one hearing-impaired employee led company recruiters to nearby Horace Mann Austin School for the Deaf. Shawmut donated educational materials for the school's proof-and-coder curriculum, and, in return, school instructors taught sign language to the bank's supervisors. A number of people trained in the program eventually came to work for the bank.

For companies willing to work with them, rehabilitation and training centers can be reliable allies. These organizations know it is in their own as well as their clients' interest to offer relevant preparation for the workplace, and the best rehab agencies will listen if companies tell them what they need. Abilities, Inc., founder Hank Viscardi, an advisor on disability issues to several United States presidents, counsels all rehab organizations to "understand the employer's point of view." Employers have "always wanted, and still want, the best, the safest, and most productive worker [they] can find...," Viscardi says. "We have to offer employers more than anyone else has offered them."

One organization that takes this principle seriously is the Woodrow Wilson Rehabilitation Institute. Located in southern Virginia, the institute is a valuable source of employees trained in architectural computer-aided design (CAD). After hearing about the institute's program for accident victims from the manufacturer of its CAD equipment, Smith McMahon Architects, a Washington, D.C. firm, hired their first Wilson graduate. "The Woodrow Wilson Institute has some excellent instructors, and the operators they train are conscientious, focused workers," says partner Bob McMahon. "[CAD] equipment is so specialized by manufacturer that finding an employee already familiar with it can be difficult. Because the young man we hired was job-ready, we saved the six months it would have taken to train someone ourselves. And in a busy, small company like ours, six months can make a big difference in our productivity."

Sheltered Workshops. Not all people in rehabilitation programs are comfortable with moving directly into mainstream jobs. Still, they can gain valuable, paid work experience in a sheltered workshop. Government agencies or private businesses often turn to these organizations for workers (accompanied by workshop supervisors) to perform specific tasks, either at the workshops or at the contracting company's place of business.

From an economic standpoint, contracting with these groups makes sense. According to companies that have used them, the sheltered workshop teams—including many individuals considered severely disabled—perform good work at a reasonable cost. The Du Pont Co., for instance, saves between 25 and 30 percent over the estimated in-house cost by hiring out to worker groups from the Wilmington (Del.) Opportunity Center to handle mail-order requests generated by magazine promotional offers.

Using these services, companies can, in effect, increase their employee base for "peak-and-valley" projects. Quaker Oats has put this concept to work in its Lawrence, Kansas, plant, contracting with a team from the nearby Cottonwood Workshop to assemble several hundred thousand bags of dog food in plastic canisters for a major advertising campaign. Quaker executives needed a supplemental crew but felt the project's 12-week duration did not justify placing extra permanent workers on the payroll. The Cottonwood team, which included 45 mentally retarded adults, met the need. Moreover, the temporary workers were well accepted by Quaker's employees. Notes J. R. Congra, Cottonwood's vocational director: "Quaker treated our employees as their own."

Likewise, San Francisco-based McKesson Industries supplements its labor force with workshop employees from Goodwill Industries. Goodwill transports both workers and supervisors to one of McKesson's 1000-employee warehouses, where they help to fill and label boxes. The arrangement helps McKesson provide its services more efficiently while saving on payroll costs.

Other Businesses Staffed by Persons With Disabilities. Other firms have started contracting with bona fide businesses staffed by persons with disabilities. Like sheltered workshops, these enterprises are tied to rehabilitation efforts. But unlike sheltered workshops, they are for-profit operations and subject to minimum wage laws. The Chicago Lighthouse for the Blind, for instance, uses trainees from its High Skills Program on competitively subcontracted jobs with companies like Western Electric, Zenith, Sunbeam, and Kraft. And General Electric has found that Abilities, Inc., a division of the Human Resource Center on Long Island, New York, offers fully competitive component parts manufacturing services.

Recruiting From Disability Organizations

Companies that successfully recruit disabled workers often turn to groups organized to represent the interests of people with specific disabilities. In recent years, some of the associations these firms have found most helpful are:

- The Association for Children and Adults with Learning Disabilities.
- Disabled American Veterans.
- The Epilepsy Foundation of America.
- The National Amputation Foundation.
- The National Federation of the Blind (which operates a nationwide, computerized employment network called Job Opportunities for the Blind, or JOB).
- The National Association for the Deaf.

There are also a number of organizations that specialize in matching qualified disabled persons to jobs. These groups are not rehabilitation agencies, though they may offer some training. Their main job, as they see it, is to bring employers, persons with disabilities, and rehabilitation agencies together so that disabled persons can meet their need for meaningful employment while businesses can meet their need for trained, dependable workers.

One such group is Mainstream, Inc., founded in 1975 as a legal resource for companies affected by new federal hire-the-handicapped laws. The organization has since broadened its focus to include training in job-hunting skills, a computerized job-placement service, and efforts to build working partnerships between businesses and rehabilitation agencies.

Mainstream's information director, Fritz Rumpel, says he has been "astounded" to hear many employers claim they "don't know how to find qualified applicants" and cites, as the cause, a lack of communication among employers, persons with disabilities, and the agencies representing them. "Rehab agencies and private-sector employment offices speak very different languages," Rumpel maintains. "Agencies teach their clients certain skills and then look for a job that 'fits,' while employers look at their business needs, and then try to find a person who can meet those needs. Preparing an applicant to work and marketing him or her to an employer are not the same thing. Our job is to bridge the communications gap."

Mainstream's job placement service, Project LINK, serves more than 400 employers in the Washington, D.C., and Dallas, Texas, metropolitan areas. Project LINK uses a computerized database known as the Search-Match System to quickly match applicants with the appropriate job openings. Mainstream has helped nine disability organizations around the country set up their own search-match programs.

Mary Jean McClellan, human resources director for Washington, D.C.'s American Security Bank, enthusiastically supports Mainstream's efforts, and she encourages area employers, particularly smaller companies, to rely on the organization's help in recruiting new employees. "With entry-level job applicants in short supply and some employment agencies charging large fees for their referrals, an organization that sends you trained people at no cost is really doing a favor for employers." Taking its endorsement a step further, the bank has hosted a number of industry meetings to allow groups like Mainstream to introduce themselves to the local banking community. These efforts have led to such initiatives as the National Association of Bank Women's mentoring program, through which members "adopt" and counsel persons enrolled in Project LINK.

Similarly, Operation Job Match, also based in Washington, D.C., helps employers fill openings with experienced people while assisting those who have become physically disabled to remain in—or return to— competitive employment. The group's job-readiness and placement program now helps persons with a variety of disabilities to adjust to their condition and polish their job-search skills. The organization does not place people directly but makes its job listings available to qualified clients. One innovative feature, used on occasion, is to provide employers with videotapes of statements by a number of applicants. Overall, the Job Match program finds jobs for some two-thirds of its clients.

The organization already has taken its 12-part job-readiness program to a dozen other cities and hopes its efforts will eventually be duplicated throughout the country. "So often, one hears that there aren't any or enough qualified candidates in the disabled sector," says program founder Diane Afes. "We say, here they are."

Recruiting at Colleges and Universities

Even with a declining young-adult population, the college campus remains a favorite recruiting site for American businesses. Already, prospective employers are finding colleges an excellent source of disabled job applicants as well. A new study by the National Center for Education Statistics reports that 10.5 percent of all students in postsecondary education have a disability, and most of these students are receptive to mainstream job offers.

Potential employers usually communicate with these students through such normal channels as the campus placement office, but some, like Hewlett-Packard, appeal to them more directly by hosting informational seminars. At its San Francisco-area Career Day for Disabled Students, Hewlett-Packard's staff leads job-hunting workshops for local university and vocational students and discusses career opportunities with the firm. Though Career Day is meant to be an educational event, the company typically invites a number of participants to job interviews.

Recruiting by Reputation

Naturally, a company that welcomes people with disabilities and treats them fairly is its own best recruiting tool. In the long run, attracting applicants from the disabled community will be easiest for employers known to offer these workers genuine equal opportunity.

But even an outstanding record cannot boost companies' recruiting efforts unless members of the disabled community know about it. Many employers solve this problem by attending or speaking at conferences likely to attract large numbers of disabled persons, by making sure that company-sponsored events are accessible to people with disabilities, and by prominently displaying the international accessibility sign on all their recruiting notices.

Businesses also demonstrate their openness to people with disabilities by targeting product advertising to disabled, as well as able-bodied, members of the population. McDonald's and Coca-Cola, for instance, have begun using visibly disabled people in their television commercials. Other firms do the same thing in their print ads. Their message is plain: People with disabilities are taken seriously here.

Advertising in *Paraplegia News, Independent Living, Careers & the Handicapped,* and similar periodicals is another way some firms gain visibility among the disabled community. IBM recruits physically disabled persons into its programmer training courses, for instance, with a printed advertisement showing an empty wheelchair next to a computer terminal. "Compatible Hardware," the caption reads. A second IBM recruiting ad simply presents the artificial hand and business card of Michael Coleman, one of IBM's data processing instructors, and describes his success with the company.

Educating and Training
Persons With Disabilities

The Education for All Handicapped Children Act, passed by Congress in 1975, brought children with disabilities into the public schools, many for the first time. The law's effect is clearly visible in the increasing numbers of disabled youngsters entering college. As a result, when young adults with disabilities go job hunting in the 1990s, they will be more likely than ever before to have had the same educational background as their nondisabled peers.

Surprisingly, however, even with satisfactory schooling, many disabled people have found one of their biggest hurdles to advancement to be inadequate job skills. In fact, according to surveys of business managers, up to two-thirds say their reason for failing to hire a disabled person was the person's lack of training.

Some managers blame schools and colleges for not placing more emphasis on course work that will prepare students for future jobs. But the problem goes deeper than this. While people with disabilities, especially those just approaching working age, have good reason to be confident about their job worthiness, many still are held back by the lingering effects of a culture that kept them isolated for so many years.

Kaiser Aluminum's Robert Cole believes these students can benefit from practical guidance on how to market themselves, once they have acquired their education and job skills. "Traditionally, disabled students have found the transition to work difficult," Cole says, "and rather than an initial opening to employment and career opportunities, their *nontransition* has become the beginning of a cycle of unemployment."

Another open question is whether standard training programs for the disabled are preparing them for actual jobs. "Right now, training is often out-of-date, geared toward jobs that do not exist or are on their way out," insists American Security Bank's Mary Jean McClellan. "The quality of training is going to make a big difference in the opportunities that will become available to disabled individuals in the future."

A number of companies have concluded that schools and training programs cannot reflect business' actual needs unless business itself becomes involved. We showed in Chapter 5 how corporate participation in public schools and skills-training programs has increased disadvantaged youths' job readiness. In much the same way, employer assistance has helped prepare disabled young people for work.

Academic and Career Counseling

Success in the work world (for disabled as well as nondisabled youth) begins with setting off in the right direction. When disabled young persons understand the importance of acquiring not only technical skills but also practical knowledge about finding and keeping a job, they usually become more confident, better trained, and ultimately more valuable to the companies that hire them.

Hewlett-Packard is one of a growing number of employers that helps to provide this direction, on a one-on-one basis, to college students with disabilities. Through its mentor program, the company pairs participating students with veteran employees working in the students' specific areas of interest. Mentors spend at least two hours a month coaching students in corporate organization and operations, advising them about career choices and academic preparation, and helping them to land summer jobs at Hewlett-Packard or other companies.

The Employer's Role in Training

In an effort to expand the ranks of persons with disabilities who are job-ready, a few companies, as we noted earlier, have helped shape existing training programs to good effect by sharing their needs and expectations with local rehabilitation agencies. Other firms have decided to go into the training business themselves.

Compatible Hardware: Computer Training and the Disabled. The widespread use of computers has changed the way most companies do business and the way most of their employees do their jobs. So, too, have computers broadened career choices for physically restricted persons, allowing them to move away from rote, unskilled occupations into more rewarding, intellectually challenging jobs. A number of firms are helping speed this transition by teaching disabled people job skills in a classroom setting.

At the head of the pack is computer giant IBM, which has offered programmer training courses for severely disabled persons since 1972. Working with the federal government, state rehabilitation and education agencies, and other private companies, IBM helps set up local programs and serves as an advisor until the programs are ready to operate independently. Since the venture began, more than 2500 disabled persons have graduated from 38 IBM-sponsored training centers around the country. And the company boasts that 80 percent of current graduates are placed in jobs starting at $20,000 a year or more.

"We try to gear our curriculum to meet the real needs of the job market," explains Jack Honeck, IBM's former equal opportunity manager for disability programs. Honeck points out that students completing the program find jobs not only with IBM but also with other participating firms. Corporate director of community programs Juan Sabater says program graduates "are making valuable contributions as topflight computer programmers in business and industry. We view this activity as a means for returning something to our communities, and we are committed to it for that reason and for the long run."

Another large computer firm, Control Data Corp., brings its computer training program directly to mobility-impaired persons. Taking computers into homes and apartments, rehabilitation centers, hospitals, and nursing homes, Control Data trains students in programming and other business applications. After graduation, the new programmers move into full-time jobs they can perform from home or other alternative work sites.

Of course, organizing this kind of large-scale effort demands a bigger investment of time and money than many companies can afford on their own. Thus, a few firms have taken the lead in assembling groups of employers to fund and manage training programs for the disabled. Among them is northern New Jersey's Public Service Electric & Gas Company (PSE&G), which helped create a computer-training course at Goodwill Industries for severely disabled persons. A business advisory council, set up by one of PSE&G's vice presidents, oversees the project. As with similar programs, graduates often obtain jobs with sponsoring companies.

Another employer-sponsored program, cited by the Reagan Administration as a "model private-sector initiative," is a year-long programmer training course called Business Information Processing Education for the Disabled (B.I.P.E.D.). In 1981, some 40 New York, Connecticut, and New Jersey corporations—Xerox, GTE, and Reader's Digest among them—raised more than $200,000 to launch the program. Today, staffed by a large contingent of volunteers and a few salaried employees, B.I.P.E.D. trains a dozen or more physically disabled persons at a time at each of its two facilities. Some 90 percent of its graduates have found positions paying at least $18,000 to $20,000 a year.

While most rehabilitation programs receive some training grants from the federal, state, or local governments, B.I.P.E.D, says its executive director Joe LaMaine, is funded entirely by business. "Because this is a private-sector endeavor," LaMaine points out, "the burden on the government and the taxpayer is alleviated. And after being accepted, there's no red tape for the disabled person.

"This is a program *by* business *for* business," LaMaine continues. "In a way, it's a college for the handicapped sponsored by the corporations. Our facility is an extension of their office building."

On-the-Job Training. Employers with broader job requirements than computer programming also sponsor or support vocational training efforts. These programs, usually held on the company's premises, train persons with disabilities in specific job-related skills. Trainees earn wages, paid by their referring agency, the employer-sponsor, or a combination of the two. Program graduates often find jobs with the company that trained them.

Cleveland Electric Illuminating Company's 12-week program rotates trainees through a variety of positions in the company—customer service representative, accounts payable clerk, and data-entry clerk—basing assignments on both the participants' interests and the company's needs. Cleveland Electric trainees, unlike those in some other programs, do not all work together, but work instead with long-term, usually nondisabled, employees called peer counselors, who help the trainees develop good work habits in addition to technical skills.

Marriott Corp., by contrast, trains small teams of mentally disabled persons to work in its corporate-headquarters cafeteria. During their 13-week program, trainees master such tasks as refilling flatware containers; sweeping, clearing, and cleaning tables; emptying trash barrels; and replenishing supplies along the cafeteria line. At the end of the training period, the company may hire the individuals to work in a nearby Marriott facility or send them, job-ready, to their referring agency for placement with another firm. Similar training programs, as well as programs geared to other disabilities, are offered regularly in Marriott operations around the country, and have earned the corporation numerous awards from rehabilitation agencies.

Supported Employment. Supported employment is a special type of concentrated on-the-job training provided, one-on-one, by a job coach or rehabilitation counselor. The coach accompanies a trainee to the work site, helping him or her to become comfortable with the job, and then remains with the new employee as long as needed.

The Association of Retarded Citizens (ARC), headquartered in Arlington, Texas, participates actively in supported employment programs throughout the United States. Clearly, ARC is doing its part to combat the labor shortage: over the last two decades, the organization has placed more than 37,000 people in competitive jobs.

Several Washington, D.C., area businesses have taken advantage of supported-employment programs run by local ARC chapters. The District of Columbia's year-to-18-month program provides a well-rounded curriculum that focuses on clients' specific abilities and interests and teaches both practical job skills and strategies for everyday living. The program's success is visible in the numbers: in 95 percent of the cases, the association says, employers are satisfied with their new workers and keep them on the job.

Since supported employment provides many trainees with their first job, one might expect the new workers to leave for a better position at the first opportunity. Yet they tend to stay with a company much longer than other employees, says the personnel director for Woodward & Lothrop, a department store chain that has hired more than 100 people from the ARC program. One of the store's ARC-sponsored employees, for instance, has remained more than six years in a job expected to turn

ARC-trained workers also have fared well in smaller settings, such as the Willow Tree Day Care Center in Lanham, Maryland. According to the center's director, the three women currently employed (two full-time classroom aides and a kitchen worker) have been more reliable than the nondisabled persons who preceded them in the jobs. "She has a work ethic that would put most of us to shame," the director says of one of the women. "She arrives on time every day, ready not to talk on the phone or take coffee breaks or visit with the other staff members but to work....She is even-tempered and cheerful, and I've never known her to be sick. All she asks is that she be told she is doing a good job."

Instead of working with an organization like the ARC, some larger employers prefer using their own managers, as McDonald's restaurants do, for supported-employment efforts. The fast-food chain's McJobs program includes classroom instruction, along with demonstrations and supervised practice on the grill, French fry maker, and other equipment. Each manager/job coach works with five or six disabled persons during an intensive, two-to-three-month training period. The coaches develop their own training schedules and continually review and evaluate each trainee's performance.

McDonald's splits the training costs with referring rehabilitation agencies. The restaurant pays job coaches their full-time (managers') salaries; rehab agencies cover crew members' wages while in training. After graduation, participants are mainstreamed and continue working at the store where they were trained, making way for a new class of trainees. The company boasts more than 7000 McJobs graduates to date, who work in 64 stores in 32 regions of the country.

"Many people...once...considered 'unemployable'...now hold jobs of real responsibility within the McDonald's system," says the company's president, Mike Quinlan. "Their outstanding performance has disproved the myth that hiring the disabled worker is unprofitable." McDonald's disabled employees are driven by a desire to prove themselves, Quinlan says, and their persistence has become a model for the firm's crews and managers alike. "The McJobs program has helped turn sad stories into success stories," he notes. "And we're proud of each and every one of them."

Accommodating Disabilities on the Job

Mary Pat Radabaugh of IBM knows the difference between a disability and a handicap. "The individual has the disability, but the handicap resides in the environment," she explains. "We can't eliminate the disability, of course, but we can change the environment and often minimize the handicap and, in some cases, eliminate it."

Almost everywhere they go, physically disabled people face such barriers. The barriers range from narrow doors to high shelves to unamplified telephones, things that able-bodied persons encounter on a daily basis with hardly a thought. For those with mental disabilities or invisible conditions like heart disease, nonphysical barriers—inflexible time schedules or high-pressure responsibilities, for instance—can be equally handicapping. These obstructions can prevent qualified people from finding good jobs or drive experienced people from the jobs they already have.

But the workplace of the 1990s cannot be off-limits to people with disabilities and, if barriers are removed, it need not be. Elevators, wide entrance doors, ramps, wheelchair restrooms, Braille elevator controls, and a host of other accommodations are standard features in newer office buildings. Some disabilities may require extra adjustments on the employer's part but, in most cases, only minor modifications to the work environment are needed.

Indeed, virtually overnight, advances in computers and electronics have opened wide the doors of opportunity even to the severely disabled. IBM's Phil Bravin, who worked for a year as a job counselor to college graduates who are deaf and blind, says that for people with this double handicap, "the computer is the interface, the connection to the world." Former director of the Veterans Administration, Max Cleland, agrees: "The real disabled people of the future are going to be those who *don't* have a computer to use."

Equally encouraging, these technologies are reshaping occupations in the fastest-growing fields: law, marketing, information management, financial services, health care, and leisure and travel services. For disabled persons already established in careers, the new technologies have made it far easier to interact with the nondisabled business world.

Even without the new civil rights protections for disabled persons, federal law requires all but the smallest government contractors and all organizations receiving federal grants to make "reasonable accommodations" for employees with disabilities. But resourceful employers have learned that, whether or not they are mandated by law, workplace accommodations for experienced workers or promising applicants can pay off. Such arrangements often make the difference between retaining and losing a key employee. "For anyone who becomes disabled while employed with us, we would go to great lengths to maintain them at the same level of responsibility," declares one corporate official. "We'll do everything we can to keep a person whole. It's only a handicap if it can't be accommodated."

Industries whose workers face hazardous conditions know this better than anyone: "Historically, people tended to come to work for our companies early and to stay for their working lives," explains George McGowan, chairman and CEO of Baltimore Gas & Electric Company. "Our companies, more or less routinely,...adapt[ed] to disabilities as they developed....We were *accommodating* before that word came into common usage."

Firms of all sizes can easily afford most workplace accommodations. According to a 1982 survey by Berkeley Planning Associates, for example, 80 percent of all employer accommodations cost less than $500. Some cost nothing at all.

In fact—and this may come as a surprise to the uninitiated—most employees with disabilities require *no* special accommodations. Another survey, for example, reported that only 35 percent of working disabled people said their employers had made one or more accommodations for them, while 61 percent said no accommodation had been made or was needed. Even among unemployed disabled persons, only 23 percent said they would need special devices or equipment to work full-time. In most cases, a little sensitivity and common sense are all that is required.

Where adjustments do need to be made, equipping offices with specialized computers is one way, but by no means the only way, employers can adapt the workplace for disabled persons. Companies also may be able to:

- Modify the work environment.
- Adapt equipment or services to special needs.
- Modify work schedules.
- Change the job's location.
- Tailor training and supervision to the disability.
- Restructure the job.
- Provide special training to supervisors or coworkers.
- Selectively place workers in positions where no accommodation is needed.

Many employers are discovering that changes in these areas are an extremely cost-effective way of recruiting or retaining high-quality disabled workers—and far easier to implement than they had expected.

Modifying the Work Environment

Wheelchair users already enjoy fairly free access to modern buildings, since federal law now requires new commercial and public buildings to have wide entrance doors, wheelchair curb cuts, elevators with lowered controls, and at least one set of wheelchair-accessible rest rooms. Because some older buildings lack these features, however, a number of employers have chosen to make the necessary structural changes or move their offices to street level.

One company that made this type of accommodation for an employee using a wheelchair was Smith Segreti Tepper McMahon Harned (SST), a Washington, D.C., architectural firm, which modified one rest room near its office suite in an older high-rise building. Because SST's suite also had narrow hallways, the office manager arranged for the new employee to reach his work station through a special security door.

In most cases, though, all that companies need to do is keep the halls clear of obstacles and leave floors bare or covered with low-pile carpeting. Persons in wheelchairs can use conventional office desks if they are raised a few inches on wooden blocks, but employers may need to lower some office fixtures—lamps, filing cabinets, postage meters, photocopiers, and the like—so that wheelchair users can reach them. For workers with limited arm or hand movement, employers often replace the knobs on doors, water faucets, and frequently used office equipment with levers. Supervisors or coworkers also can make minor changes to tools employed on the job, so that persons with little or no finger control can use them.

These kind of accommodations allowed Toledo Edison Company lineman Jay Bostelman to regain his independence after a disabling electrical accident. Now a meterman electrician, Bostelman uses screwdrivers, pliers, and wrenches with ridged handles, devised by his coworkers, and steadies meters through the use of holes bored in his work table. Using these simple modifications, Bostelman rebuilt more than 100 meters during his first six months back on the job. Recently promoted to service dispatcher, he also has designed about 70 computer programs to help his crew monitor power outages and equipment reliability. "There are things that may be harder for me to do," says Bostelman, "but [my coworkers] compensate, and together we get the job done in the fastest amount of time."

In some cases, simply talking to disabled workers about their needs can shed light on other possibilities. One of IBM's blind employees, for instance, did not know when it was safe to cross the street separating two company office buildings. IBM solved the problem by giving the worker a device to change the traffic signal each time he needed to cross.

Adapting Equipment and Services to Special Needs

New office technologies have given people with very little mobility unprecedented freedom to work in a wide variety of occupations. This amazing machinery permits those with the minutest of motor capabilities to pass college courses, perform intricate computations, write legal briefs, or even design buildings. Some equipment, for example, allows a person to type on a computer terminal using a light pen attached to the head. Other devices can be operated by small movements like a blink, a breath, or a raised eyebrow. Practical, everyday applications for computers operated entirely by voice are just around the corner. And these products are becoming more affordable every day.

Accommodating Mobility Impairments. Hands-free telephones and voice-activated dictation machines are two common devices that allow persons who cannot use their hands to conduct normal business activities. Often they are the sole accommodation a quadriplegic employee requires. Such was the case for Vivian Berzinski, an attorney with the

Washington, D.C., law firm Arnold & Porter. When applying for a position with the firm, she asked only for a speaker phone. Other modifications to her office were equally uncomplicated. On Berzinski's desk, a small wooden stand holds a standard computer keyboard at her shoulder level; another stand positions the computer's video display screen at her eye level. She types on the keyboard with a plastic rubber-tipped pointer held between her teeth. This simple instrument also allows her to use the telephone, buzz her secretary on the intercom, and turn pages in books and documents.

IBM's Bill Jackson, who worked for the company 25 years before an accident left him paralyzed from the neck down, also performs a highly responsible job with minimal accommodation. "I've been treated as normally as you can possibly be in my situation." he says. "They put a little ramp in at the back door. I have a dictating machine with special fittings and a speaker phone. That's about it." But Jackson's employer made another accommodation, perhaps the most important thing that can be done for a valued employee who becomes disabled. Following the accident, IBM's Midwest regional manager held Jackson's position open for six months while he underwent rehabilitation. In only four months, Jackson returned to work as manager of a National Service Division branch office.

For employees who are not totally paralyzed but have difficulty moving their arms or have lost an arm, there are one-handed typewriters, automatic dial telephones (also widely used among able-bodied workers), and computer terminals operated with a single finger. And many individuals who cannot reach and bend freely, such as those suffering from muscular dystrophy or arthritis, have devised a simple tool—a stick with a magnet on the end—to help them retrieve metal items, even papers stapled or paper clipped together, from the floor or a table top.

Persons who have lost control of one side of their body after a stroke can benefit from this one-handed technology as well. George Michnale, an insurance agent who works outside Kansas City, Missouri, found it relatively simple to adjust the controls in his company vehicle for stroke victim Nancy Gibson, whom he had just hired as his driver. In the adapted vehicle, Gibson, whose left side is paralyzed, drives Michnale from appointment to appointment while he makes phone calls and prepares for the next meeting. While he's in meetings, she makes deliveries.

Telecommuting for the Disabled.   A more dramatic but highly effective means of accommodating physically restricted employees has been to change the location of the job altogether (which employers also have begun to do for their mainstream workers with family responsibilities, as Chapter 4 showed). The use of alternative work sites or full-scale telecommuting seems to make the most sense for those who cannot travel easily. Quadriplegics, for instance, may find working from home considerably more convenient than commuting to a downtown office.

One successful telecommuting effort has been American Express Company's Operation Homebound. As an experiment, the company installed word processing stations in the homes of ten disabled persons. The home workers took their assignments from a phone-operated dictation pool, typed the documents, and sent them—via telephone lines—directly from their terminals to a central control office. Control-room employees printed and delivered drafts to the authors, who then telecopied edited versions back to the typists for correction. The experiment's success led American Express to convert the home workers, all consultants, into full-time, payrolled employees.

Many telemarketing companies also use physically restricted home workers to conduct surveys and sell products over the phone. Both the Gallup and Harris polling organizations employ such home workers nationwide for telephone research. On a smaller scale, Huntsville (Ala.) Hospital recently hired a severely disabled young man to interview former patients about the service they received during their hospital stay. He conducts the survey by telephone from his home—from his bed, in fact.

Accommodating Visual Impairments. A wide range of accommodations for people with visual impairments also is available to employers. Braille and large-type or recorded materials allow these employees to read the same printed matter as sighted employees; Braillewriters even let them keep notes for their own use. If important books, manuals, or other written information are not already available in these formats, a number of volunteer organizations throughout the country can transcribe them. In addition to these options, partially sighted persons may be able to read visually by using hand-held or table magnifiers and shields to reduce white paper's glare.

Companies also can record, as IBM does, their training manuals, benefit brochures, and other major employee publications onto cassettes. And when not enough time is available to transcribe printed materials (such as when an employee takes a written test or fills out a form), employers often use sighted reading assistants.

People with visual impairments can work in technical or manufacturing settings, using machines or tools with brailled or notched markings, guide plates and stops, or electronic sound feedback. And this group has been one of the most dramatic beneficiaries of new computer technologies:

- Computers that translate typed words into Braille, one line at a time.
- Speech synthesizers that "say" the words appearing on a terminal screen.
- Braille printers.
- Laser scanners that "read" entire printed pages into computer storage, making them immediately available to blind and sighted readers alike.

Many of these devices, particularly those that can be attached to standard computers, range in price from less than $100 to nearly $3000, though the more sophisticated, self-contained systems can cost as much as $8000.

But such investments can pay off and, at Bank of America, they have. William F. Holmes, vice president and manager for equal opportunity programs, says management has already placed a number of these systems throughout the company. One experience offers a convincing example of how valuable such accommodations can be.

Soon after hiring a blind woman for a job not requiring vision, bank managers saw that she had an exceptional talent for customer relations. But to put that talent to work, the new employee would have to read customers' account information from a computer screen, a seemingly impossible task. The company solved the problem by acquiring a piece of equipment that both talks to her in synthesized speech and turns computer output into Braille. As a result, "customers who speak with her over the telephone have no idea she is blind," says Holmes, who believes her superior performance on the job more than compensates for the company's investment in a special computer. "Our philosophy has always been that if someone meets a business need for us, we should not hesitate to make appropriate accommodations to allow that person to perform his or her job most effectively."

Accommodating Hearing Impairments. Alexander Graham Bell had people with hearing impairments in mind when he invented the telephone. Since then, engineers have crafted several new ways of helping hard-of-hearing persons use this indispensable communications tool. Moreover, installing such devices as amplifiers and high frequency or visual telephone ringers is one of the simplest and least expensive ways for companies to accommodate their hearing-impaired employees. For those with more severe hearing disabilities, telecommunications devices for the deaf (better known as TDD) can be attached to standard telephones, allowing hearing-impaired employees to "talk" with other TDD users through a keyboard and small electronic display screen.

Resourceful employers are continually finding ways to adapt standard office equipment for nonhearing use. Integrated Microcomputer Systems, for example, a company employing many deaf persons and whose founder and president, John Yeh, is himself deaf, recently developed a way to use IBM-compatible personal computers to communicate by telephone through TDDs or other IBM-compatible PCs. Yeh maintains that the system can easily be installed in any business. "While [TDD] has been an excellent tool,...relatively few businesses and private individuals have [this] equipment. At the same time," he says, "we have 20 million PC owners in the U.S. today. Because our system can be run through an ordinary PC, it opens many more channels of communication between the hearing and deaf communities."

A living example of how such technology changes the way companies define jobs for the deaf is William Schwall, a telephone installer for Southwestern Bell. Schwall communicates to his customers via small note pads and calls his supervisor from their houses on a pocket-sized TDD. After installing a telephone, he checks to see that it is working with a device (produced by an amateur inventor) that translates sounds into light signals.

For business situations involving more lengthy information exchanges, such as meetings, conferences, or training sessions, companies may need to bring in sign language interpreters; several firms already do this on a regular basis. Of course, for daily activities, hiring a sign language interpreter to assist deaf employees can be costly. But a handful of companies have stretched their investment by retaining a full-time interpreter for hearing-impaired employees who work together.

This approach made sense for one of Marriott's Roy Rogers outlets, which brought in an interpreter to work with the predominantly deaf staff. And Marriott has been a leader in taking other, far less expensive steps to help bring people with hearing impairments into its work force. One Marriott facility that employs deaf laundry room workers, for instance, merely adjusted the washing machines to use flashing lights instead of a buzzer to signal the end of a wash load.

Managing Accommodation Expenses. The Berkeley Planning Associates study, mentioned earlier, found that most workplace accommodations were neither costly nor inconvenient for employers. But companies need to plan for these expenses, since chances are good that they will be relying more heavily on disabled workers as the more traditional work force shrinks.

One way companies can guarantee money is available for these accommodations is to establish a fund specifically for that purpose; doing so also sends a message of support to workers with disabilities. Bank of America started such a fund to allow managers to "help defray the unplanned costs of services and equipment that enable handicapped employees to perform their jobs better." The fund has been used for everything from hearing aids to a wheelchair user's parking fees.

Firms such as Bank of America that already have hired many people with disabilities (and expect to hire more) have few qualms about purchasing talking terminals or other specialized equipment for their employees. But many companies with less experience are hesitant to make such an investment, especially if they are worried about employee turnover.

American Security Bank found a way around the problem. A few years ago, the company wanted to hire a computer programmer who was blind. But there was a catch: the man needed a special terminal costing nearly $3000. Deciding to take a chance, the company purchased the equipment, depreciating it over two years, and told the programmer he could keep the terminal if he remained with the bank for the entire period. Both parties profited from the arrangement. American Security recouped its investment in the terminal by retaining a skilled worker; the employee acquired a valuable tool that increased his bargaining power with future employers.

Breaking Down Barriers to Understanding

These days, companies that hire people with disabilities often receive considerable public attention. This is all to the good. As with women and minority group members before them, disabled job seekers (and their supporters) are still battling the ignorance and prejudice that for years have prevented them from receiving a fair chance in the job market. Fortunately, for both disabled people and employers, the business world has come a long way toward righting these wrongs. But employees with disabilities do not become invisible just because they are inside the company's doors.

In an ideal world, employers would judge all workers by their capabilities and dependability, not by their appearance or physical condition. Some firms already have helped to bring that ideal closer. But working alongside people with disabilities still is a new experience for many employees at both the management and staff levels, and many misunderstandings and stereotypes remain.

Nondisabled persons are not the only ones who need their consciousness raised, however. Given their history of isolation, it is hardly surprising that many people with disabilities need to develop more self-esteem before they can completely blend into the workplace. Of course, the disabled population will always have its stars, but as one of its members told us, "You must remember that all disabled people are not like me. Many lack both the training and the confidence to advance in their careers. They may feel isolated from opportunities, and once they do find a job, they hold onto it, afraid to risk looking for another, even if means a chance to move up. Many look at their job as the only one they will ever have."

Employers who, through their actions, have shown good faith toward the disabled community are slowly helping to remove this last, most destructive set of obstacles. Yet even when a company actively recruits people with disabilities, there is no guarantee that these employees' supervisors and coworkers will accept them immediately. Attitudinal barriers die hard. One unfavorable experience can reinforce long-held prejudices; fear or embarrassment can result in unkind treatment or unproductive pity; and ignorance can lead to destructive stereotyping.

Ironically, these anxieties also can become excuses for not correcting obvious problems, though failure to do so could weaken a disabled employee's career potential. As one manager admitted: "We're not sophisticated enough to treat the handicapped like everybody else. We're slightly intimidated by them. It makes us feel good to be 'helping the handicapped,' but we're afraid to discipline or correct them if they're not doing their job properly. We still treat them as though they are apart from the normal work force.

"Several years ago, until minorities and women were considered a normal part of the workplace," she went on, "employers had to go through the same attitudinal changes with them. Until having disabled employees becomes the norm, we'll continue to fight this tendency. We will have succeeded when we stop looking first at a person's disability and instead look first at his or her skills."

In the meantime, the more innovative companies are taking several steps to bring that day closer.

Employee Orientation

Becoming comfortable in new surroundings takes time for anyone, whether it is the first job or the fifth. Company philosophies, office routines, and, especially, personalities vary dramatically from place to place. For employees with disabilities, adjusting to a new work environment may be even more difficult. For example, while a hearing person can learn a great deal about the company and its employees simply by listening to casual office conversations, a deaf person does not have this privilege. A blind person may not know where to find office resources—such as photocopiers, office supplies, or reference manuals—or even whether they exist, while a sighted employee could scout out the same items in a ten-minute stroll around the building. Other disabled workers find it hard to develop informal working relationships simply because they are perceived as different.

Successful managers clear up some of these problems by making sure employees with disabilities receive a thorough orientation within their first few days with the company. Supervisors often introduce coworkers and managers, one at a time, to hearing-impaired employees, allowing them to spend a few minutes with each person. Name tags, used during the first week or two, and an organizational chart also help these employees feel at home more quickly. Visually impaired workers prove able to memorize the office or factory layout more quickly when given a detailed tour during their first week on the job.

Another way companies have helped new employees feel more comfortable, whatever their disability, is by initiating a mentoring, or buddy, system to compensate for any initial lack of a peer support group. The mentor, who may be either part of the personnel staff or a member of a new employee's work group, is available to help him or her understand the company's insurance plan, employee benefits, and company policies and to answer other work-related questions. The mentor also encourages others in the company to include the newcomer in lunchtime or after-hours social gatherings.

Other firms take even more dramatic steps. Supervisors and other personnel at Jersey Central Power & Light Company, for example, take sign language courses to help them converse with deaf employees. And sign language is so commonplace at Integrated Microcomputer Systems that an observer will sometimes see two hearing employees conversing in sign.

In some cases, hearing-impaired employees themselves teach their coworkers how to communicate with them. Tom Coughlan, a biomedical photographer at Yale University School of Medicine, has informally helped his colleagues to master sign language, and Andrea Kurs, who prepares overhead transparencies for the Naval Air Systems Command, offers lunchtime courses in signing. Hearing employees, in turn, often help their deaf colleagues by being their telephone "ears." Tom Coughlan's secretary, who is fluent in sign language, directly interprets phone conversations for him. J.C. Penney staff accountant Anne Makler, on the other hand, has an associate handle her calls and discusses them with her later.

Sensitivity Training for Nondisabled Employees

Even before disabled employees come to work for the first time, good managers strive to make the job site less threatening for them. While positive day-to-day experiences will eliminate many potential misunderstandings, a few companies are taking a more direct approach to changing attitudes in the workplace. These firms are convinced that educating nondisabled employees and managers about disabilities (sometimes as part of broader diversity training programs) is an excellent way to remove negative perceptions and start the process of bringing disabled workers into the mainstream.

Reluctance to hire or promote people with disabilities typically stems from fear of the unknown: fear that they can't do the job, fear that supervising them would be too difficult, fear of offending them or of being offended *by* them. Programs like the one developed by Chicago-based Leopold and Associates replace fear with facts. Called Breakthrough, this three-hour program for human resources managers is designed to help managers understand hire-the-disabled laws, learn to interview disabled job applicants, and plan accommodations for workers with disabilities. Participants have included managers from Bristol-Myers, International Paper, Borden, Kraft, and a number of other large and small firms. One attendee said the program is effective because "it's not overly syrupy. It's very easy to feel good about hiring the handicapped by playing on people's sympathies [but] this is a really nuts-and-bolts technique."

Sensitivity training that helps workers imagine what it is like to have a disability is another proven technique for removing attitudinal barriers. Hewlett-Packard features a Lottery for Life each year at its National Barrier Awareness Day observance. During this demonstration, nondisabled employees experience disabilities by being blindfolded, using a wheelchair, or simulating a hearing impairment for part of the day.

Quiet Success Stories

Stephen Hawking, the British physicist, was in many ways the "Man of the Year" in 1988. Proclaimed the most brilliant mind since Einstein, the theorist of black holes and other new-frontier discoveries appeared on the cover of *Time* magazine, authored a book that headed the *New York Times* best seller list for much of the year, and added more fundamental understanding to science than perhaps any other living human being.

Of course, anyone who has seen a picture of Hawking knows he is no ordinary genius. Severely disabled by Lou Gehrig's disease, he has lost control of both his arms and legs and speaks with such difficulty that only his closest associates can understand him. Only by using a special machine that translates his eye blinks into typewritten words can Hawking share his knowledge with the world. Ironically, were Hawking not so extraordinarily gifted, he might well have been ignored by universities and employers who didn't bother to take a second look.

Hawking's millions of less well-known disabled counterparts also have talents they can put to good use. When companies look carefully at job applicants' *abilities* rather than their *disabilities,* the benefits often prove striking. Those benefits may not be obvious right away; a person needs to spend a little time on the job before an employer knows it has made a good match. And, like any other group of employees, some people with disabilities will make outstanding workers; others, adequate workers; and still others, poor workers. But by treating each of these employees individually and avoiding generalizations, firms that are short of workers are finding that disabled persons with the capability, drive, and determination to succeed do so as well as any nondisabled employee.

Many firms are justifiably proud of the achievements their disabled workers have made in the face of severe personal hardship and persistent attitudinal barriers. That pride has led some to share their stories with the public, by means of company publications, speeches, or the news media. For example:

- Andrea Godwin, a stenographer in Du Pont's Chemicals and Pigments office, joined the company in 1980. Suffering from multiple birth defects, she had undergone 32 major operations by the time she was 14. Today, she walks with crutches. A 1982 brochure reports that "since she began her present assignment in March of 1981, Andrea hasn't missed a single day of work. Her supervisor notes, 'I can always count on Andrea. She's the first one in when it snows.'" This young woman had a positive attitude, and Du Pont gave her a chance. "People respond to you based on how you feel about yourself," says Godwin. "I don't feel handicapped."

- At San Francisco television station KPIX, a hearing-impaired woman named Kane Chinn joined the staff as a secretary but decided she would like to become an editor. On her own time, she worked hard to pick up editing skills, little by little, asking managers and producers for help. Eventually, Kane became an award-winning editor for two popular children's programs, *Hot Streaks* and *Mac and Mutley.* Though she has since left the station, Chinn has parlayed her experience there into a free-lance business, editing national stories for other stations throughout the state.

- Another KPIX success story is Jana Overbo, a wheelchair user with only limited hand movement but with a strong desire to work in television. KPIX made no special accommodations for Jana, but her manager, sensitive to the intern's challenges and personal desire to succeed, gave her as much guidance as she could. Following the internship, Overbo became an entry-level production assistant. She has since helped produce *Bay to Breakers* and other KPIX special projects.

■ Charles Reichardt joined IBM in 1978, five years and more than 2000 letters after beginning his job search. After graduating from college in 1972, Reichardt, blind from birth, sent résumés to 1000 potential employers. Only one, a company looking for someone to relocate to a distant state, wanted to interview him. Reichardt returned to school and earned his masters degree. Again, he mailed out 1000 résumés without a single encouraging reply. Discouraged, he shared his story with contacts on his ham radio, one of whom was married to a manager at IBM. The company interviewed and hired him, and today he is an information systems analyst.

During his employment interview, IBM managers learned that, in addition to ham radios, Reichardt had another hobby—repairing automobiles. As a high school student, he had earned money fixing cars, on a free-lance basis, when local businesses would not hire him for summer jobs along with the other teenagers. IBM recognized that this kind of experience and drive would be an asset to the company. Reichardt remembers: "Through my avocation, they saw that I had an analytical mind and they examined it....I appreciate the fact that the interviewing team had the foresight to look at all of me and not throw out that uniqueness in me."

Reichardt has worked in a number of areas at IBM and says his employer "has been very responsive" to his needs by providing him with a talking computer and a Braillewriter. He was instrumental in making IBM's PROFS (Professional Office System) more usable for the blind and is listed as a resource for both the American Association for the Advancement of Science and the American Foundation for the Blind. His contributions also include a directory of services and specialized equipment for the physically disabled and training on IBM systems for blind employees and customers.

Men and women like Godwin and Chinn, Overbo and Reichardt are not Stephen Hawking. But, in many ways, they are much more. They are people who, without the benefit of extraordinary intellect or worldwide attention, have overcome disabilities to make a success of their lives. They are just a few of the many quiet success stories to be found in the disabled community. Like most nondisabled employees, they have one clear goal: to do the best job they possibly can.

And for businesses desperate for high quality workers, the best news is this: There are millions more just like them, waiting to be hired.

8
When Old Isn't

The television spot is called New Kid. The day begins, a bright spring morning. A good-looking, gray-haired gentleman leaves his house and takes off down the sidewalk at a brisk pace. On the way, he encounters a few of his friends, who ask him to go fishing with them. He apologizes, but says he can't.

The scene switches to a neighborhood McDonald's restaurant: "I hear there's a new kid starting today," says a young crew member. "I hope he's cute," her coworker sighs. Just then, they hear a knock on the store's locked glass door. It is the man from the first scene. The workers signal that they're not yet open, but when the old man displays a paper cap, they realize that *he* is the new kid. The next time the man appears, he is waiting on customers, surrounded by attractive, cheerful teens, as the good-time theme plays in the background.

This low-key yet revolutionary advertising approach is not meant just to sell hamburgers. It is designed to sell the company as well—as a first-rate place to work. And it has done wonders for McDonald's reputation among older adults. "Seniors have to feel that they're welcome," explains Stan Stein, the firm's senior vice president for personnel. "We have to break through the image that we're just for young people."

Ten or fifteen years ago, this commercial probably never would have been conceived, much less left the drawing board. Fast-food establishments (and most retail businesses, for that matter) had more young applicants than they could put to work. Now, many are struggling for whatever workers they can get, regardless of age.

What happened between the mid-1970s and the late-1980s, of course, is that the largest generation of all time grew up. Even its most junior members, the babies of 1964, are now in their mid-twenties, most well beyond the entry-level positions of their teens. And those following behind will not come close to meeting the next decade's demand for workers. Before the year 2000, the number of 20- to 24-year-olds in the labor force will fall by nearly 2.5 million and the 25-to-29 age group will decline by almost 3 million. At the same time, the number of workers aged 45 and above will *increase* significantly.

The population as a whole is growing older too. Medical progress and healthier life styles have helped make today's elderly population the largest ever. The most recent numbers show 30 million Americans over the age of 65, with forecasts indicating that 5 million more will join them by the turn of the century.

With demographic projections like these, conventional ways of looking at older Americans as nonworkers will have to be retired. Otherwise, to put a new spin on the old ballad's lament, the 1990s will be a time of "workers, workers everywhere, nor any a person to hire."

A New Way of Thinking

Understandably, firms that have built their success on a young work force view these forecasts with trepidation. It is, after all, much simpler to use existing recruiting methods that have worked in the past than to devise entirely new and unproven ones. But many company managers, like McDonald's Stan Stein, look on the aging of the work force as an invitation to strengthen the company's base of employees by extending recruiting and training efforts beyond the traditional applicant pool. "Over half our crew today is nontraditional," Stein told us. "We've been changing very consciously, not waiting for the crunch."

The shortage of younger talent also has prompted a number of firms to reject early retirement policies and, instead, to offer older employees incentives to remain on the job as long as possible. "Pushing for early retirement is like shooting ourselves in the foot," observed one corporate vice president. "We need to make it attractive for valuable older workers to stay. Once you let people go, it's very hard to get them back."

Numbers aside, there are plenty of good reasons why businesses are beginning to abandon the "workers, workers everywhere..." mentality and to seriously view older people as a mainstream labor source. Several managers told us that investing in these workers has helped increase the overall stability of their work force. Satisfied employers also report that their older workers are highly motivated, quality-conscious individuals with good attendance records, good safety records, and excellent work habits.

The data support their claims:

- In a recent survey by the Cornell Hotel and Restaurant Administration, food-service managers gave older workers "above average" scores on their overall job performance, with particularly high marks for dependability, attitude, emotional maturity, guest relations, and work quality.

- Aging in America, an employment referral organization for persons aged 45 and above, reports that turnover is extremely low for the older workers it places: 94 percent remain on the job for a year or more, and 85 percent stay for at least five years.

- Almost three-quarters of the 400 firms questioned in a 1985 survey by the American Association of Retired People (AARP) rated their older workers' on-the-job performance as "excellent" or "very good." An even higher proportion of respondents said their older employees demonstrated better-than-average attendance as well as punctuality, commitment to quality, and practical knowledge.

- Another study, which looked at more than 1 million workers' compensation records in 30 states, concluded that older workers have fewer occupational injuries than younger workers.

Without abandoning their quest, or even their preference, for young recruits, many employers are realizing that older employees have a unique advantage: their maturity. "Younger workers haven't seen enough business cycles and have a greater tendency to knee-jerk reactions," maintains Victor Buzachero, vice president of human resources at the Birmingham, Alabama, Baptist Medical Center. "Older ones take a broader view and offer a stability and loyalty that youth has yet to learn."

For all their strengths, older people, like members of the other nontraditional groups we have discussed, often must overcome attitudinal and other barriers in the workplace before they can fit in. Senior citizens may be penalized for working more slowly than their younger counterparts, for example. Some may have slight physical disabilities that need accommodating. Others may lack the necessary training: those returning to work after several years of retirement may find once sophisticated job skills have become obsolete.

In most cases, employers can remove these small obstacles easily, just by showing a little flexibility. But businesses' greater challenge, in labor-short times, will be in finding ways to bring productive older people back into the workplace—and then giving them a reason to stay on the job.

Attracting Older Workers

Unlike most other members of the new work force, retirees typically are *not* looking for a job. They may be perfectly content (and financially able) to pursue leisure activities full-time. On the other hand, while wanting to return to work in some form, they may be unwilling to give up *all* their newfound free time. Or they may worry about keeping up with younger employees trained in the latest technology, or be concerned that reemployment would jeopardize their pensions and Social Security benefits.

At McDonald's, Attitude Counts

Despite these difficulties, a number of imaginative companies are successfully drawing retired people back to the workplace, many by offering training, Social Security and benefits counseling, and flexible scheduling. But an even more powerful recruiting tool, one that multiplies the effectiveness of individual recruitment programs, is a company's positive attitude toward older workers. Firms that value seniors' experience and talents transmit their confidence in these workers to employees, potential applicants, and customers alike. And that creates a loyalty and interest that other, more indifferent employers cannot begin to match.

McDonald's Corp. is an acknowledged leader in recruiting, hiring, and training older people: "rehirement," in the corporate lingo. Personnel chief Stein explains that the company's success in this area stems from a sincere, top-down commitment to hire as many qualified older workers as possible. That dedication manifests itself in corporate long-range planning and in management's continual efforts to create a hospitable workplace for seniors. But while putting senior citizens on its front line can only help McDonald's overall public image, Stein downplays that aspect of rehirement. "This is not a public relations program," he declares. "It's a program to get employees."

And the plan is working. McDonald's now employs nearly 3500 workers over the age of 55. And with crews reflecting both ends of the age spectrum, Stein says, many stores have become recruiting notices in themselves: "If you attract four or five seniors, you have built a solid nucleus. Then the progress becomes self-perpetuating. You can walk down to our competitors and see them looking for help, while our store is fully staffed."

The company's rehirement efforts revolve around McMasters, a program similar to the corporation's successful McJobs program for people with disabilities. McMasters' participants follow a four-week course that includes classroom instruction, demonstrations, and one-on-one training from experienced job coaches. Local service agencies often pick up a portion of the training costs. After "graduation," the trainees become part of the restaurant's regular crew, and many older workers eventually move on to part-time management positions.

Other Firms Turn to Seniors

McDonald's is not the only large-scale employer to ask older workers to fill in the gaps left by a shrinking teenage work force. Using its founder as an example (the late Colonel Harland Sanders got his start in the business at age 66), another fast-food enterprise, the Kentucky Fried Chicken Corp., has built a solid reputation for employing senior citizens. The Colonel's Tradition program places older people in part-time managerial positions, at competitive salaries, where they are trained in various aspects of the restaurant's operation. Flexible hours, generous benefits, and the opportunity to move into more responsible positions add to the program's appeal.

Nor are fast-food businesses alone in responding to the birth dearth in this fashion; the hotel and motel industry has also begun to eagerly recruit older workers. Days Inns, an Atlanta-based chain, employs nearly 50 senior citizens at its central reservations office. These employees are patient and courteous with customers, managers say, and "they don't mind doing what you ask them to do." The company clearly values these workers (several have earned promotions), and the loyalty goes both ways. "Aside from my church and my family, my job here means everything to me," says one older woman. Like Days Inns, Marriott and Ramada hotels regularly seek out and train older workers—with comparable success.

Tailor-Made Jobs

Companies that have made a serious commitment to hire older workers often begin their efforts by examining existing jobs to see if any can be made more accessible or appealing to older persons. For instance, many offer special training or even redesign certain positions to include shorter hours or less physically demanding tasks.

One of the main concerns older workers and employers share is the increasingly technical nature of today's workplace. Many retirees, of course, have sophisticated skills that require only minor updating. But rapid advances in workplace technology may have so eclipsed the way things were done in their last job that some seniors are wary of even trying to rejoin the work force. Employers are helping to remove obstacles like these with job-specific training that bridges the technology gap. For instance:

- Aetna Insurance offers a personal computing workshop for its retirees.

- Boston's Shawmut Bank trains older workers in computer bookkeeping and word processing and supports a community training program for seniors called Operation Able.

- Kelly Services, Manpower, Inc., and other temporary-help firms emphasize in their recruitment ads that they train reentering office workers—including older workers—on state-of-the-art word processing systems before placing them with an employer/client.

Even simple job modifications can significantly increase the chances that senior citizens will apply for job openings, as one major retailer has found. Recently, Builders Emporium eliminated the heavy lifting requirements for store clerks, making such work more appealing to older applicants. Now, the western-states hardware chain brings in younger night crews to restock the shelves, while daytime personnel concentrate on service and selling. The company is delighted with the new recruits, who relate well to customers and tend to know more than younger clerks about the merchandise. Turnover rates also have declined by more than 30 percent since Builders decided to mature its work force.

Other firms, equally committed to the view that age is no barrier to productive employment, have taken different approaches to bring more seniors into their work force. Control Data Corp., for example, has reenlisted some of its recent retirees to work from their homes on company-installed computer terminals. And Minnesota Title Financial Corp. has converted its full-time messenger jobs to part-time, attracting a number of retirees to the firm. Supervisors now assign each job to a pair of workers who, together, draw up a job-sharing schedule. Attendance rates are high in these positions, and, when someone is absent, substitutes are readily available.

Expanding Recruitment Sources

Not every company's budget can handle the polished advertising campaigns and the continuous, nationwide training programs that have made McDonald's such a leader in recruiting older workers. But fortunately for smaller-scale employers, senior citizens interested in working are easy to find—if a company knows where to look for them.

As Americans live longer, healthier lives, a number of job placement services for older people have begun to spring up around the country. Local governments and private industry councils sponsor many of these groups. While large companies tend to build up their own recruitment channels, many smaller firms are finding these local organizations a welcome answer to their recruiting needs. Seniors Inc.!, for instance, has sent Denver, Colorado, florist Selma Jultak some of her most reliable delivery drivers: "Everyone is work-oriented. You can hardly get them to take a day off. I think it's great."

Also in Denver, historic Zang Mansion has found several top-quality workers through a local JTPA (Job Training Partnership Act) program. Director Ron Gremer, who employs a pair of job-sharing octogenarians, says he prefers "more mature" workers because they're less likely to fall victim to the "whims of opportunity."

Religious organizations, senior citizens clubs, and adult education programs also offer good prospects for companies seeking to recruit older workers. Kelly Services, Inc., the national temporary-services agency, has found members of these groups very receptive to its appeals for part-time receptionists, secretaries, accountants, paralegals, computer programmers, and even engineers. Likewise:

- McDonald's sends recruiters to some of these associations (and to local government agencies) and then invites the organizations' leaders to tour its restaurants and see "gold-collar workers" in action. The company often ends up with several new recruits for its McMasters program.

- Bank of America recruiters occasionally visit retirement communities.

- Marriott Corp. has sent letters to senior citizens organizations across the country to promote job openings at its Roy Rogers restaurants.

A company's own customers may be another good source of potential employees. Georgia Power Company, for instance, has hired a number of retired customers with building experience to weatherize homes for low-income seniors. Bank of America places recruiting flyers at teller stations, where older customers will see them.

At Days Inns, the star recruiters are the older workers themselves. Recently, several enthusiastic members of the hotel chain's reservation center staff planned, promoted, and ran a job fair for area senior citizens. "I enjoy working here so much that it is a pleasure to tell others about my Days Inns experience," proclaimed one of the event's organizers.

Making Employment More Attractive Than Retirement

Slowly, the practice of encouraging early retirement is being replaced by organized incentives to *stay* in the company work force:

- At Xerox Corp., older, unionized workers may bid for less stressful or physically demanding assignments and then split any salary reduction with the company. The program has helped Xerox retain a number of productive employees who were considering retirement.

- Grumman Corp. has always encouraged its employees to work past the age of 65. Phased retirement is common, and the company routinely calls on retirees to help with new defense contracts. Asserts Grumman's Daniel Knowles: "Companies are not concerned about older workers out of the milk of human kindness. We're pragmatists."

Xerox and Grumman know their success in producing high-quality machinery depends on keeping older workers on the team. Yet, ironically, many modern employers still expect workers past a certain age to make room for their upwardly mobile juniors. Even with federal law now prohibiting mandatory retirement policies, many firms actively encourage their employees to retire at age 65, 62, or even earlier. Why? Because, they say, older people work more slowly than younger ones and, sometimes, their skills and knowledge are out of date. Businesses facing plant shutdowns or other belt-tightening measures often see early retirement as a way to keep involuntary layoffs to a minimum.

A recent Conference Board survey estimates that nearly two-thirds of all United States corporations offer early retirement, while only 4 percent provide any incentives to delay retirement. These policies may help explain why less than one-third of today's over-55 population is employed (compared with nearly one-half the members of that age group 60 years ago), even though many are in good health and can expect to remain healthy and active for at least another 10 to 20 years.

What's more, most prospective retirees say they would be happy to stay on the job a few more years—if the conditions were right. A recent study by the Cornell Hotel and Motel Administration, for example, found that most older workers would choose to postpone retirement as long as they could switch to part-time positions or less stressful duties.

Given many older Americans' interest in continuing to work—at least for a while—encouraging early retirement in an era of skilled-labor shortages seems dangerously shortsighted. Realizing this, many companies are finding ways to make retirement something more than an all-or-nothing proposition.

Benefits and Incentives

Traditionally, retirement pay and benefits are seen as rewards for loyal service to an employer. But what if a company wants to reward an older employee without having to sacrifice his or her experience and talents? Adopting a policy rooted in Asian rather than American culture, some businesses are conferring positions of special honor or respect to top retirement-age performers. Monetary benefits may be part of this incentive package, although that is not always the case.

To discourage key technical employees from retiring, for instance, the New York-based Corning Glass Works created a senior associate program. The advisory position, which includes a pay raise, allows experienced employees to continue sharing their knowledge while avoiding the headaches of day-to-day management. "Corning conveyed the message that there was something else besides the end of the road for me," says product engineer Roger Whitney. "At other companies, you hit 55, and bingo, you're gone....Maybe we can't all be hotshot managers, but this senior associate program is a nice little carrot."

Likewise, Instron, a Canton, Massachusetts, manufacturer of materials-testing equipment, recruits its older employees to help novice salespersons learn how to do their jobs better. In their sales emeritus program, coaches accompany the younger people on sales calls and critique their on-the-job performance. Even without maintaining the work load they carried as young salesmen and saleswomen, these older employees know they are making a valuable contribution to the company's productivity.

Teledyne Continental Motors, a Michigan engine manufacturer, operates a more structured program. There, veteran hourly workers become eligible for Golden Bridge benefits at age 58. From that time until retirement, the company increases their insurance, pension, and surviving spouse benefits. Employees also may take extra vacation days or convert them to postretirement payments. Teledyne has been pleased to find that most program participants choose to forego the time off.

Easing the Transition to Retirement

For a person who has spent some 60,000 hours of his or her life at work, full-time retirement can be an unsettling prospect. Even seniors with many outside interests may feel unprepared to suddenly drop out of the work force. "I may be ready to stop putting in 40 hours at a desk—and 10 on the road," says Andy Hopkins, who founded A & B Line Haul Services in Orange County, California, at the age of 61. "But it will be a long time before I'm ready to quit altogether."

For today's employer, these feelings couldn't be more welcome. By encouraging older workers to retire *gradually,* businesses are finding they can stretch their investment in experienced employees. And most older workers say this is just what they want. Several studies indicate that most employees nearing retirement age would like to stay with their current employer rather than start anew somewhere else.

Phased retirement or retirement rehearsal policies are an option some firms have adopted to permit older workers to ease toward retirement status rather than making the transition all at once. Such plans allow companies to retain their older employees' skills while giving them an opportunity to "taste" retirement—and even start developing outside pursuits—before deciding whether to leave the work force.

One of the most innovative of these programs is sponsored by the Polaroid Corp. An unpaid, six-month leave of absence lets older employees preview retirement up to five years before actually quitting work. Or employees simply may choose to reduce the number of hours they put in and continue earning prorated salaries and benefits. Of those who take advantage of the leave program, about one-half eventually decide to come back full-time.

Varian Associates, a high technology firm in California's Silicon Valley, allows workers aged 55 and older to phase into retirement over a two-year period. Participating employees typically work a four-day week during the first year and a three-day week during the second, but they sometimes can modify the plan, provided they work at least 20 hours a week. While on these part-time schedules, the employees continue to receive prorated salaries, benefits, and vacation periods.

Managers must take nonsupervisory assignments when they enter the Varian Associates program, but other workers—including assemblers, clerical workers, technicians, engineers, and scientists—are not expected to change jobs. At the end of this transitional period, a significant number choose to go back to work full-time rather than retire.

The program also has prompted a number of retirees to come *back* to work. For example, the company rehired veteran microwave test tube technician Bill Ames when skilled-worker shortages caused production to lag a year and a half behind schedule. He was happy to go back to work part-time after three years of leisure. "How many times can you mow the yard?" he says.

Casual Employment

Casual—that is, temporary or occasional—employment is proving to be another excellent way for businesses to keep in touch with retirees and put their experience to good use. Retail stores and businesses that cater to tourists, for instance, have long relied on extra help during peak seasons. Manufacturers often need to build up their labor force temporarily when an unusually large order comes in. And accounting firms inevitably use extra workers at tax time.

By viewing their own retirees as a pool of substitute labor, a number of businesses have been able to save much of the time and expense of hiring and training new workers. Consulting relationships with retiring employees and job banks are two low-cost, high-return techniques being used to find skilled labor on short notice.

The Travelers Insurance Corp.'s successful retiree job bank got its start in 1981 when corporate recruiters threw an "unretirement" party for former employees. The response was impressive: more than 300 retirees said they were available for temporary and part-time assignments with the firm. But before long, recounts one official, demand for these reliable employees exceeded their supply, and the company had to start enlisting other firms' retirees as well.

The job bank now fields temporary clerical, administrative, research, and underwriting assignments for 750 experienced workers. Because only about 250 are on the job in a typical week, job bank members maintain a satisfying balance between work and leisure. They also receive paid training on computers and word processing equipment—an important perquisite for retirees who have been out of the work force several years.

The Travelers pays job bank workers hourly wages at the midpoint of each job category: $6.46 for clerical help, $14.82 for executive secretaries, and so on. And the company has modified its pension program to double the number of hours recipients may work without jeopardizing benefits; to help out in this regard, the payroll office monitors each member's earnings to ensure that they do not exceed Social Security–imposed limitations. These new policies have saved the company almost $1 million a year in fees to temporary employment agencies. "You can't find a negative in the program," asserts Director of Employment Don DeWard. "We get people who are anxious to work, who know the job, whose productivity is terrific. They make more money than they could otherwise, and we get help for less. It's a win-win situation."

Southern California's Aerospace Corp. is another company that believes casual employment is the best way to protect the company's investment in workers who have retired. Personnel Director Robert Rubenstein explains: "For people with highly marketable skills, it would be possible for them to leave our company, take our retirement benefits, and then go to work for somebody else. That wouldn't make any sense. So why not give them the opportunity to work here?"

Aerospace brings back almost 100 former employees each year to fill in on special projects and during especially busy periods, and 20 to 30 percent of every retiring "class" choose to continue their association with the company. Returning retirees may work up to 1000 hours a year without losing their pension benefits.

Volunteer Assignments

Retirees who are willing to share their experience and skills with others but don't want the added responsibility of a paid job may be receptive to volunteer assignments with their former employers. Because volunteers are often more flexible than full-time employees, they can be ideal helpers for customers or employees with disabilities or other special needs. For example, Blue Cross/Blue Shield of Indiana's Ambassador Corps visits older customers in their homes to help them understand their insurance coverage. The program uses volunteer helpers who have retired from insurance, accounting, or teaching careers.

Older volunteers also can become involved, on the company's behalf, in academic or career-oriented school programs. The Travelers, for instance, arranges for retirees to volunteer as tutors and aides in the Hartford Public Schools. Not only do these efforts bolster the company's image in the community, but they also help build the future labor force for this high-growth area. Likewise, in Detroit, Michigan, retired machinists teach young adults valuable workplace skills at Focus: HOPE's Machinist Training Institute.

Managing an Older Work Force

When employers first become serious about hiring senior citizens, they often discover that recruitment and management techniques tailored to young people do not work as well with people over age 60. This shouldn't be surprising: older and younger workers often have vastly different needs, expectations, and work styles. The prospect of integrating seniors into a youth-oriented labor force, in fact, is one of the main reasons many employers are slow to take advantage of this large potential source of skilled workers. But even the most tradition-bound employer can't beat back demographics for long. The changing composition of the population and work force means that management practices ultimately will have to change anyway. And the sooner those changes are made, the more effective the new techniques will be as a recruitment and retention tool.

Oldsters as Newcomers

Sensitivity training, like the popular courses many employers have used to educate mainstream employees about the special needs of working with the economically disadvantaged, minority group members, immigrants, and people with disabilities, also is becoming a valuable training aid for making the transition to an older work force.

Kentucky Fried Chicken, McDonald's, and other firms accustomed to a very young work force now are beginning to teach their managers how to motivate and reward older employees. All line managers at Kentucky Fried Chicken, for instance, are asked to attend a day-long awareness-training seminar that not only offers ideas about recruiting, training, and managing older people but also allows managers and workers to confront, together, what training director Flo Barber calls "the myths and realities of using older employees as a significant resource."

McDonald's corporate staff also offers guidance and answers questions from the chain's owner/operators about managing older workers. One popular training tool is a series of videotapes that feature senior citizens talking about their on-the-job experiences.

Personal and Career Development

In his popular book *The Three Boxes of Life and How to Get Out of Them*, career-development specialist Richard Bolles discusses how most people separate life's main activities into three distinct parts: the learning phase, which takes place in youth; the working phase, which takes place in early- through mid-adulthood; and finally, the playing phase, which is reserved for the retirement years. Bolles goes on to describe how a person can learn to *blend* learning, working, and playing throughout one's life—especially in the lengthening years of senior citizenship.

For forward-looking employers, helping workers achieve this balance is rapidly becoming more important. Today's workers have a good chance of changing jobs—even careers—several times before retirement. The current midmanagement crunch makes it even more likely that, without fulfilling alternatives, those at the height of their productivity will burn out and leave their employers. And the older ones might opt for early retirement out of sheer frustration.

Knowing this, several companies are taking preventive steps to bolster preretirement-age workers' motivation and loyalty.

Planning Ahead.   Some firms, including Control Data Corp., Ford Motor Company, and IBM, offer preretirement employees specific instruction in "life-path" or "life-span career" planning. Such programs often include seminars or individual counseling on:

- Financial planning.
- Continuing education or retraining.
- Psychological aspects of aging.
- Alternatives to full retirement, including part-time, consulting, or volunteer work.

Taking a Break From the Rat Race.   For companies that can afford to offer them, sabbaticals and extended leaves of absence help to restore talented but weary midcareerists' productivity, enthusiasm, and loyalty. For years, the academic community has used these regular breaks in the institutional routine to promote rejuvenation, learning, and creative thinking. Now the business world is taking a look at this not-so-new idea. Employer-sanctioned breaks from work are more widespread in corporate America than one might think. Nearly 14 percent of all United States companies offer their employees regular sabbaticals.

Although academic sabbaticals are traditionally year-long breaks at regular intervals, in the business world they are often just a few weeks or months in duration, and sometimes are allowed only on a limited basis, such as once in a career. These breaks can be either paid or unpaid. For instance, Tandem Computer, a San Francisco Bay area firm, offers its workers paid six-week sabbaticals. They are the company's "most popular benefit," according to Tandem executive Patricia Becker. "The benefits that the company gets back are tremendous," she adds. "People return to work renewed. It's wonderful what time to reflect and think can do for a person."

Employees who have worked at least ten years at California's Wells Fargo Savings Bank may apply for a three-month, fully paid "personal growth leave." One woman in her fifties, a former Olympic swimmer, took advantage of the program to train for and compete in an international swimming competition in Australia. She won two events in her class and told *Fortune* magazine Associate Editor Anthony Ramirez: "I feel very, very loyal to Wells Fargo." Her reaction is typical of employees in the program, now in its twelfth year.

Wells Fargo employees also may opt for up to six months of paid community-involvement sabbaticals. During this time, the company essentially loans the workers to nonprofit agencies. One man spent his six months organizing and promoting recreational programs for disabled people; another helped set up a child-abuse prevention center. Like

Wells Fargo, Xerox Corp. occasionally donates its employees to worthy causes and has done so for up to a year at a time.

Education and Retraining. Companies that are reluctant or unable to part with employees for such a long period still can foster their personal and professional development through training programs. Such training is especially important for older workers. "You *can* teach an old dog new tricks, and doing so increases the level of commitment and loyalty on both sides," says Victor Buzachero of the Baptist Medical Center. "That will pay big dividends in the long run."

Control Data Corp. is one employer for whom "age is invisible in the training process," according to Joanne Larato, Control Data's manager of internal communications. Age-neutral training, she adds, takes into consideration that "there are certain types of knowledge you can't develop through the training process"—getting along with people, critical thinking, and the commonsense good judgment that comes after many years of day-to-day living.

The corporation provides a wide range of training, including in-house courses and tuition aid for classes taken elsewhere. Program management is decentralized and flexible enough to reflect individual workers' needs. If an employee's regular performance appraisal suggests a need for improvement, his or her supervisor may suggest a training or retraining program. "There is definitely an advantage to retraining older workers," Larato told us. "It is in the company's business interest to keep its work force up to date technologically." And without question, it is less expensive and disruptive than recruiting, hiring, and training a new team from scratch.

IBM goes one step further, promoting its employees' educational development even after they retire. The corporation's Retiree Education Assistance Program (REAP) gives employees and their spouses up to $5000 in tuition aid during the three years before and two years after retirement—increasing the skill levels of this growing rehirement pool.

Old Isn't

The positive experiences of an increasing number of companies relying on older workers have put to rest much of the conventional wisdom about older employees:

- Companies no longer can view the usually minor adjustments required for older workers as too expensive, without considering the difficulty of finding enough younger workers to fill their job openings and the costs of training them.

- Firms no longer can view older workers as demanding too great an investment of management's time, without considering the many decades' worth of valuable skills and knowledge that most older workers possess.

- And companies no longer can view an older work force as necessarily less flexible, without considering the possibility of part-time work, casual employment, or job restructuring as ways to match good workers with unfilled positions.

Those companies that take seniors seriously—and take specific steps to attract, retain, and retrain older workers—are finding themselves far better equipped than their competitors to deal with the coming skilled-labor shortages. The corporate programs profiled in this chapter demonstrate that it *is* possible to keep older employees in the work force—and to bring them back once they retire. These steps also help foster the impression of a corporation committed to hiring and retaining older workers, an image that in itself can be a powerful recruiting tool.

But for the future, what is needed more than anything else is a simple change in attitude. In earlier times, senior citizens were thought of more in terms of retirement communities than company workplaces, more in terms of outpatient rolls than payrolls. Old age was synonymous with a life of leisure, estate planning, slipping health, and the writing of wills. Old age was—well, old age.

That's in the past now. In the era of long lives and short hiring queues, old simply *isn't*. Not anymore.

9
Managing the New Work Force

Imagine taking off on a drive without your glasses, trying to negotiate a treacherous mountain road, able to see little more than blurred images. Imagine that it has just started to rain, making the trip even more difficult. Now imagine that you are racing for time against motorists who *are* wearing glasses. To say the least, your chances of winning the race—or even finishing it in one piece—are not very good.

Yet many thousands of businesses are in this same position as the labor shortages of the 1990s approach. To be sure, most successful firms have learned to look far down the road before making decisions about acquiring and managing capital, raw materials, suppliers, and market niches—the whole range of factors that influence which products and services to offer, how to produce them, and how to sell them. Long-range, or strategic, planning has become the map guiding choices in these areas, and most large companies wouldn't even consider embarking on a major project without consulting this map.

It is surprising, then, that so few businesses have begun to apply the same farsighted thinking to acquiring and managing their most important resources—their *people*. A large majority of firms appear to be trapped in a cycle of *reacting* to labor force trends, rather than *anticipating* them. Yet even the most skillfully drawn business plan can miss its mark if the human factor isn't adequately taken into account. A company that fails to make careful plans for its future work force may find that it has to:

- Delay production lines for months or years when it cannot find enough of the right kind of workers.

- Miss new market opportunities because its labor force isn't trained well enough to adjust quickly to new technologies or production processes.

- Watch large numbers of employees with children defect to a nearby competitor that offers on-site day care.

- Lose valuable foreign-born employees after a supervisor, unfamiliar with cultural subtleties, unintentionally offends them.

- Find once dependable training or recruitment methods suddenly overwhelmed by an unexpected shift in available workers' skill levels.

- Scramble to salvage its public image after a business downturn forces the layoff of hundreds of workers in their prime earning years, and then unsuccessfully attempt to bring these employees back on board when business picks up again.

There is a way to avoid many of these pitfalls: by making strategic human resources planning a regular part of the high-level corporate planning process. In Chapter 3, we introduced this concept as 20/20 Management. Companies will be able to prosper in the 1990s, we said, only if they can clearly visualize their options for work force recruitment, training, and deployment in the years ahead—and then act on that insight before the competition does.

The next five chapters described some techniques that the more far thinking firms are using to reach nontraditional workers: women (especially women with children or elderly dependents), minority group members and the economically disadvantaged, cultural minorities (including recent immigrants), people with disabilities, and older workers. This chapter ties these ideas together and discusses, in addition, general management strategies that innovative companies have adopted to forecast and respond to their work force needs.

These strategies are the soul and substance of 20/20 Management. They should be viewed not so much as a wish list or a mere conversation piece, but rather as a set of *ten commandments for competitiveness*. They are:

1. Make human resources an equal partner on the corporate team.

2. Develop a strategic work force plan.

3. Explicitly forecast the company's work force needs.

4. Make the case for change.

5. Become an inclusive employer.

6. Manage for retention.

7. Train and retrain.

8. Promote, promote, promote.

9. Think small.

10. Become a community fixture.

Wanted: The Right Attitude

Of course, commandments must be followed to be effective, and that makes attitude perhaps the most critical aspect of 20/20 Management. If companies are going to beat—even profit from—the coming worker shortage, senior executives and line managers alike need to begin thinking about the human element of their operations in a new way.

First, companies have to stop looking at their workers as a cost of production and start looking at them as assets. They are an investment, as much of an investment as high tech machinery or updated computers are. A business wouldn't dream of letting these costly pieces of equipment rust or remain idle for lack of needed repairs. So why should a company allow its workers—the most valuable part of its production "processes"—to go without educational or training "repairs," or the kind of daily management "maintenance" that will keep them satisfied and dedicated employees?

Second, businesses of all kinds need to become more avid collectors of information on improving the way they recruit, train, and manage their work forces. They need to have what RJR Nabisco Chairman Louis V. Gerstner, Jr., calls a "thirst for what works." That doesn't mean managers should abandon old ways of doing things just because they are old. But it does mean being receptive to change when it's called for and prepared with ideas for making that change. The techniques described in this book are only a start. Hundreds more are waiting to be discovered, catalogued, and made ready for implementation.

Closely related is a third change in attitude: businesses need to become collectors of the *right kind* of ideas. It is easy to be seduced by advances in other parts of the world (Japan's economic miracle is a prime example), but managers should recognize that what works in another country will not necessarily work here.

Jim Fallows makes this argument in his book *More Like Us.* He cites the experiences of Jared Taylor, the son of an American missionary living in Japan. One day, Taylor was discussing the country's phenomenal economic rise with an American expert on the Far East. "Do you think we need to be more like Japan?" Taylor asked his friend.

"Hell, no," the friend replied. "We need to be more like us."

What Taylor's friend meant was that companies should search for those aspects of American culture that strengthen the United States economy—and then build upon them. That's a lot more difficult than simply grafting Japan's—or any other country's—management structure onto our own. But Americans, for better or worse, differ sharply from other people in many ways. Only programs that respond to the attitudes, expectations, and life styles of our *own* workers will motivate them to join up, learn as much as they need to, and work as productively and cooperatively as they can.

The fourth, and final, change in attitude is so straightforward that it is sometimes overlooked. After assessing its situation and the improvements it can make, a company has to *act*. Managers can't wait around for someone else to do the job. The days are long past when a business could wait to conduct a two-year feasibility study every time it needed to upgrade its work force.

Certainly, there's a risk in taking the lead. After a firm invests $5000 or $10,000 in training a worker, that person may well go to another company. A promising program may have to be redesigned several times before it works exactly right. But businesses that depend on capable workers will have to take these risks. There's no other choice. Nor is that choice necessarily an unpleasant one. The moral of the examples we've highlighted here, and hundreds of others like them, is this: Investment in workers *works*. But it will work only if employers plan ahead, commit themselves to difficult changes in corporate priorities, and then act.

If all this sounds like a lot of hard work, it is. No one ever said economic survival was easy. But, then, neither is being bypassed by those more eager to compete.

Make Human Resources an Equal Partner on the Corporate Team

The first step in competing for good workers is organizational: making the company's human resources function an equal part of the corporate management team. A top-notch human resources (HR) staff is critical to implementing the many types of work force strategies described in this book, but even the best HR professionals won't be able to do the job if they don't have the credibility to influence corporate decision makers. Unfortunately, personnel and related departments traditionally have commanded only superficial respect from those on the operational side of business, who often consider the HR department's focus on people trivial when compared with the more "serious" tasks of directly producing goods or providing services for paying customers and clients.

As corporate leaders begin to confront the shrinking, demographically changing work force, many are starting to rethink their skepticism about the business of work force development and management. Once content to limit personnel and allied departments to distributing paychecks and keeping employment records, an increasing number of firms are now turning to their human resource professionals for answers to such perplexing questions as:

- How to find enough workers to fill entry-level jobs.
- How to find educated, trained people for technical positions.
- How to prevent trained workers from leaving for other companies.
- How to keep a culturally diverse group of workers motivated and productive.
- How to stay ahead of changes in benefits and employee regulations.

The trends spurring these questions have forced many companies to admit that recruiting and retaining good workers is much more critical—and difficult—than it once was. These firms, concludes a study by Kearney Management Consultants, have made their human resources departments full partners in designing and implementing corporate policy. However, many companies still fail to include human resources specialists in corporate long-range planning, perhaps because they think the worker shortfalls other firms are experiencing will never touch them. "The rubber simply doesn't hit the road until there are actual shortages," one corporate equal opportunity specialist confided to us. "That's why many major companies still don't use human resource planning at all."

A Short Course in Increasing HR's Influence

Increasing the HR department's influence within a company almost always requires an explicit, affirmative decision on the part of top management. At a minimum, the lead HR officer is assigned the same rank as other key corporate officials. If finance, administration, and marketing department heads are called "vice president" and report directly to the chief executive officer, for instance, then the same is true for the top HR official. A number of firms have done at least this much: nearly 43 percent of the 379 companies surveyed in 1984 by the American Society for Personnel Administration (ASPA) say that their top human resources manager is a corporate vice president.

Upgrading HR's status in this way allows the department to play a direct role in long-range planning, rather than being forced to filter its ideas through another department with parochial interests of its own. But if the change is merely cosmetic, little will be gained. Hence, ensuring HR's direct involvement in the strategic planning process has also led the more progressive companies to:

- *Make sure the HR staff has the requisite technical training.* In firms where human resources planning is a key part of the overall planning process, HR professionals are more than good people managers. They are experts in a range of technical areas, such as skills assessment, forecasting, information management, and cost-benefit analysis. Companies typically either train their existing staff in these areas or bring people into the department with the necessary skills.

- *Expose HR leadership to the broad base of company operations.* The HR departments that best serve as partners in the planning process are well aware of what is being planned *for*—what kind of jobs and skills the company's operations require, how future production plans may change, and so on. It is usually not enough for senior HR managers to have worked in different areas in the HR function. One survey of senior HR professionals, for instance, revealed that most would not allow a person to move into a top HR job without extensive operational and line-management experience.

- *Involve other departments in human resources assessment.* Just as HR professionals in successful firms are made aware of other corporate operations, these firms also make sure top managers in other departments understand the HR process and its requirements. Many companies make human resources and equal employment opportunity (EEO) goals an important part of all managers' performance reviews. Gannett, for example, bases bonuses in part on EEO progress. In corporations like these, affirmative action hiring plans and other HR efforts are not zero-sum games in which one employee's gain is another's loss, but a vital part of work force development throughout the company. As IBM's Don Devey told us in describing IBM's recent successes in modernizing the corporate view of human resources, HR responsibilities are "everyone's concern; they aren't just centralized in one person."

- *Organize for efficiency.* In the most successful human resources programs we uncovered, the majority were both unified and decentralized. They were unified in the sense that they integrated such tasks as recruitment, personnel management, employee relations, training, salary and benefits, and affirmative action/equal employment opportunity within a single corporate unit and also coordinated human resources operations with the company's other productivity-related functions. Yet these programs were decentralized in the sense that the various HR policies could be implemented as local (that is, site or departmental) conditions warranted, rather than being constrained to some inflexible, companywide standard.

- *Develop a positive corporate attitude toward human resources.* Effective human resources planning starts from the top down, with active interest and involvement on the part of senior management. Among other things, executives in worker-oriented firms openly express their support for sophisticated HR planning and regularly raise HR planning issues at board meetings and other policy-making sessions.

- *Keep the HR department strong.* Such firms recognize that, like good workers, money spent on HR planning is not an expense, but an investment. They increase the HR budget as needed. And then they maintain it, even during business downturns, because that is often when creative work force planning is most needed if future (usually resurgent) production goals are to be met.

Develop a Strategic Work Force Plan

Once the organizational machinery for addressing future work force needs is in place, there are two ways to use it. One is by operating *reactively,* relying on the HR staff to devise solutions to work force problems as they arise. In years past, when such problems tended to be limited to spot worker shortages, special training needs, or occasional labor union troubles, the reactive approach was usually sufficient. A good argument could be made that assessing and developing plans for every contingency would have been more costly than occasionally being blindsided.

That, of course, is no longer the case. Impending, persistent labor shortages make a *proactive* approach essential to meeting a company's worker needs. And the heart of the proactive approach in the human resources area, just as in any other business domain, is strategic planning.

Unfortunately, strategic work force planning appears slow to catch on among corporate decision makers. While no specific data are available on this issue, there are worrisome signs. For instance, a recent special analysis of the Dun's 5000 data by the Center for International Research on Economic Tendency Surveys revealed that most corporations, including five-sixths of both the smallest and the largest firms, still casually assume that their employment levels will change very little from one year to the next. One suspects that few of the companies responding in this way have gone to much effort to devise plans for dealing with potential work force changes they don't even foresee.

But even those companies that do realize their work force is changing (and give more than passing attention to planning for these changes) often do so in an ad hoc fashion. A common practice is to consider work force needs on an individual project or division basis but then to ignore the issue with respect to the company's overall capabilities. "It's a little like a baseball manager who always has his line-up card ready for the next game," complains one analyst. "But he never sits down to think about how he's going to fill the roster for the next *season.*"

Since no successful firm we know of raises *financial* capital in this haphazard way, it's hard to see how this approach can be relied upon to build a superior work force as labor markets become as competitive as debt and equity markets. Rather, company managers who have already grappled with this problem report that a detailed work force plan can be even more critical than a financial plan. After all, banks are always willing to loan money if the price is right. But determining the benefits and management styles required to secure good workers is vastly more complicated than plugging a few numbers into a financial model. Often, say the managers, you can't even ask the right *questions* without a work force plan in place.

Building a Strategic
Work Force Plan

What should a good strategic work force plan look like? There are several important features. First, the plan should be written down. It should be a document, not just a discussion, so that it can be frequently referred to and the results of recruitment, training, and other work force efforts measured against it. Second, the plan should be *specific,* with work force needs and goals spelled out in detail, so the firms' executives and managers can see how far they have progressed toward their objectives—and how far they have yet to go. Finally, the plan should be regularly revised to take account of both changes in company goals and changes in the local work force.

Human resources specialist Joann L. Milano has found that the most successful strategic work force plans involve six steps. The plans:

1. *Define the need,* including the number and types of workers that will be required and those likely to be available.

2. *Formulate a concept* for meeting these needs.

3. *Develop a specific program* that makes the chosen concept concrete.

4. *Create a strategy for securing "buyoff"* (that is, either active support or reduced resistance) from executives and workers.

5. *Outline a plan for implementing* the program.

6. *Develop contingencies* for maintaining and modifying the program as changing conditions require.

Some useful sources of information for carrying out these tasks are already becoming available. The American Society for Personnel Administration (ASPA), for instance, has inaugurated an Issues Management Information System to help monitor and evaluate issues critical to developing strategic work force plans. The ASPA data base contains information in five areas:

1. Education, training, and retraining.

2. Demographics.

3. Work and family issues.

4. Productivity and competitiveness.

5. Employer/employee rights and responsibilities.

In the end, however, individual firms must take it upon themselves to decide which work force strategy will best meet their needs. "Work force plans are like a good pair of pants," says one observer of business' struggles with labor shortages. "You can ask the advice of every tailor in the country, but you won't know if they fit until you try them on."

Explicitly Forecast the Company's Work Force Needs

Most obviously, a strategic work force plan has to include some mechanism for regularly forecasting the number and type of workers the company will need, and the characteristics of the labor market in which it will have to compete for them. The most critical aspect of these forecasts is that they be *long-term*. While many of the recruitment and training ideas we've cited can produce immediate gains, others are not expected to yield significant results for several years. Their sponsoring companies know that the long payback alone is no reason *not* to undertake them, but they cannot make that decision intelligently without looking a considerable distance into the future.

Elements of Successful Forecasting

What are the elements of a successful long-term forecast? Planners generally agree that the following must be included:

- Projected corporate growth and its implications for work force levels and skills requirements.
- Possible changes in the company's organization and management structure.
- Anticipated demographic changes in the local population.
- Projected education and skill levels in the local labor force.
- Likely competition for workers from other local employers.
- Potential developments in the local and national economy, technology, and government regulations.
- A long-term planning horizon, usually five to ten years.

In making these forecasts, a company's objective should not be to predict the exact course of events (an impossible task in any case) but merely to prepare the organization to cope with a range of probable and possible outcomes. Management expert James O'Toole, in his book *Vanguard Management,* advises planners to engage in a series of "if-what?" exercises, laying out all reasonably possible developments, even those that could be considered unlikely (the "if" part), and then deciding ahead of time how to respond to or preempt each possible such development (the "what").

The Hudson Institute's Bill Johnston calls this approach "scenario-based forecasting" or "bracketing the range of possibilities." In its most sophisticated form, this technique allows forecasters to associate each potential outcome, or scenario, with the specific likelihood of its occurring; at a minimum, it's a method for keeping from being caught unawares. Either way, managers armed with such forecasts develop a clearer vision of the labor force trends their companies will confront and have in hand the options from which they can choose the best response.

Tips for Forecasters

But planners must use caution to avoid turning work force planning into a mechanical administrative drill. Perhaps the most important caveat with regard to this kind of forecasting, says Johnston, is to evaluate *all* possibilities, not just the most obvious ones, and to be willing to challenge the so-called conventional wisdom. He cites rising pay levels as a development that has been particularly vexing to many fast-growing firms. Built around flexible, nonunionized work forces, such firms traditionally have assumed they won't have to worry about periodic demands for higher wages. While that may have been true at one time, it no longer is. Since 1983, yearly compensation gains for nonunion workers have been consistently higher than for union members; while union members, on average, still earn more, the pay gap is rapidly disappearing.

Companies that don't make allowance for these and other "unexpected" possibilities risk being grievously unprepared. For instance, of the Dun's 5000 firms that, in 1982, predicted no significant work force changes in 1983, only one-third were close to the mark. *Two* of every five were off by more than 25 percent in their estimates. Clearly, incomplete forecasting can end up misleading more than informing.

Just as essential, companies must remember that they are not alone. It's an obvious but too easily forgotten admonition when surveying the labor force landscape: *Remember the competition.* Many companies—not just one's own—will be competing for the same workers. Hence, an apparent labor surplus could abruptly turn into a shortage if the number of new businesses suddenly shoots up. The Naisbitt Group's John Elkins warns that, with the record formation of new businesses and shrinking barriers to their creation, this is a growing possibility—but a predictable one, if planners will stop a moment to think about it.

The message of forecasting, then, is as basic as the Boy Scouts' motto: *Be prepared.* No firm can look into a crystal ball and predict its future work force environment with perfect precision. But, in the 1990s, few firms will remain competitive in the race for good workers if they don't at least try.

Make the Case for Change

"Develop the best idea that you can for recruiting or training. Do the long-range planning, put together all the budgets, even assemble your implementation team. But that's still not enough. If you don't get the support of senior management," laments one training director, "the idea is going nowhere."

Virtually everyone who has spent some time working for a large corporation knows this kind of frustration. But when it comes to putting new recruitment and training ideas in place, corporate work force planners have more to worry about than "jumping through all the hoops."

It's still all too common for operational managers to distrust their company's human resources department. Line managers often worry that HR is trying to appropriate some of their power or programs, while top management may stereotype the HR staff as too narrowly focused to know what is best for the company as a whole.

As William Zeigler, Aetna Life & Casualty's director of management education and general skills development, cautions: "It's one thing to bring skill levels up or to bring women with children into the work force with flexible hours or day care. But it's another to get managers to go along with the changes. A big part of the problem is communication— bringing people up to the point of reality."

Still, as senior and line managers become more comfortable with the work force strategies we've described here (and can measure their effectiveness in dollars and cents) they should gain respect for human resources officials and their proposals. Ultimately, one hopes, they will take up the banner of work force planning on their own, as some far-sighted executives already have done.

Until then, the experts tell HR specialists, don't wait to be invited. Insists management analyst Martha Finney: "Human resource managers who want to contribute to the company's strategic profile...must simply do it."

Making the case for change—to both management and workers—is the most critical part of taking the initiative. Perhaps the most troublesome chore HR planners face is justifying a large financial investment in their plans, especially when other departments may be scrimping. And even where money is not at issue, the mere fact of change, even if attractive in theory, may make some people uncomfortable. As the old saying goes, we're all in favor of progress, provided we can have it without change.

Overcoming Obstacles to Change

To overcome these obstacles, argues Michael LeBoeuf, a professor of management and organizational behavior at the University of New Orleans and author of *Imagineering*, proponents should concentrate on documenting the need for change among those in the company with decisionmaking authority. This is the essence of achieving "buyoff," and involves four key points:

- *Make people aware of the problems that exist.* Information like that in Chapters 1 through 3 helps make the general case about the approaching worker shortage, but more compelling still will be statistics and examples that relate to a firm's own work force situation.

- *Warn people about the consequences of nonchange.* Too often, work force planning advocates speak in detached terms about the long-term dangers of inaction. Absorbed in more immediate, day-to-day problems, corporate decision makers may see human resource plans as unproductive academic exercises. Hence, advocates should relate the hazards of ignoring the firm's work force needs directly to the company's financial well-being and market position.

- *Stress the benefits of change to the people whose approval is needed.* HR officials need to show the operations side of the firm that there *is* a payoff, says Stan Stein of McDonald's, who has been successfully doing just that for several years. Executives and managers concerned with the bottom line, he contends, need to understand that "we're only going to continue to grow if we have highly motivated people" and that new ways of recruiting and training workers will contribute significantly to the company's productivity.

- *Make it clear why the proposed change, for all the discomfort it may cause, is likely to be effective.* Even if colleagues and supervisors agree that a problem needs to be solved, this doesn't assure their support for the particular remedies proposed. Hence, it's just as important to show a direct link between the problem and the suggested solution—and the specific benefits this solution will bring to the company.

Of course, winning approval is only the first step. Those advocating specific changes must be ready to put them in place as quickly and in as cost-effective a manner as possible and then to see them through. As more than a few eager young managers have learned, support once tendered has an unseemly habit of evaporating if results don't start appearing within the promised time.

Become an Inclusive Employer

If there is one overarching theme to all that has come before, it is this: In the emerging labor shortage, there won't be a single qualified worker to waste. To be successful, senior executives and HR professionals alike must become dedicated to the idea of inclusive employment. Affirmative action will no longer be a matter of finding and hiring workers *because* they belong to a protected or nontraditional employee group; it will be a question of finding and hiring workers *regardless* of the demographic group to which they belong.

Former Citicorp CEO Walter Wriston, who knows as well as anyone the importance of good workers to a company's performance, puts it this way: "...the only game in town is the personnel game....If you have the right person in the right place, you don't have to do anything else. If you have the wrong person in the job, there's no management system known to man that can save you."

And officials with direct responsibility for recruiting, training, and developing top-quality workers have as much to gain—or lose—as the companies themselves. As James G. Parkel, IBM's director of personnel plans and programs and ASPA's 1988 chairman, recently reminded a group of the country's leading HR managers: "The human resource manager will be judged, to some degree, on his or her ability to secure a competent work force, whether," he emphasized, "it is made up of retirees,...part-timers," or others not traditionally part of the mainstream work force.

Making these decisions is not always easy, though. Conflicting mandates often place those charged with work force development in a difficult position, forcing them to make an apparent choice between too few workers and too few *good* workers. Sometimes, there may be no choice at all. Robert Harloe, director of training and manpower for Dunkin' Donuts, admits that it's tempting, when recruiting efforts are going slowly, to settle for any applicant "who can maintain a normal body temperature. But when you bring in someone bad just because you need someone, that becomes part of the [company] image. At the other extreme, some managers will hire only the ideal candidate....You're not looking for a winner, just someone who is trainable."

The Art of Inclusive Employment

Finding the balance—and avoiding preconceived notions about the ideal worker—is the key to the art of inclusive employment. Chapters 4 through 8 demonstrated how a growing number of companies are becoming innovators in putting inclusive employment to work. But these firms are more than idea factories. They are also characterized by their:

- Commitment to reaching out to nontraditional worker groups, rather than waiting for the workers to come to them.
- Willingness to experiment with novel approaches to recruitment and training.
- Insistence on paying competitive wages, recognizing that the short-term expense pales beside the long-term costs of employee dissatisfaction and applicant shortfalls.
- Commitment to providing attractive and creative benefit packages.
- Flexibility with regard to divisions of labor and working hours.

- Willingness to recruit workers from other cities and states, even foreign countries, if necessary.

- Openness to radical change, such as relocating a plant or division, if doing so will enhance recruiting potential.

- And, most of all, an ability to see things from the worker's point of view.

Inclusive employers also are quick to consider restructuring work to fit workers, rather than searching endlessly (often fruitlessly) for workers to fill a rigid job description. These firms typically:

- Emphasize which *skills* (not occupations) are needed and in what time frame.

- Break down jobs into their component parts before deciding how to fill them.

- Decide which tasks are most crucial to the company's success and which can be foregone or modified.

- Teach employees to perform a variety of functions, rather than limit the employees to narrow skills and job descriptions, so that they can move smoothly into positions where shortages threaten.

- Consider contracting out some activities to groups with disabled members, home workers, or other businesses.

- Try to eliminate positions that are restricted by tradition to a certain age, sex, or educational level and reassess whether the jobs could be performed by workers in different categories.

- Examine each job to determine whether on-the-job training could substitute for predetermined educational levels and work experience.

Building a Good Reputation

Finally, inclusive employers never forget that reputation can have a powerful effect—both positive and negative—on recruiting efforts. Dunkin' Donuts' Bob Harloe recounts the story of two of the firm's stores that were a mile and one-half apart. One store was desperate for workers, while the other was turning them away. The problem, he says, was apathy. Because fast-food establishments had never had a problem replacing disgruntled employees, corporate management was paying too little attention to how well individual franchises were run. But today, Harloe says, the would-be workers have their pick of jobs, and they will choose the place "that's most pleasant to work. If a particular unit has a lousy reputation, the kids in that area know what's going on. Word gets around. They know where the good places are to work."

For businesses in this situation, Keith Robinson, personnel director for Mervyn's department stores, has some advice. Employers should do a little introspection, he says, mercilessly analyzing their current management practices. If a firm is having trouble, it should first ask itself:

- Is our compensation fair?
- Does management treat employees with dignity and respect and give them appropriate recognition?
- Do we effectively promote the idea that the company is a great place to work?
- Do we encourage current employees to bring in new applicants?

Only after truthfully answering these questions should a company undertake an aggressive recruitment campaign. For if it hasn't done some probing first, Robinson contends, then it all could be pretty much "a waste of time."

Manage for Retention

"Employers search high and low to fill entry-level positions," declares a recent article in *Training* magazine. "But the real trick is keeping them filled." And what's true at entry level is, increasingly, even more true in the higher ranks. A recent study by the Center for Management Research in Wellesley, Massachusetts, found that "job satisfaction for middle managers has dropped so precipitously that it is now close to the abysmal levels reported by clerical and hourly workers." The survey also noted a decrease in commitment to the corporate organization and goals, diminished career aspirations, and a "dwindling sense of job security."

With worker shortages on the way, the last thing most employers want is to have to *replace* employees; looking for new workers to meet expansion needs or cope with normal attrition is hard enough. And so many businesses are beginning to think seriously about adopting explicit management-for-retention strategies.

More than anything, managing for retention demands an understanding of what makes good workers stay with a firm. As David Jamieson, president of the Los Angeles-based Jamieson Consulting Group, points out, "The employer used to be able to say, 'Here's your salary; your soul is ours.' We're past that now." Rapid shifts in technology and markets combined with the profusion of job openings in several fields have made job security per se both less critical and more difficult to guarantee. In its place, Jamieson says, a growing contingent of workers judge employers on their ability to meet "value needs," such as how willing they are to accommodate employees' family responsibilities or contribute to their intellectual enrichment.

Fortunately, many dissatisfied employees still maintain feelings of loyalty toward their current employer, and this loyalty can be solidified by wise management. Pollster Daniel Yankelovich has discovered that about one-fifth of all working Americans between ages 25 and 40 feel they are giving everything they can to the job and another one-fifth don't want to contribute more than the little they are now giving. But the remaining three-fifths, he found, say they would give much more to their work "if there were more in it for them: more recognition, more opportunity, a bigger stake in the results of their effort."

Furthermore, when asked how they viewed work in general, more than one-half of those questioned said they had "an inner need to do the very best job I can, regardless of the pay." And when asked what the "good life" means to them, more than 3 out of 5 included in their descriptions: "A job that's interesting."

Cultivating Worker Motivation

How can employers make the most of this modern work ethic and keep their best employees on the job when other offers beckon? For one thing, they can make clear from the beginning (as firms with high-retention rates invariably do) their interest in a long-term relationship with their employees. James Vonderhorst, assistant corporate training manager for the Southland Corp., parent company of the 7-11 convenience store chain, has found that, "for new employees, the most critical time is the first 30 days on the job. If you don't manage them properly from the start, you can kiss those folks goodbye."

And when things go wrong and employees do leave, firms with high-retention rates do more than shrug their collective shoulders and call up their local newspaper's classified advertising department; they find out what went wrong. The Hyatt Corp., for instance, steps up its exit interviewing, including questions about training and management responsiveness, whenever managers notice "a rotating door" developing.

Those firms with the most success in retention also are discovering creative ways to motivate and challenge employees. Because of the limited promotion opportunities in some down-sized, flattened-out corporations, many workers have grown less eager to put themselves on the line if an organization cannot promise them substantial career growth.

Ownership: An Old Idea Gets Better

This situation has led to the emergence, in recent years, of a corporate "motivation movement." At the movement's leading edge, reports one survey of firms grappling with the problem, is employee ownership. Workers care more about a company's fortunes, advocates say, if they have a say and a stake in where the firm is headed.

The concept of employee ownership is nothing new, of course. For years, it has been embodied in a stock-distribution arrangement called employee stock-ownership plans (ESOPs), currently in force at some 9000 companies around the country. While advocates recognize that ESOPs are not a panacea for corporate motivational problems, the plans have had some beneficial effects. A study by the National Center for Employee Ownership concluded that, all else being equal, a firm would grow 40 percent faster over a ten-year period with employee ownership than without it. For instance, at the Brunswick Corp., headquartered in Skokie, Illinois, sales per employee have risen almost 50 percent since the company established an ESOP.

But employee ownership is not restricted to stock ownership plans; it can mean anything from an equity share in profits to just a worker's sense that he counts. Among the most innovative employee-ownership and management strategies are these:

- Rochester Products of Coopersville, Michigan, makers of fuel injectors for General Motors cars, solicits advice from workers on who should be promoted to supervisor and also asks them to help evaluate potential parts and materials suppliers.

- Xerox, 3M, and Honeywell help finance small business start-ups by employees who have promising product or service ideas in return for a minority share in the new company.

- The SEI Corp. of Wayne, Pennsylvania, is one of a number of firms promoting "intrepreneuring": dividing its 1100-employee company into individual entrepreneurial units, in which groups of workers are given a 20 percent financial interest.

- The GM-Toyota joint production operation in Fremont, California, and the new Saturn auto plant in Spring Hill, Tennessee, actively involve workers in a wide range of management decisions.

- Ford, Xerox, and a number of steel companies have developed similar arrangements directly with the employee unions, not only boosting worker motivation but lessening the adversarial relationship between labor and management.

- Even the old standard, profit sharing, can be given a creative spin. The New York-based freight-hauler Guaranteed Overnight Delivery uses instant-feedback profit sharing, giving bonuses to drivers for beating their daily average of deliveries and to handlers for errorless sorting.

Holding On to Good Workers

In addition to motivating current employees, the smarter firms also tend to hold on to workers when cold economic calculations might argue otherwise. "One of the things we can learn about companies that are good workplaces," writes Robert Levering in *A Great Place to Work*, "is that they don't vary their commitment to their people when times get tough." For instance:

- Control Data Corp. relies on "rings of defense" to avoid layoffs, including the introduction of advanced new products during economic downturns, conversion of some workers to temporary part-time or contractor status, or institution of job sharing and reduced work weeks.

- Motorola goes one step further, specifically defining contingency plans ahead of time and informing job sharers that, if demand slumps, they may be temporarily placed on reduced work weeks. Using this method, the company was able to weather the 1980–1982 recession without significant layoffs, while competitor Texas Instruments was forced to hand out pink slips to more than 3000 workers.

- After a planned downsizing, the Dallas division of Mary Kay Cosmetics located a local firm, Digital Switch Corp., with a similar corporate culture, and loaned its surplus employees to Digital to help meet a surge in that company's work load. When the 12-week experiment ended, Mary Kay sent the same employees to Apple Computer for ten weeks. Eventually, the workers returned to Mary Kay. A short time later, when the Apple plant closed down, Mary Kay's business had begun to pick up and the cosmetics firm was able to return the favor by offering temporary positions to a number of former Apple employees.

These and other techniques are part of the growing collection of companywide strategies designed to make sure that workers, once hired, choose to stay. Deciding *which* technique to use remains pretty much a matter of intelligent guesswork. But, ultimately, what is most needed is a firm corporate belief in good ideas that make sense. As IBM's Jack Carter told us, "[Our corporate] officers have accepted on faith for a number of years that if we help an employee with a problem...we will have our investment repaid in morale, productivity—and commitment."

"So far," he says, "it has worked."

Train and Retrain

Chapters 5 and 7 described companies' efforts to train less-skilled minority group members, the economically disadvantaged, and people with disabilities, many for their first jobs, and to use such programs as a recruiting technique. Chapters 4 and 8 also showed how firms upgrade the skills of returning women and retirees in order to draw them back into the work force. But training is more than a stopgap solution to poor quality education or a discontinuous work history. It is, instead, becoming a lifelong process.

And not just for those without skills. Rapid technological changes are already forcing the restructuring of large numbers of jobs every few years. Thus, every working American—from executives to clerical staff, from specialists in highly technical fields to those with more general capabilities—will be subject to regular retraining just to keep up.

Officials at the U.S. Labor Department predict that, as a result, many people will have to be retrained from six to ten times in their lifetimes. Many will stay within their profession, adapting along with it; others will leave their field entirely for second, third, even fourth careers. The bottom line is this: As many as 50 million people will have to be trained or retrained before the turn of the century.

Are We Training Enough?

Most major corporations, of course, have long realized this need for training. Even by the start of the 1980s, the American Society for Training and Development could report that nearly all large firms provided training for their workers, some three-quarters of which was devoted not to remedial efforts for entry-level personnel, but to programs for white-collar employees. These trends have persisted. In recent years, for instance:

- AT&T, one of the corporate world's top spenders on training, devoted more than $350 million annually to motivation, training, and development, offering employees some 3500 different courses.

- Motorola's single-year plans called for spending $50 million on training.

- By the late 1980s, more than two dozen major firms and associations were offering academic degrees. Among them: Wang, Northrop, Arthur Andersen, Humana, and the Rand Corp.

And yet these efforts, estimated to cost anywhere from $60 billion to $210 billion each year, still may not be enough. One study conducted in 1982 determined that United States firms devoted an average of 35 hours of retraining and education per worker each year. But that compared to *65 hours* of training per worker each year in Japan—and the gap has widened since then.

If only to improve their position in the global marketplace, then, most companies will have to strengthen their commitment to education, training, and retraining. But beyond the obvious economic gains, such programs often increase worker motivation and loyalty as well. One particular plus is that, in a more fluid economy, many workers have begun looking for *employment* security rather than the more traditional *job* security. The firms that keep their workers *employable* often find they have an edge in keeping their *workers,* period.

But perhaps the best argument for aggressive retraining and education is its effect on recruitment. "Offer a rewarding program of training, and many jobs will sell themselves," says Elizabeth Clark, training director at the Naval Postgraduate Institute. "But fail to offer training, and you may have a big selling job on your hands—and sometimes an impossible one."

Help Schools Do Their Jobs

Of course, the most effective training is usually that provided by secondary and postsecondary schools themselves—certainly, the easiest worker for business to train is the one who comes to a company with at least his or her basic skills intact. But schools are having an incredibly difficult time accomplishing even this much, which is one of the reasons, as Chapter 5 discussed, that an increasing number of corporations are stepping in to help schools educate their students. But beyond giving direct aid to schools, companies can take one more step: they can help prove to students that studying and achievement are worthwhile.

Amazingly, business is not doing much along these lines now. According to a 1987 survey by the National Federation of Independent Business (NFIB):

- Only 16 percent of federation members ask job applicants with a high school education or less to report their grade point average.
- Only 14 percent ask these young people for a high school transcript.
- Only 3 percent look at aptitude or achievement test scores.

- A negligible proportion use scores from such tests as the basis for top-down hiring.

In fact, notes Cornell University economist John Bishop, studies show that high school grades and performance on achievement tests matter so little once a student goes out to look for work that these performance measures have no effect on the wages or probability of finding a job while in high school, essentially no effect on the wages of jobs obtained immediately after school, and only a small impact on wages even 4 or 5 years afterward. As a result, Bishop concludes, students who work hard in school, learn a lot, and score well on achievement tests "must wait many years to start benefiting," and even then the financial rewards are incredibly small. In this light, one must ask, is it any wonder that noncollege-bound students study no harder than they do?

Fortunately, this situation is starting to change. A group of several hundred American companies, under the leadership of the American Business Conference and the National Alliance of Business, has announced plans to create a new standardized test for high school graduates that would "measure an array of basic skills and academic achievement." Says Roger W. Johnson, chief executive officer of Western Digital Corp. in Irvine, California: "It's a great opportunity for business to...signal to young people that there are benefits to doing well and penalties for not doing well in school. We never sent that signal before except to college-level people."

If companies are to help schools bring an end to their graduates' skill shortages, signals like these will have to become much more prominent in the future.

Promote, Promote, Promote

Whenever labor force researchers examine what keeps good workers motivated, they discover that opportunities for advancement are a key factor. "When workers know they have a good chance to move up within the company," observes Julia Chlopecki, a congressional labor force analyst, "they are invariably more committed to proving themselves worthy, and that goes straight to the bottom line—more productivity, fewer absences, higher-quality work effort, and lower recruitment costs."

In an era in which experienced, highly skilled workers will become as scarce as entry-level workers are today, the lesson for employers is clear: Treat all employees as potential candidates for advancement.

The Push for Promotion From Within

With this in mind, many companies have adopted promotion-from-within policies, with considerable success. But rather than relying only on employees' initiative for building up the skills and experience that will make promotions possible, many companies are becoming actively involved in directing promising employees along training paths that mesh with the company's long-term needs. The worker benefits too. After completing the recommended curriculum, the employee becomes a first-among-equals candidate for promotion.

Management consultant Eli Ginzberg recommends that firms even make applicants' promotion prospects a key consideration in the initial hiring decision. Such prospects are more a question of attitudes than of skills. For instance, Ginzberg advises firms to be wary of selecting candidates who are "allergic to learning"; he would prefer a less well-trained but eager learner over a well-trained person with little interest in self-development. In any case, he contends, firms that focus on applicants' potential for growth will be much better able to implement promotion-from-within policies for years to come.

Promotion Based on Performance

Promotion based on performance rather than on seniority is another useful technique for increasing productivity and attracting and retaining good workers. Bank of America is a leading advocate of this approach. Says Bill Holmes, the bank's vice president and manager for EEO programs: "Experience is the key. Those who want to succeed will have to work their way up. We don't have a seniority system at B of A; instead, we focus on the development of high-potential people. When we identify employees like that, we stretch their assignments to allow them to progress even faster."

Ultimately, simply knowing that one *can* progress can be an effective motivator. In Chapter 5, we discussed the notion of career paths, which many firms are using to assure entry-level minority and disadvantaged workers that their first jobs aren't dead ends. The same approach can work for employees at all levels. In setting out specific career paths, both the company and the workers gain—the company, because it can begin job-specific training early for future supervisors and managers; and the workers, because they have a clear idea of what they need to do to advance up the corporate ladder.

Think Small

E. F. Schumacher's *Small Is Beautiful* and Kirkpatrick Sale's *Human Scale*, underground classics of the post-Vietnam era, argued that small-scale social and economic organizations should be preferred over large-scale ones. Partially as an outgrowth of this philosophy, the corporate decentralization movement, led by John Naisbitt, Tom Peters, and others, was born. Now a corporate religion in many sectors, decentralization has become a buzzword even in the most top-heavy conglomerates. In fact, the ASPA study cited earlier in this chapter found that decentralization, especially in the human resources area, has emerged as one of the top management priorities in a large share of the firms it surveyed.

But another type of thinking small has an equally important role to play in strengthening company fortunes. Although high-visibility programs like cafeteria benefit plans, on-site day care, and employee retraining are often essential to securing a capable work force, simple, usually cost-free, methods of making workers feel they are valued members of the corporate team—people whose ideas and efforts count—can be just as effective in building employee dedication and morale.

According to Robert Levering in his survey of the best places to work in America, companies often can achieve these objectives simply by relying on common sense. For instance, most of his highly rated employers take such simple but effective steps as:

- Using informal performance reviews to recognize workers' special skills and accomplishments throughout the year, rather than mechanically running through a performance checklist every six months.

- Eliminating unnecessary distinctions between executives and line workers, such as special dining rooms, parking spaces, and other ostentatious perquisites.

- Making clear, when celebrating company successes, that credit goes not just to the top executives, but to the individual workers involved.

- Treating employee complaints fairly, even if it means overruling a supervisor.

- Above all, using good faith in all dealings with their workers.

The Benefits of Communication

Probably the biggest small step, however, has proven to be regular communication between management and the rest of a company's work force. "In an industry as complex as ours," says Michelle L. Bagley, an employee communications specialist with Southern California Gas Company, "communication is obviously essential to keeping people up to date on what they need to know to do their job well. But it's just as important for showing them that management considers them part of the corporate team."

A recent IBM-sponsored survey came to the same conclusion. Questioners asked 785 opinion leaders in the human resources field what they thought were the most effective elements of a good human resources policy. "Open communication" topped the list.

At a number of companies, openness and swift complaint resolution have long been a regular part of corporate policy. For example:

- McDonald's Corp. hosts brown-bag luncheons at which company officials and line employees exchange ideas and concerns. And on the firm's annual Store Day, company executives work alongside store crews, flipping hamburgers, making milk shakes, and waiting on customers.

- Bank of America conducts a survey of all its employees every two years (and supplements it with a scaled-down 25,000-worker poll in the off years). The surveys focus heavily on employee concerns and ideas for improvements within the company. The results are distributed to managers, who share them with employees and then develop plans to put agreed-upon changes into place.

- IBM keeps an open door to the company's chairman, whose staff is required to resolve any employee grievance within 15 days. As a result of this process, says Equal Opportunity Program Manager Don Devey, "most difficulties are cleared up inside," with only a tiny fraction leading to complaints filed with outside agencies.

- The Federal Express Corp.'s Guaranteed Fair Treatment Procedure involves a five-step grievance process, culminating in an appeals board that includes the CEO and the vice president for personnel.

"Nice to Have"—Or Necessary?

Open communications and other "small things" may be nice to have, but are they really that vital? Robert Levering thinks so. Almost all of the "best places to work," he found, are characterized by openness rather than office politics. They are, in his words, "more like a family than a rivalry."

Business consultant Jeffrey Hallett, based in Alexandria, Virginia, is even more insistent on the importance of "thinking small." If managers want to attract and keep a high-quality work force, he says, they have to "honor, respect, and care for their employees....No workers...want or deserve to be treated like just another part of the machine. We either believe that our success depends on our people," he concludes, "or we don't."

Become a Community Fixture

Since the 1960s, community involvement has been a hallmark of many of the country's most successful businesses, although corporate executives often view such projects as something to be done *outside* of the normal sphere of operations, a social obligation with no direct effect on profit making. Management expert Peter Drucker describes three generally perceived purposes of corporate social action:

1. Enforcing high standards of business ethics.
2. Being charitable to the less fortunate.
3. Supporting culture (the arts, museums, and the like) and other community causes.

Usually, corporate officials expect such activities to benefit business only through the nebulous process of enhancing the firm's public image. But increasingly, as the examples in previous chapters have shown, the more enlightened firms are finding that community involvement can strengthen a business' bottom line as well by increasing access to a well-trained and educated work force. As Shawmut Bank's Maurice Wright told us, "Helping kids helps our business too. They are both potential employees *and* potential customers."

Corporate America appears to have the money to carry out this mission. One report indicated that corporate philanthropic giving rose from $2.3 billion in 1980 to $4.3 billion in 1985, most of it directed to human services and education. Even by the mid-1980s, the value of corporate contributions already had outstripped that of private foundations by nearly 3 to 1. The challenge for business, over the next decade, will be to make these funds do triple duty:

1. Help the community.
2. Help the less fortunate.
3. Help the company build up a skilled labor pool.

How should such a program be structured? To use the old saw, there are as many good programs as there are good companies. But a few of the common characteristics of the best community involvement efforts are that they are:

- Developed within the strategic planning process (and, in particular, within the strategic *work force* planning process), not outside of it.

- Assigned specific, quantifiable objectives and goals (such as to raise community awareness by 20 percent or to increase the qualified recruitment pool by 30 percent).

- Operationally integrated with the company departments they are meant to serve.

- Strongly supported by management, with both senior executives' interest and adequate corporate funding.

- Frequently evaluated to ensure that programs are meeting their stated objectives and, where they are not, promptly modified or replaced.

Community involvement, in short, doesn't have to be painful for those concerned with company finances. But it does have to be well *planned.* And, for those firms in the 1990s that wish to make the most of their philanthropic efforts, involvement in the community also has to be well *respected* among corporate decision makers. It has to be seen as just one more way of ensuring that workers will be there when they are needed.

Turning 20/20 Management Into a Way of Life

Embarking on 20/20 Management means realizing that worker recruitment and development no longer can be an ad hoc process of opening the doors and waiting for job applicants to find their way in. In the future, worker recruitment and development must be planned for—at all levels of the corporation—just as every other facet of business is planned. For the most part, workers will come through the doors only if they are invited; they will stay only if they are made to feel welcome, and wanted.

As reasonable as this sounds, it is a revolutionary approach for many firms. For too long, business analyst Joseph F. Coates has argued, "human resources planning in the American corporation has been second

fiddle; other business decisions are made and human resources follow."
In the future, this notion must change. Human resources planning will
have to become *first fiddle,* a given, a way of corporate life.

This is the ultimate managerial implication of the worker shortage:
People will have to rise to a par with *production.* Coates expresses it perhaps best of all: "I do not think there can be any doubt," he says, "that
human resources must move to parity with other forms of business
planning in the corporation. People are a fundamental factor, not a secondary factor, in corporate vitality and survival."

10
Beyond the Company's Doors

The decade of the worker shortage will be an immensely difficult time for most companies in America, but the problems it poses for employers, managers, and entrepreneurs need not be insuperable. As the foregoing chapters have shown, there is much that farsighted businesses can do—right now—to beat the coming labor shortages, from innovative recruitment strategies to job-specific training, from grow-your-own talent pools to the creative accommodation of workers' special needs. All it takes is the right mix of foresight and fortitude. If an employer wholeheartedly commits itself to 20/20 Management, puts its forecasting glasses on straight, and is willing to take a few high-payoff risks, there is every reason to expect to *thrive* amidst the worker shortfalls of the 1990s, while less prepared competitors are desperately trying just to cope.

Still, there are limits to what even the most dedicated, future-thinking businesses can do. Money aside, there remain many possible roads that simply cannot be taken because of the constraints of government policies and regulations. Employers must depend to a large degree on existing school systems, for instance, because state laws almost universally require young persons to attend accredited elementary and secondary schools. Nor can companies legally offer below minimum training wages to the hard-core unemployed, even if that might prove a cost-effective way of moving people with few job skills out of the drug markets and into the labor markets. And even the most labor-short businesses cannot recruit workers from across the nation's borders if national immigration laws prohibit these people from entering the country.

Such laws and others like them mark the boundaries of corporate flexibility, and they often leave firms to face less-than-ideal conditions for recruiting and retaining the kinds and number of workers they need. But laws can be changed—and, in many instances, they must be changed—if American businesses are to remain competitive, both at home and in the global market.

Companies can help mold these legal and regulatory environments for the better by becoming enlightened advocates for change. The key word is *enlightened*. Many corporations and trade associations have devoted their public education efforts over the years largely to defending their own special interests, both in Washington, D.C., and in the 50 state capitals. But special privileges, protections, and subsidies for specific businesses or industrial sectors will not end the worker shortages of the 1990s. While individual firms can—and should—compete on their own behalf for employees, they will need more broadly beneficial *national* policies behind them if they are to do more than fight among themselves for shares of a shrinking pool of qualified applicants.

To enlarge this pool beyond what their own efforts can achieve, companies will need to help build a nationwide consensus to revise or replace policies that hamper the country's ability to deal with worker shortages. One can argue late into the night over the extent to which ill-conceived laws and regulations are responsible for such tragic social conditions as spreading illiteracy, unconscionable school-dropout rates, inadequate work skills, and double-digit minority unemployment in the face of unfilled jobs. But there comes a point at which such arguments are academic. In so many work force-related public policy areas, the status quo *just isn't working*. Current government policies will need to be changed—even revolutionized—if all employers, not just the most exceptional employers, are to make their way through the coming labor shortfalls.

In this larger struggle, businesses need to be just as farsighted as they are in designing company-level recruitment, training, and retention strategies. They must, in short, be ready to look beyond the company's doors. That means pressing politicians to:

- Open their eyes to the tight labor-market conditions American firms are and will be facing.

- Do more than just talk about the problem or give more money to programs that aren't doing the job.

- Take the bullet-biting steps needed to keep American business competitive in the 1990s and beyond.

There are at least a dozen major areas where help is needed, and scores of minor changes that would do a considerable amount of good. But what follows are the six areas of labor force-related public policy where we believe immediate action is essential—and where we think publicly minded corporate citizens could best invest their political capital over the next few years. These six tasks are:

1. Promote educational quality.

2. Expand participation in advanced education and training.

3. Make the unemployment system a *reemployment* system.

4. Maximize mobility among jobs.

5. Turn the welfare state into a *work force* state.

6. Break down barriers to immigration.

We don't profess to have all the answers in any of these areas and would not have the space here to discuss them even if we thought we did. But the following ideas should serve as a starting point for employers interested in creating the best political context for beating the worker shortage and for making sure such devastating shortages do not occur again.

Promote Educational Quality

"Public education in America is in a widely recognized shambles," one of the current authors wrote in the mid-1980s. He shared the hope of millions that this growing recognition would lead, at last, to some dramatic improvements in the nation's elementary and secondary school systems. It hasn't. What the National Commission on Excellence in Education found in 1983 is still true today: "The educational foundations of our society are...being eroded by a rising tide of educational mediocrity that threatens our very future as a Nation and as a people."

Correcting this situation must be "job one" in America, to borrow from the popular television advertisement. The country cannot produce a talented, educated work force if the schools—the main instruments of worker education—are failing. If students leave their teen years inadequately educated, no conceivable collection of business or government training programs can compensate for 12 years of lost learning. In many cases, the training "repairs" we can make will be minor indeed.

But what do we do about the schools? Clearly, the two most popular proposals—more money and reforms around the edges—are not, in themselves, enough. According to data from the U.S. Department of Education's National Center for Education Statistics, combined federal, state, and local spending on education already totals in excess of $300 billion—more than the country's entire defense budget. Most schools aren't suffering from a lack of money in the aggregate. And while small-scale reforms like added homework and merit pay for teachers are helpful, they don't get to the heart of the problem. Even in Texas, the state that has enacted the toughest set of school reforms in the nation, SAT verbal and math scores combined crept up a mere 13 points (on a scale of 1600) by the mid-1980s before starting to fall again.

What is needed instead is a literal *revolution* in the direction and management of the nation's schools—the kind of institutional remaking that can come only at the local level. This is precisely the type of effort in which business can become most directly involved. Not only do locally based firms stand to benefit most from improved student performance, but they are likely to have more credibility than federal officials when it comes to bringing together the often antagonistic political forces that influence a community's educational policy. And, as the dominant taxpayers in many localities, they have the clout to do so—if they choose.

Xerox Chairman David Kearns and the respected education scholar Denis Doyle have written a brilliant little book called *Winning the Brain Race* that sets forth a bold agenda for making schools centers of learning once again. We encourage the interested reader to examine the book in detail for a complete description of Kearns' and Doyle's recommendations, but here is the core of what they propose:

- Public schools should compete with each other, with students and teachers able to choose the schools they want to attend. Disadvantaged students in particular should be given government aid in the form of vouchers to allow them to enroll in the public school of their choice, rather than being confined to drug- and crime-ravaged neighborhood schools where little real learning takes place.

- Schools should be reorganized as magnet schools, be open year-round, and be managed by principals and teachers.

- Teachers should have much greater control, commensurate with their status as professionals, than they currently do. For instance, they should be able to establish their own curriculum and classroom standards.

- Academic standards overall should be raised, and students held strictly accountable to them, with promotions to higher grade levels made contingent upon acceptable performance.

- The ethical, moral, and religious underpinnings of democratic society should be explicitly taught and discussed in school.

- While the federal role in education necessarily will remain limited, the federal government should be more creative in discharging its special responsibilities, such as in promoting research to identify successful educational techniques.

To be sure, steps like these won't be easy to swallow for an educational establishment that has grown comfortable with current institutional arrangements. But they must be taken—and taken now—if the United States is to avoid losing yet another generation of youngsters to ignorance and illiteracy.

Expand Participation in Advanced Education and Training

If the nation is to have the highly skilled work force it will need for the 1990s, many more young persons must go on to college and advanced training than are doing so today. A number of obstacles, however, stand in the way of increasing participation in postsecondary education, including:

- Sky-high student loan defaults.
- Years of punishing debt burdens for those students who do repay their loans.
- Inadequate government assistance to the neediest.
- The inability of millions of families to save for rising college tuitions.

If these obstacles remain in place, several billion dollars in additional investment would be required to dramatically boost participation in higher education—money that, at a time of triple-digit budget deficits and steep taxes, simply can't be had. Instead, a streamlined higher education financing system is needed, one that expands the total pool of funds for education and training without significantly raising the cost to taxpayers.

One mechanism that would accomplish this goal has been put forward by former Assistant Secretary of Labor Roger D. Semerad. The core of this approach is a new financial instrument called the Education and Training Trust Account (ET Trust Account). The proposed trust accounts would be tax-exempt savings accounts with these key features:

- Students or their parents could set up these trusts at any financial institution (just as they would a regular savings account) at any point in the student's life. Tax-free contributions to the account could be made by the intended beneficiary, his or her parents, or third parties, such as community organizations, charitably minded individuals, or the person's employer.

- The beneficiary could withdraw funds from the account at any time, tax-free, as long as the monies were used for education, training, or retraining.

- In cases where the student's savings could not cover the full cost of the education or training, the trust account could serve as a temporary debit account for these expenses, up to a fixed "credit limit." Student borrowers would pay market interest rates on the outstanding balance, and, after completing their education or training, would make regular monthly payments into the account—just as with a credit card account or a personal line of credit.

- To minimize the students' debt burdens, repayment schedules would be calculated so that borrowers never would have to spend more than a small, fixed percentage of their earnings on monthly repayments.

- To ensure collection, repayment information would be integrated into the income tax system, as child-support information now is.

With these features, the ET Trust Account would go a long way toward increasing participation in postsecondary education and training. The tax provision would promote financial preparation for college and training throughout a student's life (as well as charitable contributions to individual students), actions that today receive no tax benefit. The gradual repayment provisions would ensure that even students from poor families could receive quality education and training, without fear of prohibitive debt burdens. And the collection mechanism would virtually rule out the kind of widespread defaults that have plagued the existing federal Guaranteed Student Loan program.

Perhaps most important, this program would replace existing grant and student loan programs, including federal interest subsidies and mounting bad debts. It therefore would represent a substantial investment in the education and training of the American work force at little or no additional cost to the taxpayer.

Make the Unemployment System a *Reemployment* System

The federal unemployment compensation system, one of the most universally supported government programs, is also one of the programs most at odds with the nation's ability to beat the coming decade's worker shortage. As one writer bluntly puts it, "the current system of warehousing claimants without providing them access to programs to upgrade skills or other alternatives to long-term unemployment is [literally] wasting the productivity potential of America."

In fact, there is considerable evidence that the unemployment compensation system, as now structured, actually *promotes* unemployment—a truly perverse effect in an economy in which many firms are already desperate for workers. For instance, one recent study found that as much as one-third of adult male unemployment is caused by the relative attractiveness of benefits offered to unemployed workers—people are sometimes less aggressive in looking for work and more inclined to turn down job offers they do not like. The same study found that more than one-fifth of unemployment occurs because the compensation system encourages companies to lay off employees rather than retain them during slack times. Worse yet, displaced workers who enter a retraining program to prepare for a new job often *lose* their unemployment benefits altogether.

The basic problem with the current system is straightforward: It pays people *not* to work and *not* to be retrained. This approach may have made sense in the Great Depression, when jobs were almost impossible to find, but it certainly did not make sense in the 1980s and it makes much less in the 1990s, when it will be workers—not jobs—that are most scarce.

Thus, instead of encouraging nonwork, the unemployment compensation system should be transformed into a *reemployment* system that encourages *work* by paying recipients to train for new jobs. Under this approach, those people actively engaged in full-time retraining would receive the same dollar value of benefits as under the existing compensation system. But those who chose *not* to upgrade their skills and chances for employment would no longer be subsidized.

Turning unemployment compensation into *reemployment compensation* would help the nation close its skills gap even as it spurred workers to increase their own job qualifications. But there is another potential advantage: federal reemployment assistance could be paid directly into the worker's Education and Training Trust Account, greatly simplifying the unemployment system's management. Such consolidation should reduce errors (currently, more than 1 in every 4 unemployment benefit claims is for the wrong amount) and pare down administrative costs, leaving more money to be spent on actual benefits.

Most critically, by directly linking this assistance with the training account, federal unemployment policy would take a 180-degree turn—from a passive system that often leaves the jobless idle and isolated until their benefits run out into an active effort to overcome the nation's worker and skills shortages.

Maximize Mobility Among Jobs

During times of economic growth, large numbers of workers switch jobs, either to secure higher wages, to obtain more interesting work, or to move into an occupation that conforms more closely to their family situation or life-style. Job switching will become even more common in the 1990s, for two reasons:

- The relative scarcity of labor will produce more aggressive corporate competition for good workers.

- The faster pace of technological change will promote more rapid creation of new businesses and employment opportunities.

Employees' ability to move at will into the jobs they prefer will be vital to American productivity in the 1990s because, trite as it may sound, happier workers are generally more productive workers. Yet, in many respects, United States policy has increasingly restricted workers' mobility. For instance, a growing number of states (most prominently California and Minnesota) are limiting employers' ability to terminate workers without specific cause. Similar legislation under discussion in Washington, D.C., and in a number of state capitals includes mandatory 60 days' advance notice of plant closings, mandated parental leave, mandated severance pay, and mandated health insurance or other benefits.

While these provisions sound at once innocuous and humane, they are neither. From business' standpoint, they substantially raise the cost of hiring new workers and prevent companies from easily adjusting their work force to accommodate technological changes or new market opportunities. For example, the termination restrictions might prevent an employer from installing new equipment that would require the layoff of 50 assemblers, even if the change would raise plant productivity and lead to the hiring of 100 machine operators, quality assurance specialists, and finishers.

From the worker's perspective, such policies could reduce the number of jobs available, especially in lower-skilled categories. As the Hoover Institution's Edward P. Lazear pointedly notes, "imagine an extreme case of requiring 60 days' notice for [terminating] migrant farm workers. Since the cost of employing those workers would be prohibitive, farms would alter their harvest techniques to get around the law." Or, if they couldn't do that, they would merely go out of business, destroying the jobs the law was meant to protect. This might ease the worker shortage, but in a most perverse and unintended way.

To prevent these consequences from occurring, it is important that such mobility-restricting legislation be consistently opposed. Where policymakers feel these laws' objectives need to be pursued, they should find more economically sound ways of achieving them.

But business and political leaders also should look for more positive means to enhance worker mobility, especially among much-in-demand older workers. Because the nation's pension system ties most retirement benefits to the job itself, employees risk forfeiting their benefits if they leave their jobs after a few years. A midcareer job change, under this arrangement, could cost a person tens of thousands of dollars. But unhappy workers who are effectively biding their time until retirement could be even more costly to their employers.

To loosen up this inflexible system, the federal government should modify the tax code and other unduly restrictive laws. For instance, relatively modest changes in tax deductibility could promote earlier vesting and greater portability of pensions. And IRAs, Keogh accounts, and similar retirement savings plans should be enlarged and encouraged, not capped and discouraged as they were in the 1986 tax reform act.

Turn the Welfare State Into a *Work Force* State

Over the last generation, long-term welfare dependency has increased at an alarming rate. Today, nearly three-fourths of all unmarried women who first join the welfare system before age 25 spend at least five years on the rolls, and they stay there an *average* of more than nine years. Low-income men, generally ineligible for welfare, may be unemployed for similar lengths of time. In a stagnant, job-short economy, this situation would be cause enough for concern. But when jobs are going begging, there are both moral and practical reasons why it should not be allowed to persist.

Unfortunately, the conventional answers to these problems, job training and workfare, are not sufficient. Government-funded job training is sometimes helpful, but it isn't the solution to long-term welfare dependency and idleness. As New York University professor Lawrence M. Mead has shown, though training is often needed for advancement and higher wages, the lack of training, in most instances, is not a barrier to getting a job. The best training for work, he points out, is work itself.

Indeed, government training programs have done little to increase employment levels among the poor. Even the most sophisticated job training programs have barely made a dent in the welfare rolls. In Massachusetts, administrators of the state's celebrated Employment and Training Choices program could claim only a 6 percent net drop in the welfare rolls between 1983 and 1988, a time of vigorous statewide economic growth. Similarly, in New York, a state with equally comprehensive training programs, the welfare caseload fell by a mere 4.5 percent over the same period. And even the best workfare schemes have increased job-holding among welfare recipients by no more than 10 percent.

Why aren't work levels higher among the poor? Among the most prominent explanations:

- Many of the long-term poor are in the central cities, while the most rapid job growth is in the suburbs.
- Many of these people have been discouraged by training programs that trained them for jobs that did not exist.
- Many poor persons can earn almost as much on welfare as they can in entry-level jobs.
- Many economically disadvantaged youngsters grow up in communities where regular employment is not the norm, and so do not develop an orientation toward persistent work effort.
- In many such communities, lucrative opportunities in drug-dealing, theft, and other crimes are widely available.

Perhaps most important, however, is that the gulf between welfare dependency and idleness on the one hand, and productive, full-time work on the other, is often too wide to be easily crossed. As Chapter 5 suggested, work can be a frightening, forbidding experience for people who may have been socially and economically isolated for years. Rather than helping the poor break out of this trap, welfare only perpetuates their isolation. Yet strict work requirements, a favored response to this dilemma, may teach the poor that work is a punishment rather than an opportunity, certainly not the message society wants to convey.

What is needed, instead, is an approach to helping the poor that minimizes their isolation by ensuring that they face essentially the same choices and constraints as the nonpoor do—namely, that they *can* work if they want to, and, from a financial standpoint, that they feel a *need* to work if they want to support themselves and their families. The most direct way to bring this situation about is for the government to replace welfare with a guaranteed opportunity to work.

In the 1990s, a private-sector job probably will be available for almost anyone who wants to work—even someone with limited skills. Government can help out by assisting the poor with their job searches, upgrading their skills, even subsidizing transportation to work sites. But as a last resort, for those people still unable to find work, government should offer not welfare checks but the opportunity to work in constructive public-sector jobs.

In one stroke, this approach would replace the current system's disincentives to work with a new guarantee: that anyone who wanted a job to support his or her family would be able to find one. And the program could be easily augmented to ensure that every wage was a living wage merely by raising the federal Earned Income Tax Credit (EITC) and conditioning it on family size, a step Congress took in part in 1988.

But the greatest potential benefit of such a change is this: Replacing welfare with work would be a compassionate and effective way to start moving the economically disadvantaged and long-term unemployed into the economic mainstream. And that, perhaps more than any other public action, should help to enlarge the pool of available, work-ready job seekers in the 1990s.

Break Down Barriers to Immigration

"America has long been a sanctuary for those fleeing oppression abroad," writes Doug Bandow in *The Wall Street Journal*. "But the legendary open door is now barely ajar." For instance, Soviet Jews are being permitted, under *glasnost,* to leave the Soviet Union in record numbers—more than 19,000 in 1988, compared to only about 900 two years before. Yet after years of pressuring Moscow on this matter, the United States routinely denies hundreds of Jewish émigrés refugee status. Likewise, while President Reagan was publicly accepting responsibility for the families of the *contras* who had been forced out of Nicaragua, the U.S. Immigration and Naturalization Service was rejecting nearly one-half of Nicaraguan applications for asylum.

As difficult as matters can be for refugees wanting to move to the United States, the situation for nonrefugee immigrants is even worse. The Immigration Reform and Control Act of 1986 cracked down hard on illegal immigrants. How effective the law will be over the long-term is unclear, but one thing is certain: It has encouraged employers, wary of government-imposed sanctions, to discriminate against people seeking work just because they look or sound foreign. And it has also established a benchmark for how the country should view foreigners who want to enter the country, especially those looking for jobs: They are to be seen as a threat to the economy and to the country's prosperity.

But is this really the case? In the worker-short 1990s, it makes sense to reexamine the conventional prejudices about immigrants before permanently sealing the borders. As it turns out, the worst fears about immigration are remarkably far off base:

- The so-called hordes of illegal Mexican immigrants in recent years have amounted to only about 100,000 to 300,000 a year, just one-sixth to one-half the level of legal immigration, with net increases in the resident undocumented population near zero for some years.

- A Rand Corp. study has determined that Mexican immigration in southern California has actually stimulated total employment in the area, increased local economic competitiveness, lowered prices of some goods and services, and generally had no harmful effects on wages or job availability for native-born Americans.

- Members of most major immigrant groups, especially those from Asia, are already highly skilled and quickly come to earn their own way, contributing to rather than drawing from the nation's tax base.

- Immigrants in general receive less in government services, except for money spent on their children's education, than they pay in taxes. This is true both for illegal immigrants, who tend to avoid social service agencies, and for permanent legal immigrants.

Moreover, a convincing case can be made that the United States' historical commitment to liberty demands that fewer restrictions be placed on immigration; foreign lineage is, after all, the heritage of the vast majority of now native Americans. But even if more open immigration weren't morally correct, it is certainly economically sound. It makes no sense, when American companies are in desperate straits for employees, for the country to be locking out the very people who could become valuable additions to the work force.

At a minimum, the United States should substantially increase its legal immigration ceilings and clear away the red tape that prevents political refugees from freely entering the country. Over the longer term, politicians and business leaders alike should consider whether a country that depends so heavily on human capital for its future economic competitiveness can afford to turn away anyone, regardless of country of birth, who is able and willing to work.

Time to Get Started

"The work force challenge is clear," says RJR Nabisco Chairman Louis V. Gerstner, Jr. "It's here now and it will get worse. The leading companies in America in the mid-'90s will have addressed it *seriously*. The losers will not. They will only have given it lip service, and will have failed to change."

As this book has shown, the companies of today will be among leading firms of tomorrow, both in the nation and throughout the world, only if they do change. It *can* be done. Front-line employers all across the country are demonstrating that there are scores of effective techniques for making the work force revolution work. All that is needed is the foresight to know these strategies are necessary and the fortitude to stay with them until the returns come in.

It shouldn't take long to start seeing results. In just the past few years, management revolutions have turned many American firms, from automobiles to electronics, financial services to computer chips, into world-class competitors again. The same thing can happen with revolutions in work force policy, on both the corporate and national levels.

But whatever the course chosen, the country cannot wait, because neither technology nor foreign competitors will be standing still. If United States firms want to be in a position, a decade from now, to watch their foreign counterparts struggling once again to match *American* standards, they must dedicate themselves to one hard, long-term pursuit: to making their company the best place to work in the 1990s, and American firms the best-staffed workplaces in the world.

Achieving this goal won't be easy, but neither have any of the other uniquely American accomplishments of the last two hundred years. The only difference is that, this time, there will be a lot more runners in the race. There's no sense in waiting until they are miles ahead of us before we wake up.

It's time to get started.

Notes

Except where a secondary source is specifically identified, the information in this book was derived from interviews with company officials or from documentation provided by the companies themselves.

Chapter 1: Snapshots of a Shrinking Work Force

Page 1. The international unemployment comparisons are reported in Louis Richman, "Tomorrow's Jobs: Plentiful, But...," *Fortune,* April 11, 1988, p. 42.

Page 2. The Goldstein reference is Mark. L. Goldstein, "Tomorrow's Workforce Today," *Industry Week,* August 16, 1988, p. 41.

Page 2. Anne Ironside is quoted by Mark Czarnecki, "Help Wanted," *Canadian Business,* June 1988, p. 60.

Pages 2–3. Examples of how worker shortages already are affecting businesses around the nation are cited in George J. Church, "Behind the Help-Wanted Signs," *Time,* July 20, 1987, p. 55; Sterling North, "Help Wanted," *New England Business,* January 5, 1987, p.23; and Barbara Rudolph, "All Hands on Deck," *Time,* July 18, 1988, p. 43.

Page 3. Examples of employers' extraordinary methods of recruiting workers are found in Goldstein, loc. cit.; North, loc. cit.; John A. Byrne, "Jobs, Jobs, Jobs Galore," *Business Week,* April 18, 1988, p. 26; "The Jobs Conundrum," *The New Republic,* November 30, 1987, p. 7; Church, loc. cit.; Terry Stephenson Supple, "The Coming Labor Shortage," *American Demographics,* September 1986, p. 34; and "A Temporary Approach to Staffing Woes," *Insight,* November 14, 1988, p. 22.

Page 4. The Wendy's restaurants example is cited in Supple, loc. cit.

Page 5. Examples of recruiting techniques at fast-food franchises are found in Richard Corrigan, "Calling All Kids," *National Journal,* March 8, 1986, p. 558; Jeffrey L. Kovach, "Danger: Worker Shortage Ahead," *Industry Week,* March 3, 1986, p. 44; interview with John Elkins, "The Changing Nature of the Workforce," *The Journal of Business Strategy,* Fall 1987, p. 5; and Elsa C. Arnett, "Hungry for Help," *The Washington Post,* Washington Business, October 9, 1989, p. 1.

Page 5. John Merritt is quoted by Corrigan, loc. cit.

Page 5. The National Restaurant Association survey is cited in Harry Bacas, "Desperately Seeking Workers," *Nation's Business,* February 1988, p. 20.

Page 5. David R. Murphy's observation appears in Anthony Marshall, "Hoteliers Must Address the Employee-Shortage Problem," *Hotel & Motel Management,* February 22, 1988, p. 22.

Pages 5–6. The discussion of hotel chains' recruiting difficulties comes from Dale

Feuer, "Coping With the Labor Shortage," *Training*, March 1987, p. 68; and Marshall, op. cit., p. 17. The Anthony Marshall quote is from ibid.

Page 6. Innovations at Von's supermarkets are described by Rudolph, loc. cit.; Byrne, loc. cit.; and Meghan O'Leary, "Labor Shortage Turns Grocer to Automation," *PC Week*, July 11, 1988, p. C17.

Page 6. Examples of how worker shortages are affecting food production and distribution come from Stephen Koopp, "Rotten Shame," *Time*, June 27, 1987, p. 49; and Jeff B. Copeland et al., "Wooing the Migrant Farmer," *Newsweek*, June 29, 1987, p. 47.

Page 6. Additional discussions of worker shortages in various industries are found in Bacas, loc. cit.; Agis Salpukas, "Trucking's New Labor Problem," *The New York Times*, July 25, 1988, p. D1; North, loc. cit.; Byrne, loc. cit.; Roger D. Semerad, "An Education and Training Trust," *Testimony before the Joint Economic Committee of the U.S. Senate and House of Representatives*, December 14, 1988, p. 4; and "Labor Shortages Are Here," *Management World*, December 1987, p. 6.

Pages 6–7. Worker shortages in the skilled manufacturing and construction trades are described in Steven W. Setzer, "Labor Shortages Grip Several Cities," *ENR: The McGraw-Hill Construction Weekly*, September 25, 1986, p. 19; and Joani Nelson-Horchler, "Demographics Deliver a Warning," *Industry Week*, April 18, 1988, p. 58. Steven P. Tocco's comment appears in ibid.

Page 7. Louis V. Gerstner, Jr.'s remark comes from his "Enhancing the Curriculum" speech before the *Fortune* Education Summit, Washington, D.C., September 27, 1988, p. 6.

Page 7. The quotes from David T. Kearns, James E. Burke, and *The New York Times* come from Edward B. Fisk, "Impending U.S. Jobs 'Disaster': Work Force Unqualified to Work," *The New York Times*, September 25, 1989, p. A1.

Pages 7–8. Examples of how skills deficiencies are affecting entry-level hiring appear in Aaron Bernstein, "Where the Jobs Are Is Where the Skills Aren't," *Business Week*, September 19, 1988, p. 105; U.S. Departments of Labor, Education, and Commerce, *Building A Quality Workforce*, July 1988, p. 13; and Kovach, op. cit., p. 45.

Page 8. The Labor Department study is U.S. Departments of Labor, Education, and Commerce, loc. cit.

Page 8. McDonald's effort to deskill is from Elizabeth Ehrlich and Susan B. Garland, "For American Business, A New World of Workers," *Business Week*, September 19, 1988, p. 118.

Page 8. Chemical Bank's lowering of hiring standards is described in Bruce Nussbaum, "Needed: Human Capital," *Business Week*, September 19, 1988, p. 52; and Bernstein, op. cit., p. 102.

Page 8. The reference to U.S. Army recruits comes from Ron Zemke, "Training in the '90s," *Training*, January 1987, p. 48.

Page 8. The Domino's pizza reading program is cited in Christine Gorman, "The Literacy Gap," *Time*, December 19, 1988, p. 57.

Page 8. IBM's math courses at its Burlington, Vermont, plant are described by Nussbaum, loc. cit.

Page 8. The study by New York's Center for Public Resources is described in Dale Feuer, "The Skill Gap: America's Crisis of Competence," *Training*, December 1987, p. 30. Jerry Janka's remark is also included in ibid.

Page 9. David Kearns is quoted in ibid., p. 27.

Pages 9–10. William Brock's characterization of *Workforce 2000* comes from "The First Annual State of the Work Force Speech," *Labor Law Journal*, November 1987, p. 679.

Page 10. The comment on *Workforce 2000* appears in "The Future Work Force," *The Futurist*, March–April 1988, p. 44.

Chapter 2: The New Worker

Page 12. The introductory quote is from Czarnecki, loc. cit.

Page 12. Clifford Ehrlich is quoted by Aaron Bernstein et al., "Help Wanted," *Business Week*, August 10, 1987, p. 48.

Page 14. The *American Demographics* reference is Martha Farnsworth Riche, "America's New Workers," *American Demographics*, February 1988, p. 34.

Page 15. The New England drug store chain is described in "Low-Level Jobs Remain Unfilled," *The Washington Post*, Washington Business, November 25, 1985, pp. 1, 26–27.

Pages 15–16. Aaron Mittelman is quoted in Gary Putka, "Fading Miracle: Massachusetts Suffers as Its Revenues Lag and Route 128 Falters," *The Wall Street Journal*, February 8, 1989, p. A1.

Page 16. The Gladys Cerruto quote is from North, loc. cit.

Page 16. Nassau and Suffolk Counties' economic forecasts appear in "LI Job Opportunities to Outnumber Workers," *Long Island Business News*, August 24, 1987, p. 3.

Page 16. Population data and predictions here and subsequently in this chapter come from Howard N. Fullerton, Jr., "Labor Force Projections: 1986 to 2000," *Monthly Labor Review*, September 1987, pp. 19 and 22; William B. Johnston and Arnold H. Packer, *Workforce 2000: Work and Workers for the 21st Century*, Hudson Institute, Indianapolis, 1987, pp. 76, 92–93; Vernon M. Briggs, Jr., "The Growth and Composition of the U.S. Labor Force," *Science*, Vol. 238, October 9, 1987, p. 178; Gordon W. Green, Jr., "Lifestyles and Economic Well-Being in the United States," presentation before an *American Demographics* conference on "Managing Consumer Change," Hollywood, Fla., February 12–14, 1986, pp. 6 and 12; U.S. Bureau of the Census, *Current Population Reports*, Series P-25, No. 990, 1987; and personal communications.

Page 16. Labor force data and predictions here and subsequently come from Johnston and Packer, op. cit., pp. 77–78, 85, 89, 93; Ronald E. Kutscher, "Overview and implications of the projections to 2000," *Monthly Labor Review*, September 1987, p. 3.; Ronald E. Kutscher, "An Overview of the Year 2000," *Occupational Outlook Quarterly*, Spring 1988, p. 4; Fullerton, op. cit., p. 25; Council of Economic Advisers, *Economic Report of the President*, U.S. Government Printing Office, February 1990, Table C-36, 335; Elkins, op. cit., p. 5; Briggs, loc. cit.; and various U.S. Bureau of Labor Statistics press releases.

Page 17. Examples of high starting wages are found in Susan B. Garland et al., "Why the Underclass Can't Get Out From Under," *Business Week*, September 19, 1988, p. 123; Bernstein et al., "Help Wanted," op. cit., p. 48; North, loc. cit.; and Koopp, loc. cit.

Page 17. Rogert Zagami is quoted by Putka, loc. cit.

Page 17. The quote on the shortage of young workers is from Keith McKnight, "U.S. does little to train idle young people," *The Akron Beacon Journal*, September 6, 1987, p. 11.

Page 18. Andrew Sum is quoted in Corrigan, loc. cit.

Page 19. Examples of retirees who have returned to work appear in McKnight, loc. cit.; Bacas, loc. cit.; Bernstein et al., "Help Wanted," op. cit., p. 50; and Ehrlich and Garland, loc. cit.

Page 20. The likelihood of older or middle-aged workers accepting transfers is presented in U.S. Bureau of the Census, *Current Population Reports*, Series P-23, No. 138, Table 4-6, p. 40; and National Commission for Employment Policy, *The Education,*

Training and Work Experience of the Adult Labor Force From 1984 to 1995, U.S. Government Printing Office, June 1985.

Page 21. Sandra Gunn is quoted in "Where Women Are Succeeding," *Fortune,* August 3, 1987, p. 80.

Page 21. Samuel Preston's observation appears in Supple, op. cit.

Page 21. The Gallup poll results are reported in Johnston and Packer, op. cit., p. 87.

Page 22. The Du Pont poll is reported in Dan Oldenburg, "Worker/Family Poll," *The Washington Post,* January 11, 1989, p. C5.

Page 23. The estimated number of workers over 40 providing in-home care to their parents is from Ehrlich and Garland, op. cit., p. 113.

Page 23. *Business Week's* report that elder care responsibilities are linked with productivity losses appears in ibid.

Page 23. The Employment Benefit Research Institute study is discussed in Goldstein, op. cit., p. 43; and Ehrlich and Garland, op. cit., p. 114.

Page 23. The Roberts T. Jones quote is from Roberts T. Jones, "The Year 2000 Worker," *Association Management,* June 1988, p. 16.

Pages 23–24. The quoted corporate executive is Louis V. Gerstner, Jr., in "The Workforce Challenge," remarks at The American Express Company Senior Management Conference, Tucson, Ariz., October 13, 1988, p. 7.

Page 24. The data on minority group labor force participation are from Fullerton, loc. cit.; and Briggs, loc. cit.

Page 25. The interview with the young drug dealer is from Ehrlich and Garland, loc. cit.

Page 25. The Bureau of Labor Statistics report is cited in C. Emily Feistritzer, "Will American Workers Be Ready for the 21st Century?" *The Washington Post,* August 7, 1988, p. H12.

Page 26. The scholarly report is Oxford Analytica, *America in Perspective,* Houghton Mifflin, Boston, 1986, p. 20.

Page 27. U.S. Census Bureau data on families speaking a language other than English are cited in Briggs, loc. cit.

Page 27. The literacy levels of nonnative English speakers is reported in Roger D. Semerad, "The United States: A Post-Industrial Nation With Problems & Opportunities," *Archon,* Spring/Summer 1987, p. 4.

Page 27. The Cambodian refugee and custodial service owner are quoted in Chris Spolar, "New Working Class in the Making: Foreigners Take Jobs That Few Americans Want," *The Washington Post,* December 15, 1987, p. A1.

Page 27. References to the nurses shortage are from Ehrlich and Garland, loc. cit.; and from Arnold H. Packer, "Work Force 2000: What to Expect," *Provider,* February 1989, p. 8.

Pages 27–28. The Hyatt Hotel, 7-11, and language-training firm examples are cited in Feuer, "Coping With the Labor Shortage," op cit., p. 66.

Page 28. The Kovach story is from Kovach, loc. cit.

Page 28. The former president (of American Express Company) referred to is Louis V. Gerstner, Jr., and is quoted in Gorman, loc. cit.

Page 29. Skills and literacy requirements for entry-level jobs are discussed in the Business Council for Effective Literacy's April 1988 newsletter; U.S. Departments of Labor, Education, and Commerce, op. cit., p. 11; and Johnston and Packer, op. cit., p. 98.

Page 30. James D. Howell is quoted in Kovach, op. cit., p. 46.

Page 30. The William H. Kohlberg quote is from Cheryl M. Fields, "Need to Retrain People in Changing Fields Confronts Colleges With Creative Challenge," *The Chronicle of Higher Education,* September 17, 1986, p. 37.

Pages 30–31. High school dropout and college attendance rates are from U.S. Department of Labor, *Labor Market Shortages: A Report of the Secretary of Labor,* January 1989, p. 5; "Change in America," *The Chronicle of Higher Education,* September 17, 1986, p. 1; and Brock, loc. cit.

Page 31. Worldwide literacy rates are cited in Arnold H. Packer, *Reducing Functional Illiteracy: Research for Action,* Hudson Institute, Alexandria, Va., July 17, 1986, p. 1; U.S. Department of Labor, loc. cit.; Zemke, loc. cit.; and Semerad, "An Education and Training Trust," op. cit., p. 3.

Page 31. United States capabilities in mathematics are described in U.S. Departments of Labor, Education, and Commerce, op. cit., p. 15; H. Ross Perot, "Wake Up, America! We're Wasting Our Future," *The Washington Post,* November 20, 1988, p. D1; and Nussbaum, loc. cit.

Page 31. The Department of Labor survey on skills shortfalls is cited in U.S. Department of Labor, op. cit., p. 2.

Page 31. Secretary of Education Lauro F. Cavazos is quoted in Barbara Vobejda and Colette T. Rhoney, "Cavazos: Students 'Not Learning Much' Science and Math," *The Washington Post,* December 7, 1988, p. A19.

Page 31. Estimates of the number and type of workers who will need their skills upgraded are from Arnold H. Packer, *Retooling the American Workforce: The Role of Technology in Improving Adult Literacy During the 1990s*; background paper prepared for the Project on Adult Literacy of the Southport Institute for Policy Analysis, December 1988, p. 1; and John D. Ong, "Workplace 2000—Managing Change," *Vital Speeches of the Day,* May 15, 1988, p. 473.

Page 32. Secretary of Education Lauro F. Cavazos is quoted in Barbara Vobejda, "Priorities Lie With Disadvantaged," *The Washington Post,* November 22, 1988, p. A10.

Page 32. Jule M. Sugarman is quoted in Barbara Vobejda, "Panel Warned of Weaknesses in Work Force," *The Washington Post,* December 15, 1988, p. A18.

Chapter 3: The Work Force Revolution

Page 33. Montana's population-building efforts are described in T. R. Reid, "Montana's Calculated Effort to Add People," *The Washington Post,* April 1, 1989, p. A3.

Page 34. The Fallows reference is to James Fallows, *More Like Us: Making America Great Again,* Houghton Mifflin, Boston, 1989.

Page 34. Tom Peters' ideas on change are set forth in his book, *Thriving on Chaos: Handbook for a Management Revolution,* Alfred A. Knopf, New York, 1987, p. xi.

Page 38. The Office of Technology Assessment data are from U.S. Office of Technology Assessment, "Computerized Manufacturing Automation," cited in U.S. Department of Labor, op. cit., p. 12.

Page 38. Sar A. Levitan's remark appears in his article, "Beyond 'Trendy' Forecasts: The Next 10 Years for Work," *The Futurist,* November–December 1987, p. 29.

Page 38. The analysis of technology's effect on jobs is from Jerome A. Mark, "Technological Change and Employment: Some Results From BLS Research," *Monthly Labor Review*, April 1987, pp. 27–28.

Page 38. The Canadian study is cited in "Tech Change and the Job Market," *Au Courant*, Summer 1987, p. 3.

Page 39. Figures on worker productivity in the United States are from Fallows, op. cit., p. 55.

Page 39. Productivity and job growth in the financial services industry are discussed in Richard I. Kirkland, Jr., "Are Service Jobs Good Jobs?" *Fortune*, June 10, 1985, p. 43.

Page 39. Job growth in the accounting and computer industries is cited in Mark, op. cit., pp. 29 and 42.

Pages 39–40. Figures on projected nationwide job growth are from Johnston and Packer, op. cit., p. 54.

Page 40. Information on technology's effect on the number of low-level jobs is from a study by the management firm Arthur D. Little, cited in Dale Feuer, "Coping With the Labor Shortage," op. cit., p. 65.

Page 40. Projected skill levels for future jobs are from Arnold H. Packer, *Retooling the American Workforce*, op cit., pp. 8 and 10; and William B. Johnston et al., *Civil Service 2000*, U.S. Office of Personnel Management, Washington, D.C., June 1988, pp. 10–11.

Page 41. A discussion of the United States' lost technological advantage is presented in Perot, op. cit., p. D4.

Page 42. Joseph Duffey's quote is from Joseph Duffey, "Competitiveness and Human Resources," *California Management Review*, Spring 1988, p. 93.

Page 42. Representative Lee H. Hamilton is quoted by Hobart Rowen, "A New Economic Player Suits Up," *The Washington Post National Weekly Edition*, January 23–29, 1989, p. 5.

Page 42. The Marc S. Tucker quote is from Elizabeth Ehrlich, "America's Schools Still Aren't Making the Grade," *Business Week*, September 19, 1988, p. 135.

Pages 42–43. Semerad's quote is from Roger D. Semerad, "2000: Labor Shortage Looms," *Industry Week*, February 9, 1989, p. 40.

Page 43. Felice Schwartz is quoted by Goldstein, loc. cit.

Page 43. The Louis V. Gerstner quote is from "The Workforce Challenge," op. cit., p. 1.

Chapter 4: Women and Work

Page 45. The Naisbitt and Aburdene reference is to John Naisbitt and Patricia Aburdene, *Reinventing the Corporation*, Warner Books, New York, 1985, p. 242.

Pages 45–46. Marvin Cetron is quoted by Stephen G. Minter, "Workplace 2000: The Shape of Things to Come," *Occupational Hazards*, October 1985, p. 111.

Page 46. The figures on women's employment and wage levels come from the U.S. Bureau of the Census, *Male-Female Differences in Work Experience, Occupations, and Earnings*, 1987, Tables 1 and 2.

Pages 46–47. The U.S. Bureau of Labor Statistics supplied the ratio of women's to men's earnings by means of personal communication.

Page 47. The Gallup survey is cited in "Women Executives Feel That Men Both Aid and Hinder Their Careers," *The Wall Street Journal*, October 25, 1984, p. 35.

Page 47. The article on the glass ceiling is by Carol Hymowitz and Timothy D.

Schellhardt, "The Glass Ceiling: Why Women Can't Seem to Break the Invisible Barrier That Blocks Them From the Top Jobs," *The Wall Street Journal*, March 24, 1986, p. D1.

Page 47. Statistics on the small percentages of women in upper management are found in Thomas Burdick and Charlene Mitchell, "'Glass Ceiling,' Keeps Women From the Top," *The Washington Times*, May 5, 1988, p. C2.

Page 47. Two Baylor University researchers recorded 348 male executives' feelings about working for a woman. The survey's results are cited in David Wessel, "The Last Angry Men," *The Wall Street Journal*, March 24, 1986, p. D20.

Page 48. Kim Friedman is quoted by Laura Landro, "Real-Life Struggles," *The Wall Street Journal*, March 24, 1986, p. D12.

Page 48. The survey results on childless men and women in corporate management are included in Helen Rogan, "Executive Women Find It Difficult to Balance Demands of Job, Home," *The Wall Street Journal*, October 30, 1984, p. 33; and in Roy Rowan, "How Harvard's Women MBAs Are Managing," *Fortune*, July 11, 1983, pp. 58–72. High-level corporate women's comments about their home responsibilities also are reported in Rogan, loc. cit.

Page 48. Research by the Boston University School of Social Work is cited in the Bureau of National Affairs, *Work and Family: A Changing Dynamic*, Washington, D.C., 1985, p. 11.

Pages 48–49. Working women's responsibility for elderly dependents has been documented by The Travelers Insurance Company in its June 1985 Care Giver Survey, and by Anthony Gajda of the employee-benefits firm Mercer-Meidinger-Hansen. Gajda's figures are cited by Elizabeth Ehrlich, "For American Business, a New World of Workers," *Business Week*, September 19, 1988, p. 113.

Page 49. Information about sexual harassment in the workplace comes from Barbara Gutek's (Claremont Graduate School) survey, cited in Ellen Graham, "My Lover, My Colleague," *The Wall Street Journal*, March 24, 1986, p. D25; and two studies mentioned in the Bureau of National Affairs, *Working Women: Past, Present, Future*, Washington, D.C., 1987, p. 388: Katherine MacKinnon's "Sexual Harassment: The Experience," 1982; and Dierdre Silverman's "Sexual Harassment: Working Women's Dilemma," 1976.

Page 50. Reuben Mark's quotation and the information on Colgate-Palmolive's family programs come from Cindy Skrzycki, "Corporate Group Finds the Family Is a Hot Issue," *The Washington Post*, March 14, 1990, p. F4.

Page 53. A description of the 1982 Bureau of the Census study and David E. Bloom's observation appear in Ehrlich, "For American Business, a New World of Workers," op. cit., p. 114.

Page 54. Mervyn's recruiting strategy is described in Bacas, op. cit., p. 21.

Pages 54–55. USAA's success in recruiting military wives ebbed when the firm's claims office moved from Arlington, Virginia (near Washington, D.C.), to a new building about 10 miles further south. Recruiters are now focusing more on nonmilitary returning women, older persons, and high school and college students seeking part-time employment.

Page 55. The Charlotte Perkins Gilman quote appears in D. Hayden, *The Grand Domestic Revolution*, MIT Press, Cambridge, 1981, pp. 197–198.

Page 56. Information on recent congressional efforts to implement mandated parental leave legislation comes from Don Phillips, "Panels Back Minimum Wage, Parental Leave Bills as Labor Agenda Advances," *The Washington Post*, March 9, 1989, p. A15; and Macon Morehouse, "Senate Democrats Are Stymied on So-Called 'Family Issues,'" *Congressional Quarterly*, October 8, 1988, p. 2822.

Page 56. The argument that eliminating jobs through automation could be more economical for businesses than complying with mandated parental-leave laws appears in Walter E. Williams, "Uncle Sam's Postpartum Policies," *Venture*, October 1987, p. 16.

Page 58. Estimated numbers of private-sector and federal workers participating in flexible hour arrangements, as well as a discussion of the Bureau of Labor Statistics study, are provided in Bureau of National Affairs, *Work and Family,* op. cit., p. 6.

Page 59. The Northwestern Mutual Life Insurance example appears in Robert Levering, *The 100 Best Companies to Work for in America,* Addison-Wesley, Reading, Mass., 1984, p. 242.

Page 62. The Bureau of Labor Statistics estimate and Thomas Miller's projection on numbers of home workers are cited in Margaret Ambry, "At Home in the Office," *American Demographics,* December 1988, pp. 31–32. The estimates include persons who bring work home, employees who work full-time at home, and entrepreneurs operating home-based businesses.

Page 62. A few states have labor laws governing work done at home, primarily in factory-type occupations; states without such laws fall under the jurisdiction of the U.S. Department of Labor (DOL) and the Fair Labor Standards Act of 1938. In early 1989, DOL lifted a 40-year ban on work done at home in women's apparel and five other industries. See Frank Swoboda, "Homework Ban Lifted Despite Warning," *The Washington Post,* December 8, 1988, pp. A8–9.

Page 63. The American Service Bureau example appears in Lynie Arden, *The Work-at-Home Sourcebook,* Live Oak Productions, Boulder, 1987, p. 69.

Page 64. The 1977 survey of mothers of young children, conducted by the U.S. Department of Labor, is cited in the Bureau of National Affairs, *Work and Family,* op. cit., p. 218.

Page 64. The number of people employed by temporary-help firms between 1970 and 1986 is cited in "Employment patterns in United States are undergoing changes," *Supervision,* November 1987, p. 11.

Page 64. Felice Schwartz is quoted by Ellen Goodman, "Employing Women: A Price Worth Paying," *The Washington Post,* January 24, 1989, p. A23.

Pages 65–66. Job sharing examples at TRW Vidar and medical institutions are drawn from Barney Olmsted and Suzanne Smith, *The Job Sharing Handbook,* Penguin Books, New York, 1983, pp. 157–158.

Page 66. The *Fortune* survey is cited in Rowan, loc. cit.; Deborah Phillips is quoted in Sally Squires, "Day Care: Hard to Find, Hard to Afford, Hardly Regulated," *The Washington Post,* March 6, 1990, p. Health-12.

Page 67. Employer surveys on the effects of child-care policies are cited in Ellen Galinsky (Bank Street College), *Investing in Quality Child Care: A Report for AT & T,* Short Hills, N.J., November 1986.

Page 67. Estimated number of companies providing financial assistance for child care comes from a U.S. Bureau of Labor Statistics press release dated January 15, 1988.

Page 68. The Polaroid example is cited in literature from the Service Employees International Union's 1987 conference.

Page 68. American Can Company's child-care reimbursement policy is described in Joann S. Lublin, "Courting the Couple: The Two-Career Couple Is Forcing Firms to Contend With the Role of the Spouse," *The Wall Street Journal,* March 24, 1986, p. D30.

Pages 68–69. Gordon McGovern is quoted in Albert R. Hunt, "What Working Women Want," *The Wall Street Journal,* June 6, 1986, p. 24.

Page 70. The B.E.&K. example is from Claudia H. Deutsch, "Getting Women Down to the Site," *The New York Times,* March 11, 1990, p. 3:25.

Page 72. U.S. Bancorp's and Pacific Northwest Bell's use of the Northwest Family Network is reported in "Companies begin to play key role in day care dilemma," *Daily Journal of Commerce,* November 10, 1987.

Page 73. A shift of responsibilities recently led the California Medical Center to discontinue its participation in Transamerica Life Insurance Company's sick-child day-care program, but the company is actively seeking to replace it with another health care facility.

Page 74. The Travelers employee survey is cited in the Bureau of National Affairs, *Work and Family,* op. cit., p. 63. The Michael Creedon quote is from Kathleen Teltsch, "For Younger and Older, Workplace Day Care," *The New York Times,* March 10, 1990, p. A1.

Page 74. Data on the elderly population's growth come from the American Association of Retired Persons (AARP) research office.

Page 75. The remark by the corporate personnel chief (James Davis) about how worry over elderly dependents affects a person's on-the-job performance appears in Nina McCain, "Corporate Help for the Caregivers," *The Boston Globe,* August 12, 1986, p. 15.

Page 75. The information on the Stride Rite program comes from Teltsch, loc. cit.

Page 76. Harold E. Johnson is quoted by Glenn Collins, "Many in Work Force Care for Elderly Kin," *The New York Times,* January 6, 1986, p. I15.

Page 77. According to a 1985 survey by relocation consultants Runzheimer International Ltd., cited in Lublin, loc. cit., nearly one-half of 151 large corporations provided spouses with job-hunting assistance, up from just one-fifth in 1984.

Page 78. The Baxter Healthcare Corp. example appears in The Conference Board, *Corporations and Families: Changing Practices and Perspectives,* 1985, p. 39.

Page 80. The comment about Du Pont's Personal Safety Program comes from Joseph Ignar, director of personnel relations and development, quoted in a 1987 company fact sheet.

Page 80. Du Pont's Mary Lou Arey is quoted in "Corporate Concern for Victims of Rape," *The New York Times,* October 15, 1987, p. C7.

Page 80. Merck & Company and other employers offering affirmative action training are cited in Wessel, loc. cit.

Page 80. Data on women-owned businesses were provided by the Small Business Administration's advocacy office.

Page 81. The Citicorp example, including the quote by Walter Wriston, appears in Levering, op. cit., p. 47.

Chapter 5: Unemployment Rolls to Payrolls

Page 89. The *Workforce 2000* quotes are from Johnston and Packer, op. cit., pp. 114 and 91.

Page 92. The costs of Aetna's basic skills program are cited in Gorman, op. cit., p. 56.

Pages 92–93. Training programs sponsored by General Motors' Truck and Bus Group and Domino's Pizza are described in ibid.

Page 93. Arnold Packer is quoted in "How Can Businesses Fight Workplace Illiteracy?" Cathy Petrini (ed.), *Training and Development Journal,* January 1989, p. 22.

Page 96. AFSCME's program is described in Gorman, op. cit., p. 57.

Pages 96–97. Automobile dealers' partnerships with high schools in the Washington, D.C., area are profiled in Warren Brown, "Mini-Dealerships: A Career in Gear," *The Washington Post,* Washington Business, January 30, 1989, pp. 32–33.

Page 97.   Dow Chemical Company's relationship with local schools is described in Brad Edmondson, "Why Adult Education Is Hot," *American Demographics*, February 1988, p. 41.

Page 97.   Gregory Forest Products Sawmill is discussed in Gorman, op. cit., p. 58.

Pages 98–99.   Businesses that hire the hard-core unemployed are highlighted in Joel Glenn Brenner, "Area Businesses Tap New Source to Solve Severe Labor Shortage," *The Washington Post*, September 2, 1989, p. A1.

Page 103.   Herb Schervish's contribution is cited in Albert R. Karr, "Labor Notes," *The Wall Street Journal*, January 31, 1989, p. A1.

Page 106.   William Zeigler's observation appears in "How Can Businesses Fight Workplace Illiteracy?" op. cit., p. 24.

Page 109.   Larry Adams is quoted in Boyce Thompson, "Human Resources," *Building Supply Home Centers*, March 1988, p. 77.

Page 111.   The Robert Harloe quotes are from Feuer, "Coping With the Labor Shortage," op. cit., pp. 73–74.

Chapter 6: Cultural Matchmaking

Page 116.   Ghulam Safi's story is recounted in Sandra Evans, "Job Center Boosts Immigrants Over Age, Language Barriers," *The Washington Post*, Virginia Weekly, April 27, 1989, p. 1.

Page 117.   William Julius Wilson's observation appears in his book, *The Truly Disadvantaged*, University of Chicago Press, Chicago, 1987, pp. 57 and 60–61.

Page 118.   The Muller and Espenshade reference is to Thomas Muller and Thomas J. Espenshade, *The Fourth Wave: California's Newest Immigrants*, The Urban Institute Press, Washington, D.C., 1985.

Page 119.   Predictions of the immigrant population in the year 2000 come from Johnston and Packer, op. cit., p. 93.

Page 119.   Figures on the demographics of immigration are cited in Lennie Copeland, "Making the Most of Cultural Differences at the Workplace," *Personnel*, June 1988, p. 52; Muller and Espenshade, loc. cit.; and in Joel Kotkin, "Selling to the New America," *Inc.*, July 1987, p. 44.

Page 120.   The Aldoberto Perez example is from Ron Schere, "Help Wanted in U.S. Factories," *The Christian Science Monitor*, March 25, 1988, p. 3.

Page 120.   The effects of a lack of fluency in English on work force participation are reported in Cordelia Reimers, "Cultural Differences in Labor Force Participation Among Married Women," *American Economic Review*, May 1985, pp. 251–255.

Page 121.   Workplace English training for northern Virginia hotel employees is discussed in Leigh Jackson, "Arlington Brings English Classes to Workplace," *The Washington Post*, Virginia Weekly, January 26, 1989, p. 1.

Page 121.   Long Dinh's training program is described in Elizabeth Tucker, "Southeast Asians Find a Niche in Local Companies," *The Washington Post*, Washington Business, February 22, 1988, p. 1.

Pages 121–122.   The VOICES program at Digital Equipment Corp. is described by Juliet F. Brudney, "Making English Useful," *The Boston Globe*, September 27, 1988, p. 41.

Page 122.   Chuck Palid's quote appears in Feuer, "Coping With the Labor Shortage," op. cit., p. 66.

Page 122. Rudi's bakery is cited by Margaret Engel, "On the Rise in the Inner City," *The Washington Post*, May 10, 1989, p. E4.

Page 123. The SKILLPAC and other IVD examples are from Arnold H. Packer, "America's New Learning Technology," *Personnel Administrator*, September 1988, pp. 64, 67, and 132.

Page 123. For more sophisticated training uses of IVD technology, see Robert Neff, "Videos Are Starring in More and More Training Programs," *Business Week*, September 7, 1987, p. 109.

Page 123. Burke Stinson is quoted in Kerry Elizabeth Knobelsdorff, "Corporations Take Aim at the High Cost of Worker Illiteracy," *The Christian Science Monitor*, March 10, 1988, p. 12.

Page 124. Beaumont Hospital's accent-reduction program is described in Betty J. Blair, "Voice Program Puts the Accent on English," *The Detroit News*, February 23, 1988, pp. 1C and 3C.

Page 129. The Badi Foster quote comes from Badi Foster et al., "Workforce Diversity and Business," *Training and Development Journal*, April 1988, p. 39.

Page 130. The insights into possible cultural misunderstandings are taken from Sondra Thiederman, "Breaking Through to Foreign-Born Employees," *Management World*, May/June 1988, p. 22; Lennie Copeland, "Learning to Manage a Multicultural Workforce," *Training*, May 1988, p. 49; and Patti Watts, "Bias Busting: Diversity Training in the Workplace," *Management Review*, December 1987, p. 53.

Page 131. Kevin Sullivan is quoted by Copeland, "Learning to Manage a Multicultural Workforce," op. cit., p. 54.

Page 131. The Avon example appears in Lennie Copeland, "Pioneers and Champions of Change," *Personnel*, July 1988, p. 48.

Page 131. The story of Mars Market is recounted in Kotkin, op. cit., pp. 45–46.

Chapter 7: Opening Doors to the Disabled

Page 134. The estimated numbers of working and nonworking disabled persons come from the U.S. Bureau of the Census, *Current Population Survey*, March 1988, Table 12. The figures may be somewhat low, however, since many working-age people with disabilities are reluctant to identify themselves as such.

Page 134. The poll from Louis Harris and Associates is *The ICD Survey of Disabled Americans* (conducted for the International Center for the Disabled), December 1985.

Page 134. The social policy analysts quoted are Sar A. Levitan and Robert Taggart (eds.), *Jobs for the Disabled*, The Johns Hopkins University Press, Baltimore, 1977, p. 84.

Page 134. The judgment about people's chances of becoming disabled as they age is from Honeywell Handicapped Employees Council, *The Handicapped Employee in the Diverse Workforce: Report and Recommendation*, 1987. p. 19.

Page 134. George Will's comment comes from his remarks at a 1987 seminar cosponsored by the Smithsonian Institution's Woodrow Wilson Center and the National Office on Disabilities.

Page 135. The President's Committee on Employment of People with Disabilities, formerly the President's Committee on Employment of the Handicapped, received its new name by Executive Order on May 10, 1988. (See Executive Order 12640, cited in *The Federal Register*, Vol. 53, No. 92, May 12, 1988.)

Page 135. The poll cited is Louis Harris and Associates, *The ICD Survey II: Employing Disabled Americans* (conducted for the International Center for the Disabled in cooperation with the National Council on the Handicapped and the President's Committee on Employment of the Handicapped), New York, 1986.

Page 135. Sar A. Levitan's observation about employers' fears of hiring the disabled is from Levitan and Taggart (eds.), op. cit., p. 8.

Page 136. The hotel and restaurant industry survey results are reported in J. A. Schapire and F. Berger, "Responsibilities and Benefits in Hiring the Handicapped," *Cornell Hotel and Restaurant Administration Quarterly,* February 1984, pp. 58–67.

Page 136. Results of the Du Pont employee survey appear in the firm's 1982 corporate publication, *Equal to the Task.*

Page 136. The quote by Chuck Cuyjet appears in Brenner, op. cit., p. A12.

Pages 138–139. Hank Viscardi is quoted by Dick Dietl, "The Second Life of Hank Viscardi," *Worklife,* January/February/March 1988, p. 18.

Page 139. The Quaker Oats example is found in William E. Smart, "Workers With Something Extra: From the Retarded, Enthusiasm and Reliability," *The Washington Post,* January 20, 1987, p. E5.

Page 142. The Diane Afes quote appears in Dick Dietl, "Operation Job Match Helping to Fill the Worker Void," *Worklife,* January/February/March 1988, pp. 10–11.

Page 142. The figure on disabled students in postsecondary education is included in the National Center for Educational Statistics' *Profile of Students with Disabilities,* 1989, Table 1, Figure 1, pp. 6–7.

Page 143. One such survey of business managers' attitudes toward the disabled is a 1987 poll by Louis Harris and Associates, which reports that 66 percent of managers who had not hired disabled people in the preceding three years said that an important reason for not doing so was the lack of qualified applicants.

Page 143. Robert Cole made the observation about disabled students' career prospects during his address to Mainstream's 1987 Annual Conference.

Page 145. Juan Sabater is quoted in the *Forum,* the Projects with Industry newsletter, May 1988.

Pages 145–146. B.I.P.E.D.'s experience is recounted in Gordon M. Goldstein, "Corporations Back Program for Disabled," *The New York Times,* March 23, 1986, pp. XXII–1, 6–7.

Page 147. Woodward and Lothrop's experience with workers referred by ARC is documented in Smart, loc. cit.

Page 147. The observation about retarded workers at the Willow Tree Day Care Center is from the director, Judith Vaughan, "Three Terrific Helpers, and All Are Disabled," *The Washington Post,* September 20, 1987, p. C8.

Page 148. Mary Pat Radabaugh of IBM is quoted in "IBM's National Support Center for People With Disabilities," *Worklife,* Summer 1988, p. 28.

Page 149. Max Cleland's statement appears in ibid.

Page 149. The study on the cost of accommodations is Berkeley Planning Associates, "A Study of Accommodations Provided to Handicapped Employees by Federal Contractors: Final Report," U.S. Department of Labor, 1982.

Pages 149–150. The survey of working disabled people is a poll by Louis Harris and Associates, *The ICD Survey of Disabled Americans,* op. cit.

Pages 151–152. The story of Vivian Berzinski is told by Anne Swardson, "The Irresistible Force of Vivian Berzinski," *The Washington Post Magazine,* May 8, 1988, pp. 22–29, 50.

Page 152. George Michnale's working arrangements for Nancy Gibson are highlighted in Diana Lambdin Meyer, "A Lesson in Independent Living," *Independent Living*, September 1987, pp. 14–15.

Page 153. Operation Homebound is described in Board of Telecommunications and Computer Applications, *Office Workstations in the Home*, National Academy Press, Washington, D.C., 1985, pp. 8–15.

Page 153. The young man who held the Huntsville Hospital interviewing job was Daryl Smith. Smith's story is told in "Job Applicant," *Worklife*, Fall 1988, pp. 17–21.

Page 155. William Schwall's success as a telephone installer is recounted in Georgene Fritz and Nancy Smith, *The Hearing-Impaired Employee: An Untapped Resource*, College-Hill Press, San Diego, 1985, pp. 112–113.

Page 158. The observation of hearing employees conversing in sign at Integrated Microcomputer Systems comes from Jack Anderson, "Success in a World of Silence," *Parade*, January 31, 1988, pp. 10–11.

Page 158. The experiences of Tom Coughlan, Andrea Kurs, and Anne Makler are described in Fritz and Smith, loc. cit.

Page 159. The Breakthrough program is described in Gopal C. Pati et al., *Managing and Employing the Handicapped: The Untapped Potential*, The Human Resource Press, Brace-Park, 1981, pp. 296–297.

Page 161. Charles Reichardt's story is reported in Dick Dietl, "Everybody Needs a Charlie but IBM Found This One," *Worklife*, January/February/March 1988, pp. 12–15.

Chapter 8: When Old Isn't

Page 163. Numbers of people in the labor force, by age group, come from Fullerton, op. cit.; and Riche, op. cit., p. 36.

Page 163. The number of Americans over age 65, an estimate from the U.S. Bureau of the Census, is reported in Ken Dychtwald and Joe Flower, *Age Wave: The Challenges and Opportunities of an Aging America*, Jeremy P. Tarcher, Inc., Los Angeles, 1989, pp. 6 and 8.

Page 164. Employers' experiences with older workers are documented in William Pat Patterson, "Gray Can Be Beautiful," *Industry Week*, September 5, 1988, pp. 48–49; Norman Root, "Injuries at Work Are Fewer Among Older Employees," *Monthly Labor Review*, March 1981, pp. 30–34; Frederick J. DeMicco and Robert D. Reid, "Older Workers: A Hiring Resource for the Hospitality Industry," *The Cornell Hotel and Restaurant Administration Quarterly*, May 1988, p. 58; Kristin Connolly, "Older Workers Find Place in Lodging Industry," *Hotel & Motel Management*, September 28, 1987, p. 68; an American Association of Retired Persons (AARP) commissioned survey by Yankelovich, Skelly & White, cited in Anthony Ramirez, "Making Better Use of Older Workers," *Fortune*, January 30, 1989, p. 186; and Root, op. cit., p. 30.

Page 164. Victor Buzachero is quoted in Patterson, op. cit., p. 49.

Page 166. The Colonel's Tradition program at Kentucky Fried Chicken is highlighted in DeMicco and Reid, op. cit., p. 57.

Page 166. The Days Inns example appears in Connolly, op. cit., pp. 2 and 68.

Page 167. The Builders Emporium example comes from Ramirez, op. cit., p. 184.

Page 167. The Minnesota Title Financial Corp. example is cited in AARP, *Managing a Changing Work Force*, Washington, D.C., 1986, p. 16.

Page 168. Examples of senior citizens placed in jobs in the Denver, Colorado, area are reported in Ann Shrader, "Seniors' Wealth of Experience a Bonanza for New Employers," *The Denver Post,* September 20, 1987, p. B9; and Diana Griego, "Senior Citizens Wield Seasoned Hand on Job," *The Denver Post,* July 31, 1987, p. B1.

Page 168. The Kelly Services, Inc., and McDonald's examples are from Dychtwald and Flower, op. cit., pp. 197 and 182.

Page 168. The quote from a Days Inn employee appears in DeMicco and Reid, op. cit., p. 60.

Page 169. The Xerox Corp. example comes from AARP, op. cit., p. 9.

Page 169. The Grumman Corp. example is cited in Ramirez, op. cit., p. 186.

Page 169. The Conference Board survey results are reported in ibid., p. 80.

Page 169. The Cornell Hotel and Motel Administration study results appear in DeMicco and Reid, op. cit., p. 58.

Page 170. Corning Glass Works' senior associate program and Inston's sales emeritus program are highlighted in Ramirez, op. cit., pp. 184 and 186.

Page 170. Teledyne Continental Motors' Golden Bridge program is described in AARP, op. cit., p. 9.

Page 171. A 1982 survey showing that almost 80 percent of workers over 55 prefer part-time employment to complete retirement is cited in Harold Sheppard and Richard Mantovani, *Part-Time Employment After Retirement,* The Travelers Insurance Companies, Hartford, 1982. Sixty percent of those preferring part-time work in the Sheppard and Mantovani study want to stay at the same job. In another survey of older workers, reported in Lois Copperman et al., "Older Workers and Part-Time Work Schedules," *Personnel Administrator,* October 1981, pp. 35–35, about 67 percent say they would "consider" part-time work as a step between full-time work and retirement. Most of these respondents say they would prefer to stay with the same employer.

Page 171. Varian Associates' phased retirement program is described in AARP, op. cit., pp. 19–20.

Page 171. The Bill Ames quote comes from Ramirez, op. cit., p. 179.

Pages 172–173. The Aerospace Corp. and Blue Cross/Blue Shield of Indiana examples come from Dychtwald and Flower, op. cit., pp. 196 and 168.

Page 173. Older teachers at Focus: HOPE's Machinist Training Institute are highlighted in AARP, op. cit., p. 14.

Page 175. The estimate of the number of companies offering employee sabbaticals is from Dychtwald and Flower, op. cit., p. 98.

Page 175. The Tandem Computer example is found in ibid., p. 190.

Pages 175–176. Wells Fargo's sabbatical program is described in Ramirez, op. cit., p. 184; and Dychtwald and Flower, op. cit., p. 191.

Page 176. The Victor Buzachero quote appears in Patterson, op. cit., p. 49.

Chapter 9: Managing the New
Work Force

Page 180. The Jared Taylor story is from Fallows, op. cit., p. 12.

Pages 182–183. The survey of senior HR professionals is cited in Edward F. Lawler III, "Human Resources Management: Meeting the New Challenges," *Personnel,* January 1988, p. 26.

Pages 184–185. Results of the Dun's 5000 survey are cited in Joseph W. Duncan, "Businesses Are Naive Forecasters," *Dun's Business Month,* October 1985, p. 82.

Page 186. The ASPA data base is described in Catherine Downes Bower and Jeffrey J. Hallett, "Issues Management at ASPA," *Personnel Administrator,* January 1989, p. 40.

Page 187. James O'Toole's comments are from James O'Toole, *Vanguard Management: Redesigning the Corporate Future,* Berkley Books, New York, 1985, p. 244.

Page 188. A comparison of union and nonunion compensation gains appears in Janet L. Norwood, "The Future of Employment: Demography and Work," *Current,* May 1987, p. 21.

Page 188. The Dun's survey is from Duncan, loc. cit.

Page 188. The John Elkins quote is from Elkins, op. cit., pp. 5–6.

Page 189. The Martha Finney quote is from Martha I. Finney, "Planning Today for the Future's Changing Shape," *Personnel Administrator,* January 1989, p. 47.

Page 189. The four points are adapted from Michael LeBoeuf, *Imagineering: How to Profit From Your Creative Powers,* Berkley Books, New York, 1980, pp. 147–150.

Pages 190–191. Walter Wriston is quoted by Randall S. Schuler et al., "Matching Effective HR Practices With Competitive Strategy," *Personnel,* September 1987, p. 27.

Page 191. James G. Parkel is quoted in Finney, op. cit., p. 46.

Pages 191–193. Robert Harloe is quoted by Feuer, "Coping With the Labor Shortage," op. cit., p. 74.

Page 193. Keith Robinson's formula for good management is cited in Bacas, op. cit., p. 19.

Page 193. The *Training* article is Feuer, "Coping With the Labor Shortage," op. cit., p. 64.

Page 193. The Center for Management Research study is cited in Chris Lee, "The New Employment Contract," *Training,* December 1987, p. 47.

Pages 193–194. David Jamieson's views on what makes good workers stay with a firm are presented in ibid., p. 52.

Page 194. Daniel Yankelovich's findings are discussed in an interview in "Our Turn," *American Health,* September 1988, pp. 56 and 59.

Page 194. The James Vonderhorst quote appears in Feuer, "Coping With the Labor Shortage," op. cit., p. 75.

Page 194. The Hyatt Corp. example is from ibid., p. 74.

Page 195. The data on ESOPs and Brunswick Corp.'s success with employee ownership are documented in Dana Rohrabacher, "ESOP Is Not a Hoax," *The Washington Post,* June 12, 1989, p. A14.

Pages 195–196. The examples of innovative employee-ownership and management strategies are from Main, loc. cit.; Norwood, loc. cit.; and Louis Richman, "The Skilled and Unskilled Jobs of the Future," *Current,* July/August 1988, p. 21. Also see Stephen C. Brandt, *Entrepreneuring in Established Companies: Managing Toward the Year 2000,* New American Library, New York, 1986.

Page 196. The Levering quote is from Levering, op. cit., p. 132.

Page 196. The examples of employers' commitment to protecting workers' jobs are from O'Toole, op. cit., p. 25; and Alan Halcrow, "A Tale of Three Companies," *Personnel Journal,* September 1985, p. 14.

Page 197. The U.S. Department of Labor prediction is cited in Fields, op. cit., p. 42.

Page 197. The estimated number of workers who will need retraining is from Bernstein, "Where the Jobs Are," op. cit., p. 104.

Page 197. The American Society for Training and Development's figures and the AT&T and Motorola examples are from Anthony Carnevale and Harold Goldstein, *Employee Training: Its Changing Role and an Analysis of New Data*, American Society for Training and Development, Washington, D.C., 1983.

Pages 197–198. The names of employers offering academic degrees are from Naisbitt and Aburdene, op. cit., p. 195. The estimated costs of such training are taken from Elkins, op. cit., p. 7; and from Anthony Carnevale of the American Society for Training and Development, quoted by Minter, loc. cit., p. 111.

Pages 197–198. Comparisons between worker retraining and education in the United States and in Japan are found in Czarnecki, op. cit., p. 249.

Pages 198–199. The NFIB survey is John H. Bishop and K. Griffin, *Recruitment, Training and Skills of Small Business Employees*, National Federation of Independent Business Foundation, Washington, D.C., 1989.

Page 199. The observations by economist John Bishop are from John H. Bishop, "Employment Testing and Incentives to Learn," *Journal of Vocational Behavior*, Vol. 33, No. 3, December 1988, pp. 409 and 414.

Page 199. The quote about the new standardized test and that from Roger W. Johnson are from Cindy Skrzycki, "Test of High School Graduates Planned," *The Washington Post*, November 4, 1989, p. C1.

Page 200. Eli Ginzberg's recommendations are from Eli Ginzberg, *Executive Talent: Developing and Keeping the Best People*, John Wiley & Sons, New York, 1988, pp. 73–74.

Page 201. The reference to Robert Levering's findings is from Levering, op. cit., passim.

Page 202. The IBM-sponsored survey is cited in Jack J. Phillips and Anson Seers, "Twelve Ways to Evaluate HR Management," *Personnel Administrator*, April 1989, p. 56.

Page 202. The Levering quote is from Levering, op. cit., p. 150.

Page 203. Jeffrey Hallett is quoted by Bacas, op. cit., p. 20.

Page 203. The three purposes of corporate social action described by Peter Drucker appear in Peter Drucker, *Management: Tasks, Responsibilities, Practices*, Harper & Row, New York, 1973, pp. 313–314.

Page 203. Figures on corporate philanthropic giving are from Ginzberg, op. cit., p. 160.

Pages 204–205. The Coates quotes are from Joseph F. Coates, "An Environmental Scan: Projecting Future Human Resource Trends," *Human Resource Planning*, Vol. 10, No. 4, 1988, p. 235.

Chapter 10: Beyond the Company's Doors

Page 208. The author's quote is from Clint Bolick, "Solving the Educational Crisis: Market Alternatives and Parental Choice," in David Boaz and Edward H. Crane (eds.), *Beyond the Status Quo: Policy Proposals for America*, Cato Institute, Washington, D.C., 1985, p. 207.

Page 208. The commission's quote is from the National Commission on Excellence in Education, *A Nation At Risk*, U.S. Government Printing Office, 1983, p. 5.

Page 209. The test score data are from National Center for Education Statistics, *Digest of Education Statistics*, U.S. Government Printing Office, 1988, p. 111.

Pages 209–210. The Kearns and Doyle recommendations are summarized in David T.

Kearns and Denis P. Doyle, *Winning the Brain Race: A Bold Plan to Make Our Schools Competitive Again,* ICS Press, San Francisco, 1988, pp. 12–13.

Pages 210–211. Roger D. Semerad's proposal is described in Semerad, "An Education and Training Trust," loc. cit.

Pages 211–212. The criticism of the federal unemployment compensation system includes information from Raymond P. Thorne, "Paying People Not to Work: The Unemployment Compensation System," *NCPA Policy Report No. 133,* National Center for Policy Analysis, Dallas, July 1988; and William H. Peterson, "The Department of Labor and the National Labor Relations Board," in Charles L. Heatherly and Burton Yale Pines (eds.), *Mandate for Leadership III: Policy Strategies for the 1990s,* The Heritage Foundation, Washington, D.C., 1989, p. 360.

Page 213. For a discussion of governmental actions to limit employers' ability to terminate workers, see Edward P. Lazear, "The Labor Market and International Competitiveness," in Annelise Anderson and Dennis L. Bark (eds.), *Thinking About America: The United States in the 1990s,* Hoover Institution Press, Stanford, 1988, pp. 369–376.

Page 213. The Lazear quote is from ibid., p. 374.

Page 214. Statistics on young female welfare recipients are from Charles Murray and Deborah Laren, "According to Age: Longitudinal Profiles of AFDC Recipients and the Poor by Age Group," paper prepared for the Working Seminar on the Family and American Welfare Policy, American Enterprise Institute, Washington, D.C., September 1986, p. 45.

Page 214. Professor Mead's research is from Lawrence M. Mead, *The New Dependency Politics: Nonworking Poverty in the U.S.,* Basic Books, New York, forthcoming.

Page 215. The experience under Massachusetts' ET-Choices program is cited in Spencer Rich, "Dukakis' Job-Training Plan Works, Group Reports," *The Washington Post,* August 29, 1987, p. A4; and Charles Stein, "Progress in Cutting Rolls Is at a Standstill," *Boston Globe,* June 23, 1988, p. 1. Comparative numbers from other states' job training and workfare programs are found in Josh Barbanel, "New York Reduces Its Welfare Rolls," *The New York Times,* August 26, 1987, p. A1; and Judith M. Gueron, *Work Initiatives for Welfare Recipients: Lessons From a Multi-State Experiment,* Manpower Research Development Corporation, New York, February 24, 1986.

Page 216. The information on United States policy toward immigrants and refugees is from Doug Bandow, "Refugees Deserve a Better Welcome," *The Wall Street Journal,* February 13, 1989, p. A14.

Page 217. Data on undocumented immigration are from Council of Economic Advisers, *Economic Report of the President,* U.S. Government Printing Office, January 1986, pp. 217–219.

Page 217. The Rand Corp. study is Kevin F. McCarthy and R. Burciaga Valdez, *Current and Future Effects of Mexican Immigration in California,* Rand Corp., Santa Monica, 1986, p. 53.

Page 217. Immigrants' skill and income levels are discussed in Andrew Hacker, "Black Crime, White Racism," *The New York Review of Books,* March 3, 1988, p. 40.

Page 217. Data on immigrants' participation in the welfare system are cited in Lazear, op. cit., p. 395.

Pages 217–218. Louis V. Gerstner, Jr.'s comment is from Gerstner, "The Workforce Challenge," op. cit., p. 10.

Index